K. Warner Schaie, PhD, is the Evan Pugh Professor of Human Development and Psychology and Director of the Gerontology Center at the Pennsylvania State University. He has previously held professional appointments at the University of Nebraska, West Virginia University, and the University of Southern California. Dr. Schaie received his BA from the University of California–Berkeley and his MS and PhD degrees from the University of Washington, allin psychology. He is the author or editor of 26 books and over 200 journal articles and chapters related to the study of human aging. Dr. Schaie is the recipient of the Distinguished Scientific Contributions Award of the American Psychological Association and of the Robert W. Kleemeier Award for Distinguished Research Contributions from the Gerontological Society of America. He was awarded the honorary degree of Dr. phil. h.c. by the Friedrich-Schiller-University of Jena, Germany.

Jon Hendricks, PhD, is Dean, University Honors College and Professor of Sociology, Oregon State University. He earned his PhD from the Pennsylvania State University and was previously on the faculty at the University of Kentucky with a joint appointment in the UK Medical School. Hendricks is a past-president of the Association for Gerontology in Higher Education and served as chair for the Sociology of Aging and the Life Course section of the American Sociological Association, and as chair of the Behavioral and Social Sciences section of the Gerontological Society of America. He has received the Distinguished Career Contribution Award from the latter as well as the Kalish Innovative Publication Award. Hendricks is author or editor of over a dozen books, has written nearly 100 articles/chapters in social gerontology and has served as editor of two book series in social gerontology. He is currently Co-Editor-in-Chief of the Hallym International Journal of Aging and has been on the editorial boards of many of the major journals in social gerontology.

The Evolution
of the Aging Self

The Societal Impact on
the Aging Process

K. Warner Schaie, PhD
Jon Hendricks, PhD

Editors

 **Springer Series
Societal Impact on Aging**

Springer Publishing Company, Inc.
536 Broadway
New York, NY 10012-3955

Acquisitions Editor: Helvi Gold
Production Editor: J. Hurkin-Torres
Cover design by Susan Hauley

00 01 02 03 04 / 5 4 3 2 1

Library of Congress Cataloging-in-Publication Data

The evolution of the aging self : the societal impact on the aging
   process / K. Warner Schaie and Jon Hendricks, editors
        p.   cm. — (Societal impact on aging series)
   Includes bibliographical references and index.
   ISBN 0-8261-1363-X (Hardcover)
   1. Old age—Social aspects.   2. Aged—Psychology.   I. Schaie,
K. Warner (Klaus Warner), 1928-   II. Hendricks, Jon, 1943-   III.
Societal impact on aging.
HQ1061 .E95   2000
305.26—dc21   00-027398
                                                                          CIP

Printed in the United States of America

Contents

Contributors

Vern L. Bengtson, PhD
Andrus Gerontology Center
University of Southern
   California
Los Angeles, CA 90089

Dan G. Blazer, MD, PhD
Department of Psychiatry and
   Behavior Sciences
Duke University Medical Center
Durham, NC 27710

Eileen M. Crimmins
Andrus Gerontology Center
University of Southern
   California
Los Angeles, CA 90089

Dale Dannefer, PhD
Margaret Warner Graduate
   School of Education and
   Human Development
University of Rochester
Rochester, NY 14627

Freya Dittmann-Kohli, PhD
Department of
   Psychogerontology
University Nijmegen
6500 HE Nijmegen
The Netherlands

Richard A. Easterlin, PhD
Department of Economics
University of Southern
   California
Los Angeles, CA 90089

James R. Farr, PhD
Department of Psychology
The Pennsylvania State
   University
University Park, PA 16802

Du Feng, PhD
Human Development and
   Family Studies
Texas Tech University
Lubbock, TX 79409

Kenneth J. Gergen, PhD
Department of Psychology
Swarthmore College
Swarthmore, PA 19081

Mary M. Gergen, PhD
Department of Psychology
The Pennsylvania State University, Delaware County
Media, PA 19063

Linda K. George, PhD
Department of Sociology and
Center for the Study of
Aging and Human
Development
Duke University
Durham, NC 27708

Rosann Giarrusso, PhD
Andrus Gerontology Center
University of Southern
California
Los Angeles, CA 90089

Jaber F. Gubrium, PhD
Department of Sociology
University of Florida
Gainesville, FL 32611

Sarah Hall Gueldner, PhD
School of Nursing
The Pennsylvania State
University
University Park, PA 16802

Melissa A. Hardy, PhD
Pepper Institute on Aging and
Public Policy
Department of Sociology
Florida State University
Tallahassee, FL 32306

Martha Holstein, PhD
The Park Ridge Center for the
Study of Health, Faith and
Ethics
Chicago, IL 60611

Robert L. Kane, MD, PhD
School of Public Health
University of Minnesota
Minneapolis, MN 55455

Neal Krause, PhD
School of Public Health
University of Michigan
Ann Arbor, MI 48109

Sarah Matthews, PhD
Department of Sociology
Cleveland State University
Cleveland, OH 44115

Angela M. O'Rand, PhD
Department of Sociology
Duke University
Durham, NC 27708

Leonard I. Pearlin, PhD
Department of Sociology
University of Maryland
College Park, MD 20742

Erika L. Ringseis, PhD
LLB Student, Faculty of Law
The University of Calgary
2500 University Drive NW
Calgary, Alberta, Canada T2N
1N4

Merril Silverstein, PhD
Andrus Gerontology Center
University of Southern
California
Los Angeles, CA 90089

Gerben J. Westerhof, PhD
Department of
  Psychogerontology
University Nijmegen
6500 HE Nijmegen
The Netherlands

Susan Krauss Whitbourne, PhD
Department of Psychology
University of Massachusetts at
  Amherst
Amherst, MA 01003

Yan Yu, PhD
Department of Sociology
University of Maryland
College Park, MD 20742

Preface

This is the twelfth volume in a series on the broad topic of "Societal Impact on Aging." The first five volumes of this series were published by Erlbaum Associates under the series title of "Social Structure and Aging." The present volume is the seventh published under the Springer Publishing Company imprint. It is the edited proceedings of a conference held at the Pennsylvania State University, October 12–13, 1998.

The series of Penn State Gerontology Center conferences originated from the deliberations of a subcommittee of the Committee on Life Course Perspectives of the Social Science Research Council chaired by Matilda White Riley in the early 1980s. That subcommittee was charged with developing an agenda and mechanisms that would serve to encourage communication between scientists who study societal structures that might affect the aging of individuals and those scientists who are concerned with the possible effects of contextual influences on individual aging. The committee proposed a series of conferences that would systematically explore the interfaces between social structures and behavior, and in particular to identify mechanisms through which society influences adult development. When the first editor was named director of the Penn State Gerontology Center, he was able to implement this conference program as one of the center's major activities.

The previous eleven volumes in this series have dealt with the societal impact on aging in psychological processes (Schaie & Schooler, 1989); age structuring in comparative perspective (Kertzer & Schaie, 1989); self-directedness and efficacy over the life span (Rodin, Schooler, & Schaie, 1990); aging, health behaviors, and health outcomes (Schaie, Blazer, & House, 1992); caregiving in families (Zarit, Pearlin, & Schaie, 1993), aging in historical perspective (Schaie & Achenbaum, 1993), adult intergenerational relations

(Bengtson, Schaie, & Burton, 1995), older adults' decision making and the law (Smyer, Schaie, & Kapp, 1996), the impact of social structures on decision making in the elderly (Willis, Schaie, & Hayward, 1997), the impact of the work place on older workers (Schaie & Schooler, 1998), and mobility and transportation in the elderly (Schaie & Pietrucha, 2000).

The strategy for each of these volumes has been to commission six reviews on three major topics by established subject-matter specialists who have credibility in aging research. We then invited two formal discussants for each chapter—usually one drawn from the writer's discipline and one from a neighboring discipline. This format seems to provide a suitable antidote against the perpetuation of parochial orthodoxies as well as to make certain that questions are raised with respect to the validity of iconoclastic departures in new directions.

To focus the conference, the editors chose three topics of broad interest to gerontologists. Social and behavioral scientists with a demonstrated track record were then selected and asked to interact with those interested in theory building within a multi-disciplinary context.

The purpose of the conference reported in this volume was to examine the manner in which social structures impact age-related changes in self-concept. The self-concept is an integral part of an individual's sense of well-being, degree of life satisfaction, experience of life quality, as well as other issues central to understanding the lives of older persons. Hence, we felt that this topic deserved closer conceptual scrutiny and that the application of methodological sophistication was warranted.

The volume begins with a broad examination of the constructs of well-being and sense of self as well as a review of the literature of what we know and what we still need to know. The introductory chapter is then critiqued from both a sociological and psychological perspective.

The substantive chapters then examine age-related changes in self-concept in terms of broadly defined societal domains. The first of these domains is the context of the family. A prominent three-generation study of intergenerational transmission of values serves as the exemplar for this topic. The second domain is the role of work status on changing sense of self. This chapter develops the concept of personal meaning systems and uses as an exemplar a major German survey of attitudes towards work and retirement which makes use of the natural experiment of the reunification of Germany, to contrast the impact of different social systems on the development of self in East and West Germany. The third domain involves the impact of the health care system on the aging self. The impact of recent changes in the provision of health care and of the relation between the individual and health care provider on maintaining self-esteem are particularly in the frail elderly are considered.

The fourth domain to be considered is the impact of social policy and changes in policy upon the aging self. This chapter in particular addresses some of the macro-societal changes that have eventual effects upon the aging individual. The final domain is concerned with an even broader domain, less easily operationalized, that involves the impact of societal values and expectations. This chapter takes a rather positive position with respect to the future of older persons, but may be relevant primarily to the more affluent elderly. The critiques discuss the caveats that must be raised in the application of the authors' conclusions to less favored portions of the elderly population.

We are grateful for the financial support of the conference that led to this volume which was provided by conference grant AG 09787-07 from the National Institute on Aging, and by additional support from the Vice-president for Research and Dean of the Graduate School of the Pennsylvania State University. We are also grateful to Judy Hall, Melissa Beidler and Alvin Hall for handling the conference logistics, to Anna Shuey for coordinating the manuscript preparation, and to Rebecca Reed and Pamela Davis for preparing the indexes.

K. Warner Schaie

REFERENCES

Bengtson, V. L., Schaie, K. W., & Burton, L. (1995). *Adult intergenerational relations: Effects of societal changes.* New York: Springer.

Kertzer, D., & Schaie, K. W. (1989). *Age structuring in comparative perspective.* Hillsdale, NJ: Erlbaum.

Rodin, J., Schooler, C., & Schaie, K. W. (1990). *Self-directedness and efficacy: Causes and effects throughout the life course.* Hillsdale, NJ: Erlbaum.

Schaie, K. W., & Achenbaum, W. A. (1993). *Societal impact on aging: Historical perspectives.* New York: Springer.

Schaie, K. W., Blazer, D., & House, J. (1992). *Aging, health behaviors, and health outcomes.* Hillsdale, NJ: Erlbaum.

Schaie, K. W., & Pietrucha, M. (2000). *Mobility and transportation in the elderly.* New York: Springer.

Schaie, K. W., & Schooler, C. (1989). *Social structure and aging: Psychological processes.* Hillsdale, NJ: Erlbaum.

Schaie, K. W., & Schooler, C. E. (Eds.). (1998). *Impact of the work place on older persons.* New York: Springer.

Smyer, M., Schaie, K. W., & Kapp, M. B. (1996). *Older adults' decision-making and the law.* New York: Springer.

Willis, S. L., Schaie, K. W., & Hayward, M. (1997). *Impact of social structures on decision making in the elderly.* New York: Springer.

Zarit, S. H., Pearlin, L., & Schaie, K. W. (1993). *Social structure and caregiving: Family and cross-national perspectives.* Hillsdale, NJ: Erlbaum.

CHAPTER 1

Well-Being and Sense of Self: What We Know and What We Need to Know

Linda K. George

U nderstanding the nature and determinants of "the good life" has intrigued scholars for more than 2,000 years, receiving, for example, considerable attention from classic Greek scholars, including Plato and Aristotle. Although quality of life, or well-being, as it is usually labeled in the social and behavioral sciences, has always been an issue of scholarly concern, the aging research community has arguably devoted the most sustained attention to it. There are undoubtedly many reasons for the attraction of well-being for gerontological researchers. One reason is surely the knowledge that when one is studying a segment of the life course where *quantity* of life is limited, a reasonable goal for individuals, clinicians and other service providers, and public policies is maximizing *quality* of life.

The pursuit of self-knowledge has a history as long as that of well-being. The nature of the self also has intrigued scholars and philosophers since ancient times. And, indeed, the dictum to "Know thyself" originated in ancient Greece. Although the study of well-being and self-knowledge have distinct intellectual histories, the expectation that they are related is a long-held conviction. From a simple, common sense perspective, it is difficult for most of us to imagine that all can be well in our lives unless all is fundamentally well with our selves also.

The purpose of this chapter is to examine what we know, and what we need to know, about the linkages between the self and quality of life. Given that these issues have been prominent in scholarly discourse for more than 2,000 years, I obviously have had to be selective. Thus, it is useful to note from the onset what I will and will not do in this chapter. I begin with consideration of the concepts of quality of life or well-being and the self as they are most commonly used in the social and behavioral sciences. This is followed by a review of what is known about the relationships between the self and quality of life and a critical evaluation of the extent to which that body of research does justice to the links between the two. The last sections of the chapter address profitable areas for future research, with an emphasis on broader conceptualizations of some of the ways that self and well-being are interrelated. Throughout the chapter, the primary focus is on self and well-being linkages during later life.

Let me also briefly note what will not be included in this chapter. First, quality of life, which will be interchangeably referred to as "well-being," will be examined only as a psychosocial phenomenon. Broader conceptualizations that attempt to incorporate health and illness, economic resources, and other less psychosocial components of life experience are explicitly excluded from this review. Moreover, because of space limitations, not all potentially relevant dimensions of the self will be examined here. Finally, although I try to keep abreast of relevant work in both psychology and sociology, I am a sociologist; thus, my review will undoubtedly do less justice to the relevant knowledge base in psychology.

QUALITY OF LIFE: CONCEPTUAL AND DEFINITIONAL ISSUES

Two distinct traditions in the social and behavioral sciences provide the conceptual foundation upon which most quality-of-life research rests. The first tradition focuses on what is most commonly called "subjective well-being," which includes happiness, life satisfaction, and morale. This is the conceptual foundation of quality of life that is used by virtually all sociologists and by the majority of psychologists. The second, more recent approach has been labeled both "psychological well-being" and "positive mental health." This conceptualization emerged from developmental psychology and is closely linked to lifespan developmental theories. I will briefly review the major characteristics of and differences between these two traditions. Subsequently, I will consider the advantages and disadvantages of each. Although there are important differences between these two approaches, it is important to note that the two traditions emerge from a common desire to capture the full range of human experience, from the most negative to the most positive.

Subjective Well-Being

Subjective well-being, more commonly labeled either life satisfaction or happiness, depending on the specific measurement tool used, has been important in diverse areas of inquiry in the social and behavioral sciences. Subjective well-being is viewed as a useful, general, or global assessment of how people assess the quality of their lives. As such, it has been used for many purposes, including, for example, (a) determining the degree to which social disadvantage, both ascribed and achieved, affects life quality; (b) understanding the effects of varying political structures on the lives of the populations they govern; and (c) understanding the effects of role gain and loss on well-being.

Subjective well-being has been criticized as being atheoretical, but that is an unfair indictment. One conceptualization, for example, posits that perceptions of subjective well-being rest on individuals' evaluations of the actual conditions of their lives, as compared to the desired conditions of their lives. The larger the perceived discrepancy between the actual and the ideal, the lower the evaluation of life quality. The proposition that subjective perceptions rest upon actual-to-ideal comparisons has received considerable attention in the social and behavioral sciences; and though it is a simple theory, it has been a fruitful one. Both cognitive and emotional processes are involved in actual-to-ideal comparisons: determination of the discrepancy between the actual and ideal is essentially a cognitive task, but emotional investments are involved, both in defining what is ideal for one's life and in translating the discrepancy between the actual and the ideal to a rating of quality or satisfaction.

Another common criticism of subjective well-being is that the meaning of individuals' ratings of well-being is unclear because the nature of the actual and ideal is unmeasured (e.g., we do not know the referents that individuals use in imagining their ideal life conditions). This criticism is an exaggeration of the state of the research base. Although the referents that individuals use in evaluating subjective well-being are typically unmeasured, research has identified the referents typically used in such evaluations. Three related, but distinct, bodies of research have illuminated the bases on which subjective evaluations of life quality rest. First, early studies using measures of happiness and life satisfaction not only asked respondents about their level of well-being, but also how they viewed ideal life circumstances (e.g., Cantril, 1965; Gurin, Veroff, & Feld, 1960). One reason that subsequent studies do not typically ask this question is that the answers were remarkably consistent across individuals: good health, financial security, high-quality relationships, rewarding work, and, to a lesser extent, pursuit of meaningful leisure.

Similar conclusions emerge from a second body of research. Survey research has repeatedly demonstrated that ratings of well-being are largely an average of ratings of satisfaction with these specific domains of life experience (e.g., Andrews & Withey, 1976; Campbell, Converse, & Rodgers, 1976; Rodgers, 1982). Definitions of "good health" and the other bases of perceived life quality undoubtedly differ across individuals and social groups. Nonetheless, the major referents used in evaluating life quality are clear.

The third body of research tackles a different aspect of subjective well-being: how significant discrepancies between actual and ideal life circumstances are interpreted (e.g., Carp & Carp, 1982; Liang & Fairchild, 1979). Typically, when actual-to-ideal discrepancies are large, subjective well-being is dampened. Perceptions of equity and justice, however, can modify the meaning of these discrepancies. If actual-to-ideal discrepancies are viewed as fair and equitable, perceived life quality typically remains high. There is certainly a personal, idiosyncratic component of subjective well-being. Nonetheless, we understand the major patterned foundations of perceived life quality.

Substantial effort has been devoted to assessing the convergences and divergences between specific components of subjective well-being—especially the distinction between happiness and life satisfaction, which differ in two primary ways (Andrews & Withey, 1976; George, 1981). First, happiness is a more emotion-based evaluation of one's life than life satisfaction, which is a more cognitive assessment of achievements to aspirations. Second, happiness and life satisfaction are differentially sensitive to the immediate environment. Happiness tends to be quite transitory, increasing and declining in predictable ways in relation to external conditions. Life satisfaction, in contrast, is more stable over time and is less affected by the current environment, although it is responsive to changes in the major conditions of life (e.g., large changes in health and financial resources). Most investigators find life satisfaction more compatible with their conception of quality of life, and "happiness" is now seldom used outside of studies focused specifically upon emotions.

Psychological Well-Being/Positive Mental Health

Because of the similarity between the terms "psychological well-being" and "subjective well-being," from this point I will use the alternative label of "positive mental health" for the former concept. Conceptualization and operationalization of positive mental health is relatively recent, and was launched by dissatisfaction with subjective well-being as it has been conventionally used in prior research. The premier scholar in this emerging field is Carol Ryff. It is she who has provided us with the best-articulated conceptualization of positive mental health and a psychometrically tested instrument for measuring it (Ryff, 1989, 1995; Ryff & Keyes, 1995; Ryff & Singer, 1996, 1998).

A number of scholars have criticized the use of subjective well-being as the *sine qua non* of life quality. Space limitations preclude a review of the many grounds upon which their criticisms rest, but it appears to me that the common thread in these indictments is that one need not view one's life circumstances as positive in order to experience quality of life. In particular, the terms "purpose" and "meaning" are consistently used by scholars who feel that life quality should not be defined as simply feeling good about life. From this perspective, for example, one can experience substantial pain, trauma, and suffering, but so long as there is meaning in the suffering, life quality is adequate. Another way of summarizing the positive mental health perspective is to state that it emphasizes positive functioning rather then positive feelings.

The positive mental health approach rests on the theoretical underpinnings of developmental and clinical psychology. Both developmental and clinical scholars work with notions of human wellness. Developmentalists seek to identify the criteria for psychosocial competence at various stages of the life course. Moreover, many developmental theories specify optimal and "worst case" scenarios for developmental tasks, with the optimal representing psychological health (e.g., Erikson, 1959; Gould, 1978). Clinicians also must have an image of psychological wellness in order to develop therapeutic modalities that offer clients appropriate and rewarding change. The typical approach in conceptualizing positive mental health has been to extract from developmental and clinical literatures the roster of core characteristics that comprise positive mental health.

Ryff's work represents the best-articulated selection of core characteristics, accompanied by the development of measurement tools and empirical assessment of their utility. Her original measure of psychological well-being included six subscales, representing core characteristics of optimal psychological functioning: autonomy, environmental mastery, personal growth, positive relations with others, purpose in life, and self-acceptance (Ryff, 1995). Based on subsequent empirical work, she has pared the original subscales to four, two of which she views as primary and two that are "possible" and secondary (Ryff & Singer, 1996, 1998). The primary components of positive mental health are purpose in life and quality connections to others; the secondary components are positive self-regard and mastery. Ryff's taxonomy is but one possible approach to defining and measuring positive mental health, but it illustrates the general character of this approach.

Potential and Problems of the Two Approaches to Quality of Life

In general, I believe that science is enriched and advanced when important issues are investigated using multiple conceptual approaches. This general stance applies to conceptualizations of quality of life as well. It is far too early (and may never be sufficiently late) to pursue a single approach to understanding quality of life. It is useful, however, to consider the potentials and problems of defining life quality as subjective well-being or positive mental health.

The major advantages of using subjective well-being as a summary indicator of quality of life include its face validity/intuitive appeal, its simplicity, the lack of imposition of investigator values, and the broad body of meaningful research based on that approach. With regard to intuitive appeal, it is hard for most of us to believe—on experiential grounds, if nothing else—that the quality of life is high among people who are acutely or chronically miserable. At this point, there are multiple well-established and, of practical value, short instruments measuring subjective well-being that are suitable for any kind of study—thus, the simplicity. And subjective well-being, as conceptualized and measured, is based solely on individuals' evaluations of their lives. If their assessments of life quality are based on their contributions to society, so be it; if they are based on success in dominating and manipulating others, that's fine too. The disadvantage with subjective well-being is that, while we might as a society wish to nurture quality of life in general, there are undoubtedly individuals whose ideas of what it takes to have the "good life" are not aspirations we wish to collectively assist them in achieving. In a related manner, there may be life conditions that are beyond our interventions and supportive capacities. In these cases, individuals reports of life quality may have little practical relevance.

The advantages of the positive mental health approach are that we know precisely what we are measuring (i.e., individuals cannot equate life quality with winning the lottery and exacting revenge on their enemies) and that there is substantial professional consensus that the characteristics of concern are important indicators of psychological functioning. But the advantages of the positive mental health approach may also be their disadvantage—at least, for some purposes. With this approach, the investigator is clearly imposing a definition of life quality on individuals who may or may not evaluate their own lives on those criteria. Purely idiosyncratic deviations from expert opinion are less problematic than the potential for unequal "fit" of the criteria across social groups. For example, what are "age-fair" and "health-fair" definitions or measures of purpose in life?

I also see two potential methodologic problems with the positive mental health approach that are not applicable to subjective well-being. First, one of the major uses of quality of life in the social and behavioral sciences is identifying the conditions that either foster or impede it. Yet, available measures of positive mental health include components that appear to be based on a combination of life conditions and psychological functioning. I fear that there will be substantial confounding of life conditions and life quality using the positive mental health approach.

The topic of interpersonal relationships is a prime example. Many scholars wish to determine the degree to which interpersonal relationships contribute to life quality. It would be difficult to study this issue "cleanly" using measures of positive mental health in which high-quality relationships are part of the definition of life quality. Second, it is not clear to me that the positive mental health approach permits a summary assessment of life quality—or how such a summary might be meaningfully constructed. Does one need to score reasonably well on *all* core characteristics of mental health to be viewed as psychologically well? Should each component of positive mental health be weighted equally? Undoubtedly these and other issues will be resolved as work in this area continues, but for now, the lack of resolution is a limitation of this approach.

Finally, with regard to conceptualizing and measuring quality of life, the field would be greatly enriched by studies that include measures of both subjective well-being and positive mental health, yielding documentation about their convergences and divergences. It may be, for example, that "all roads lead to the same place"; that is, that individuals who rank high on subjective well-being also rank high on positive mental health. Whatever patterns are observed, however, the resulting information would help refine our understanding of life quality.

THE SELF: CONCEPTUAL AND DEFINITIONAL ISSUES

For our purposes, I will use the terms "self" and "identity" interchangeably to refer to the individual's global view of himself or herself. Some scholars restrict the term "identity" to components of the self that are based on social roles (e.g., Burke & Reitzes, 1981).

But most view "identity" in the broader sense used here (Gecas, 1982; Gecas & Burke, 1995; Stryker, 1987). Operationally, research typically focuses on specific facets or components of the self. Research on the links between the self and well-being has focused on two major components of the self: self-efficacy and self-esteem. In line with previous work, "self-efficacy" refers to perceptions that one has basic control over one's life (Bandura, 1977; Gecas, 1989; Seligman, 1975). A corollary assumption is that self-efficacy is essentially a self-judgment about personal competence. Also in line with previous work, self-esteem refers to feelings of self-worth (e.g., George, 1995; Rosenberg, 1979).

There is an enormous and rich literature on self and identity, most of which is beyond the scope of this chapter. I will focus on three related, but distinct, research traditions that are the focus of much recent and current research, and that highlight the links between the self and quality of life.

The Self as a Cornerstone of Well-Being

The most obvious research tradition is that which explicitly posits that the self is a determinant of well-being. Although it is recognized that well-being is a function of multiple causal factors, positive self-regard (e.g., high self-esteem and self-efficacy) is viewed as a critical antecedent of well-being. Although I have not seen it stated this way, work in this area suggests that positive self-regard is a necessary, but perhaps not a sufficient, condition for high quality of life.

This appears to be a simple and straightforward conceptual proposition. Nonetheless, it has sparked some controversy, focused on the degree to which positive self-regard is an antecedent of or a component of well-being. Most scholars believe, as do I, that positive self-worth is different from perceptions of life quality. For me, the compelling logic for this distinction is that I find it quite reasonable to expect that a nontrivial proportion of people who enjoy a sense of competence and self-worth would nonetheless not view their life quality as high. The potential confounding of these two concepts is especially problematic for advocates of the positive mental health approach to defining life quality. As noted above, positive self-regard is often viewed as a component of positive mental health. Clearly, if one adopts the positive mental health approach, it is inappropriate to view at least some components of the self, including self-esteem and self-efficacy, as antecedents of well-being.

The Self as a Mediator Between Social Structure and Quality of Life

A related research tradition views the self as a determinant of well-being, but also, and more importantly, as a mediator through which social structure affects quality of life. This has been especially common in studies of the effects of stressful life events and chronic stressors on both mental health (typically depression or generalized distress) and subjective well-being (e.g., Essex & Klein, 1989; Holahan & Moos, 1991; Krause, 1986; Pearlin, Lieberman, Menaghan, & Mullen, 1981). The general rationale for viewing the self as a mediator between social structure and well-being is that a strong sense of self-worth and/or competence enables cognitive reappraisals that lessen the perceived threat of stressful circumstances.

As I have previously argued (George, 1990), careful review of relevant studies suggests that there are two ways of interpreting the mediating role of the self. Although the difference in interpretation may appear subtle, it represents quite different views of the power of the self. In the first interpretation, investigators view the self as simply an intervening variable—as one step in a causal chain. From this perspective, social structure is the "driving force" under consideration; the self is simply an intermediate outcome that is generated by social structure. Investigators using the second interpretive stance view the self as a more powerful and independent predictor of well-being. From this perspective, the self is a kind of "gatekeeper" or "filter" that plays an important role in determining the degree to which social structure and other external factors are able to affect well-being. That is, the self is one means by which human agency can dampen the pressures of social structures on individuals.

The Self as a Motivating Force in Human Behavior

Social and behavioral scientists strongly endorse the proposition that the self is a major motivating force in human behavior. At the most basic level, the general expectation in this research tradition is that individuals behave in ways that are compatible with the self. At an empirical level, numerous specific hypotheses relevant to this expectation have been examined, including, among others: (a) individuals will seek occupations that are compatible with their perceptions of their interests and skills; (b) individuals will seek friends who confirm their views of themselves; and (c) individuals will develop achievement goals in line with their perceptions of their capacities.

Although the motivating force of the self has been studied in multiple specific contexts, a common assumption and/or concern seems to underlie this body of research: the major motivating force of the self is self-protection (e.g., protecting and sustaining a sense of self-worth and competence). An impressive body of research addresses the various threats and challenges that the self faces as a result of both crises imposed on individuals and the processes of maturation and aging. A large and related corpus of work focuses upon the mechanisms that individuals use to protect the self—with varying degrees of success—from those assaults. Nowhere is this emphasis on protecting the self more thoroughly examined than in aging research, where it is often assumed that (a) processes of aging and disease threaten the self; (b) age-related losses of roles and significant others place the self at risk; and (c) negative, stereotypic public images of old age, which are frequently subscribed to by the elderly as well as their younger peers, create an atmosphere in which decrements in self-regard might be expected to be the norm.

With regard to links between the self and quality of life, then, this research tradition suggests that sustaining well-being in late life will be partially a matter of protecting the self. Moreover, if threats to the self are disproportionately common in old age, efforts to protect the self should escalate in late life as well. Thus, late life should be a strategic site for examining the links between self and life quality.

THE SELF AND QUALITY OF LIFE: STATE OF THE EVIDENCE

I will later argue that both conceptual and empirical work on the relationships between the self and quality of life have been overly narrow, leaving important components of those relationships unexamined. Nonetheless, a large body of research addresses the links between self and well-being using the conceptual perspectives reviewed above. Space limitations preclude a detailed review of this large and complex research base. Instead, I will focus on the general conclusions that I believe to be reasonable on the basis of research to date.

Self as a Determinant of Well-Being

Because of the confounding between self and positive mental health, only research on the self as a determinant of subjective well-being is pertinent to this issue. Several studies have examined the relationship between components of the self and subjective well-being. And virtually without exception, moderately strong, statistically significant, and positive relationships are observed (see Higgins, 1987, for a review). People who feel better about themselves also feel better about their lives. This pattern is true not only for self-esteem and self-efficacy, but for other components of the self as well (e.g., self-direction, self-complexity). Correlations between the self and well-being have been observed in both age-heterogeneous samples and samples of older adults.

Although there is abundant evidence that components of the self are related to perceived life quality, an inference of causality requires more than correlational evidence. Unfortunately, the other criteria required for concluding that the self is a determinant of subjective well-being have yet to be documented. It is especially surprising that the issue of causal order has not received attention. There has been little effort to track the impact of changes in the self on changes in subjective well-being or vice-versa. From a theoretical perspective, the expected direction of effect would be from the self to well-being, but logical cases also can be made for quality of life affecting the self, and/or self and well-being affecting each other in a reciprocal fashion. Nor have there been systematic attempts, to my knowledge, to rule out the possibility that relationships between self and subjective well-being are the result of other factors (e.g., social status, successful role performance). Thus, on the basis of research to date, it is safe to conclude that there are meaningful relationships between the self and quality of life, but not that the self is a determinant of well-being.

Related research, not intended as tests of the self as a determinant of well-being, nonetheless offer evidence that this issue merits investigation beyond the simple strategy of correlating components of the self with measures of subjective well-being. In an ambitious study of four age groups, Fiske (1980) studied "hierarchies of commitment" in four areas of the self over a 5-year period: interpersonal investments, altruism, competence/mastery, and self-protection. Her primary focus was the rank order of these self-commitments. She hypothesized that individuals' hierarchies of commitment would change in predictable ways over time (these changes would differ across age groups because of differing developmental tasks) and that deviations from the developmental patterns would be associated with decrements in well-being. Neither hypothesis was supported. There was substantial change over time in individuals' commitment hierarchies, but there were few patterns overall or within age groups—and the commitment hierarchies were unrelated to life satisfaction. In this study, there was an unanticipated lack of relationship between a component of the self and well-being. Nonetheless, it demonstrates that the links between the self and well-being are undoubtedly more complex than can be appreciated by correlating self-esteem and self-efficacy with perceptions of life quality. Another example of relevant work that lies outside the usual approach is Whitbourne and Powers' (1994) study of the ways older women construct their lives in terms of events, time, locus of control, and affect (with the latter representing their assessment of perceived well-being). Contrary to expectations based on some developmental theories, positive life quality was associated with an external locus of control, a focus on events in the family, and a time perspective that focused on the present and future, rather than the past.

The Self as a Mediator of the Effects of Social Structure on Quality of Life

The mediating role of the self has been examined in many studies. Despite the impressive volume of studies in this research tradition, our knowledge is restricted because of the narrowness of this field. This narrowness takes two forms. First, and most important for our purposes, few of the available studies focus on the self as a mediator between social structures and quality of life. Rather, most investigations focus on the extent to which the self mediates the effects of social structures on illness. Second, the range of social structures examined has been small. Largely because most of this research, especially among older samples, has been based on the stress and coping paradigm, most of the structural arrangements examined have been problematic ones, such as living in poverty, living with chronic or disabling illness, and role loss. Consequently, caution is needed in making broad conclusions about the self as a mediator of the effects of social structure on well-being, and research that extends our understanding of this issue is of high priority.

Empirical findings concerning the mediating role of the self have been mixed. Some studies report that self-esteem and self-efficacy mediate the effects of both stressful life events and chronic stressors on subjective well-being (e.g., Elwell & Maltbie-Crannell, 1981; Holahan et al., 1984; Krause, 1986; Mutran & Reitzes, 1981; Turner, 1981). Other studies fail to support the self-as-mediator hypothesis (e.g., Ensel, 1991; Wheaton, 1985). Reasons for these conflicting results remain unclear. Most scholars speculate, however, that there is probably a level of specificity in the mediating capacities of the self that has not yet been identified. For example, self-esteem and self-efficacy may be differentially important for different stressors (and other social structural arrangements) and/or for different dimensions of well-being.

In the research just summarized, the focus is on the extent to which different dimensions of the self mediate the relationships between objective life conditions and well-being. Another, smaller body of research focuses on the self-processes that mediate between life conditions and perceptions of well-being. Heidrich and Ryff (1993), for example, examined three self-processes as potential mediators of the relationship between physical health and two methods for assessing quality of life: subjective well-being, and three dimensions of Ryff's concept of positive mental health (personal growth, positive relations, and autonomy).

The first process examined was social integration, defined as the extent to which the individual perceives she is attached to the social order via normative guidelines and participation in social roles. The second process examined was social comparisons, with the expectation that positive comparisons of self to others would lessen the effects of poor health on well-being. The final process examined was self-discrepancy, operationalized as the extent to which the actual self differed from the ideal self. Results of the study indicated that two of the self-processes—social integration and social comparisons—mediated the effects of health problems on all four indicators of well-being. Similarly, Ryff and Essex (1992) investigated the extent to which social comparisons and reflected appraisals mediated the effects of residential relocation on positive mental health. Both processes mediated the effects of relocation on selected dimensions of positive mental health.

Overall, the self-as-moderator hypothesis receives considerable, but not consistent, support in research to date. Of more concern than the consistency of findings is the fact that the scope of research on this topic is quite narrow, focused, for the most part, on illness rather than well-being, and incorporated in a stress-and-coping framework that leads to a virtually exclusive focus on life circumstances that are expected to be problematic. If we wish to better understand the full range of ways that the self intervenes between objective life conditions and perceptions of life quality, broader and more balanced inquiries are needed.

The Motivational Force of the Self

Research on the motivational force of the self in late life has had an interesting history. Initially, inquiries were based on the assumption that the conditions of late life (e.g., failing health, restricted financial resources, role loss, death of significant others) would erode feelings of self-worth and self-competence. Specific theories articulating this expectation include social breakdown theory (Kuypers & Bengtson, 1973) and Rosow's description of old age as a "tenuous role," characterized by a public status, but without meaningful rights and responsibilities (1985).

In general, empirical findings failed to support the expectation that components of the self, such as self-esteem and self-efficacy, typically decline in late life. For example, Bengtson, Reedy, and Gordon (1985) reviewed 62 studies of stability and change of self-perceptions. More than half of the studies (which included both age-heterogeneous samples and samples restricted to older adults) focused specifically on self-esteem. The overwhelming majority of studies indicated that self-esteem remains stable in both structure and level. Demo (1992) reaches similar conclusions in a more recent review, although age does not receive explicit attention. Similarly, most investigators have failed to find evidence that either self-efficacy or a related construct, locus of control, decline in late life (e.g., Gatz, Siegler, George, & Tyler, 1986; Gurin & Brim, 1984), although there are exceptions to this pattern (e.g., Mirowsky, 1995). These studies investigated age-related patterns of self-perceptions and can best be viewed as inquiries about "normal development."

Expectations that positive self-regard is at special risk during late life emerged from another research tradition in which it was speculated that, although there are unlikely to be developmental changes in self-perceptions, the conditions of late life (e.g., health problems, role loss) are likely to threaten self-esteem and self-efficacy. Empirical evidence here is more mixed. There is no evidence that role loss *per se* or the role losses most common in late life erode positive self-regard. There is no evidence, for example, that retirement and widowhood erode feelings of competence and self-worth (Atchley, 1976; Ferraro, 1985; Norris & Murrell, 1987; Palmore, Fillenbaum, & George, 1984). Indeed, retirement appears to have minimal psychosocial impact (i.e., depression and subjective well-being also are unaffected). Widowhood is associated with higher levels of depression and declines in subjective well-being, but these effects appear to dissipate quite rapidly, and there is no evidence that widowhood affects perceptions of the self.

There is evidence that social stress can lower both self-esteem and self-efficacy (Burke, 1991; Lachman, 1984; Pearlin, Lieberman, Menaghan, & Mullen, 1981). These declines tend to be modest, however, and can be averted by adequate social and personal resources. Moreover, there is no evidence that older people are more likely to experience stress-related decrements in self-regard than are their younger peers. Indeed, older adults experience fewer stressful life events than do middle-aged and younger adults (Goldberg & Comstock, 1980; Hughes, Blazer, & George, 1988). Thus, there is no reason to believe that stress-related changes in self-esteem and self-efficacy are more prevalent among older adults in community settings. Qualitative studies, however, have identified the difficulty of sustaining a sense of identity and personhood for some older adults. Gubrium, for example, has documented the difficulties in sustaining identity for persons in long-term care facilities and those who are diagnosed with dementing illness (Gubrium, 1975; Gubrium & Lynott, 1985). A high priority for future research is identifying the ways in which the motivation to protect the self affects responses to stress (e.g., how stress is appraised, choice of coping strategies, attributions about the cause of the stressor).

Given the lack of evidence that either aging *per se* or the conditions of late life place older people at excess risk for decrements in self-evaluation, social and behavioral scientists turned their attention to the mechanisms that allow most older people to sustain a positive sense of self. This has generated an interesting body of research that not only demonstrates the creative ways in which individuals protect their self-evaluations, but also reinforces the view that individuals are active creators of their lives. Although space limitations preclude a detailed review of this research tradition, examples of the self-protecting strategies revealed in previous research will be offered.

The methods people use to protect the self fall into two major categories: cognitive and behavioral. In essence, cognitive strategies are methods of discounting threats to the self. A wide range of cognitive strategies have been identified in previous research, ranging from "looking on the bright side," to "having faith," to using social comparisons in a way that reinforces one's sense of competence and self-worth. Manipulating social comparisons appears to be an especially powerful method of protecting the self, and has been documented in both quantitative and qualitative studies. Previous research has shown, for example, that older adults are able to sustain a sense of self-esteem and satisfaction, even when they subscribe to ageist stereotypes, by viewing themselves as personal exceptions to the general conditions of late life (Chudacoff, 1989; George, 1985). In a classic ethnography of life at Merrill Court, a low-income housing project for the elderly, Hochschild (1973) describes a "poor dear" approach to social comparisons that helped residents to sustain feelings of self-worth. Although all the residents were poor, and most were widowed women, they chose to compare themselves to the "poor dears" who were worse off than they were. Sometimes, the "poor dear" was another resident who was more disabled, or had no children. But if need be, one could always affirm one's competence and self-worth by comparing oneself to the "poor dears" in nursing homes.

Behavioral strategies also are often used to protect the self. For example, there is strong evidence that age-homogeneous environments help to protect the self and sustain subjective well-being. Evidence supporting this conclusion has emerged in both quantitative and qualitative investigations. Quantitative studies suggest that self-esteem and subjective well-being are higher, on average, among older adults who live in environments with a large proportion of age peers than in more age-heterogenous settings (Rosow, 1967; Ward, La Gory, & Sherman, 1988). Qualitative studies also emphasize the self-affirming qualities of relationships with age peers. Hochschild observed this at Merrill Court, where residents had great affection for their children and grandchildren, but emphasized that they felt truly themselves only in the company of age peers (1973). In addition, residents were selective in their sojourns outside of Merrill Court, expressing concern about the treatment they received from younger people, and actively seeking ways of identifying environments that were sensitive to and respectful of older adults. Matthews (1979) provides another sensitive account of the ways that a group of older women with limited resources nonetheless constructed a social world that was comfortable and self-affirming—and relatively isolated from the larger society.

Thus, despite the fact that initial theoretical expectations about the likelihood of erosion of the self in late life were not supported, the motivation to protect the self emerges clearly and in considerable detail. The motivation *per se* was expected; it is the success with which older adults meet that motivation that generated surprise.

PROTECTING THE SELF AND ENHANCING THE SELF: THE NEED FOR A BETTER BALANCE

As noted above, previous research on the motivational force of the self has focused almost exclusively on the ways that individuals protect self-esteem and other self-evaluations.This research provides rich accounts of the ability of the human spirit to protect its basic sense of self-worth despite the traumas and vicissitudes of life. Nonetheless, I believe that the single-minded focus on protecting the self has resulted in neglect of an even greater testimony to individuals' adaptive capacities: the ability to enhance the self and experience personal growth. It is standard, in descriptions of the self, to acknowledge that people are motivated to protect and enhance self-perceptions, but both conceptual and empirical scholarship focus on the former. It is as if the field has assumed, without compelling evidence, that the sole agenda for the self, especially in late life, is to protect and defend, rather than to expand and grow.

It is a central thesis of this chapter that more attention needs to be paid to the desire to enhance the self and the mechanisms that serve that purpose. Self-enhancement is not a new idea; it is a subtheme acknowledged in much of the literature on the self. Indeed, the well-known tension between the views of individuals as products of their environments and that of individuals as the active creators of their lives is one illustration of this (Lerner & Busch-Rossnagel, 1981; Thoits, 1994). My point is that, *despite* the recognition that individuals are growth-seeking as well as self-protective and proactive as well as reactive, this recognition has not translated into balanced study of the self-enhancing and self-protecting motivations of the self.

A starting point for redressing this imbalance might be to examine the conditions under which individuals choose self-enhancement and self-protection. Self-enhancing behaviors are probably riskier than self-protecting behaviors. Self-protection implies warding off potential threats to the status quo of the self, whereas self-enhancement implies opening up to new views of the self, with no guarantee that the new self-perceptions will be comfortable (the "no pain, no gain" principle). A number of interesting questions come to mind with regard to the choice to protect or enhance the self. Why is it that two people, each of whom must choose between protecting the self or enhancing it, will make different choices? Are such choices related to characteristics of individuals or of the environments in which they are embedded? Are there age changes in how individuals prioritize self-protection and self-enhancement? If so, are those changes relatively uniform, suggesting a developmental substrate, or are changes primarily a result of changes in life circumstances? I think that these are fascinating questions that represent only a fraction of the possible ways that an explicit focus on self-enhancement could yield a richer, more balanced view of the life of the self.

A limited literature, overwhelmingly experimental, has examined one rather narrow component of the choices individuals make when confronted with information that can be used for purposes of self-protection or self-enhancement. Specifically, there has been debate about how persons with low self-esteem will react when provided with information designed to increase feelings of self-worth. Persons with low self-esteem are a strategic group for examining issues of self-protection versus self-enhancement. On the one hand, self-enhancing motives should result in people eagerly internalizing information that increases feelings of self-worth. On the other hand, self-protective motives would make it likely that people will tenaciously preserve the status quo of the self, rejecting any information that is at odds with current self-perceptions. Empirical efforts to determine whether low self-esteem is more strongly associated with self-protective or self-enhancing responses to new information have been inconclusive (e.g., Swann, Griffin, Predmore, & Gaines, 1987; Swann, Pelham, & Krull, 1989). Obviously, these studies only scratch the surface of the potential of research examining self-protection and self-enhancement.

Although there has been no concerted effort to study self-enhancement in later life, extant theories and research intimate that self-enhancement is possible and perhaps typical in late life. Many of these suggestions are found in developmental theories and research. For example, the last stage of Erikson's eight stages of life is integrity versus despair (1959). His description of integrity suggests that it may be a culminating step in the growth of the self. Of particular relevance is his contention that integrity includes total self-acceptance. More recently, Markus and Nurius (1986) demonstrated that older, as well as younger, adults report cognitive and emotional commitments to desired "future selves," suggesting commitments to self-enhancement. Examples of what appears to be enhancement of the self also can be seen in a number of excellent qualitative studies. In this regard, Clark and Anderson's classic study (1967) represents one of the best illustrations of scholars who went looking for factors associated with adequate adjustment to late life, and found that some older people do much more than adjust—they grow from the experiences of old age.

Note that my description of self-enhancement in late life is very similar to notions of positive mental health described earlier. To me, it is the ideas of growth and purpose that are the most attractive features of extant conceptualizations of positive mental health. My quarrel with this research is that positive mental health, defined in terms of growth of the self, is defined as psychological well-being. It is of much greater service to the field, I believe, to reserve notions of well-being for global evaluations of the quality of one's life, and to view the self as an important determinant of those evaluations.

THE INVULNERABLE SELF

Is it possible that some people's sense of self makes them essentially invulnerable to threat, so that their entire focus is upon self-enhancement? I think that is possible, although I expect that this occurrence of invulnerability is relatively rare. What kinds of self-perceptions would characterize an invulnerable self? Such a self would have to be able to ward off threats from social disapproval, negative social comparisons, and negative reflected appraisals. Such a self could not rest upon the securities afforded by health and vigor, support from significant others, or plentiful financial resources, because all of these can be taken from one's life—or fail to appear in it at all. The invulnerable self would need to rest on self-affirming principles that are independent of the conditions of one's life. For most scholars of the self, it is a truism that the self is developed in the context of and sustained or altered by social conditions, including the messages provided by significant others, the rights and responsibilities of social roles, and broader aspects of social and cultural location. Consequently, it is asking a lot for social and behavioral scientists to conceive of a self that transcends the social environment. I think that we must consider that possibility, however.

In this section, I will consider two components of the self that have the potential to both transcend the social environment and render the individual relatively invulnerable to its potential threats to self-evaluations: the authentic self and the spiritual self. Both of these identities have received limited attention to date, but I hope to make the case that they have great potential to advance our understanding of the self and the transcendent capacity of the human spirit.

The Authentic Self

For our purposes, and compatible with previous literature, the authentic self refers to the sense that one's life, both pubic and private, reflects one's "real self" (Goffman, 1959; McGuire, 1984; Swann, 1990). The issue of authenticity has an interesting history in the social and behavioral sciences in that most scholars have emphasized the costs of authenticity and the general lack of it in the modern self. Goffman (1959) was perhaps the first to explore the life of the "public self." He came to the conclusion that the public self is usually highly nonauthentic and that this is a necessary condition for successful social interaction. More recently, Gecas and Burke suggested that "Perhaps the central problem of selfhood in modern societies . . . is the problem of authenticity" (1995, p. 57). Their support for this assertion rests on a broad body of scholarship that characterizes the modern self as fragmented, alienated, overwhelmed, and ambivalent—conditions variously referred to as the "minimal self" (Lasch, 1984), the "mutable self" (Zurcher, 1977), the "alienated self" (Schwalbe, 1986), and the "saturated self" (Gergen, 1991). Thus, it is the lack of authenticity, rather than its presence, which has led to renewed concern about this component of the self. And if we want to understand authenticity, we are going to have to study its presence, rather than its absence.

Giving priority to the authentic self has typically been viewed as a risky proposition. Beginning with Goffman's early work and continuing to the present, scholars have posited that the desire to express the "true self" can threaten the social foundations upon which other components of the self rest. Goffman (1959, 1967) suggested that presenting the true self to others puts one at risk of "losing one's audience" (i.e., of being viewed by others as lacking credibility or socially desirable traits). More recent scholars also have noted the tension between authenticity and social approval, suggesting that authentic behavior may elicit social disapproval, which in turn may undermine self-esteem (McGuire, 1984; Swann, 1990; Weigert, 1991).

This view of authenticity rests on an interesting, but untested assumption: that the authentic self is, by definition, at odds with normative guidelines concerning appropriate and/or desirable behavior. Beyond the tradition in the social sciences to see the desires and needs of society as incompatible with those of the individuals who comprise it, the rationale for this assumption is unclear. Part of the rationale may rest on the fact that much of Goffman's pioneering work focused on the management of "spoiled identities" that accompany social stigma or marginal social status. In those contexts, the benefits that result from hiding the authentic self are clear-cut. This doesn't mean, however, that the cost-benefit ratio of concealing versus revealing the authentic self is the same in other, less marginal contexts. We simply don't know the answers to a variety of questions about social reactions to authenticity: Is it true that societal members view authenticity as a liability rather than an asset? Do we not admire people with the courage to be authentic, despite potential social costs? Do we not desire to be authentic without being censored by others? Would we not grant others the right to the same treatment? Thus, an important issue for future research is to delineate the degree to which and the conditions under which authenticity puts other components of the self at risk.

Attention to the authentic self has the potential to inform our understanding of the self in other ways. For example, although reflected appraisals (Felson, 1985; Ichiyama, 1993), social comparisons (Bandura & Jourdan, 1991; Wood, 1989), and objective achievements (Gecas & Seff, 1990; Staples, Schwalbe, & Gecas, 1984) are strongly linked to self-esteem, some people are able to sustain solid feelings of self-worth despite clear messages of social disapproval or low levels of objective accomplishment. To date, explanations for this "deviant" pattern have focused on self-protection strategies, such as attributional styles and defense mechanisms (Markus & Wurf, 1987; Mehlman & Snyder, 1985; Rhodewalt, Morf, Hazlett, & Fairfield, 1991), as well as selecting one's social environment and audiences (e.g., Rosenberg, 1979). Another possibility, however, is that these people's self-evaluations rest on foundations other than the reactions of others or performance levels as evaluated by others. Commitment to the authentic self is a possible alternative.

The effects of aging on a sense of authenticity may take a variety of forms. One can make a case that one's sense of authenticity is likely to decline in later life. The major losses that are common in old age may make authentic behavior problematic because the environments or interactions that formerly provided an arena for expressing the true self are no longer available. Health problems may disrupt or make difficult one's ability to live from a sense of authenticity. But a case also can be made for the opposite hypothesis. For many older adults, late life offers unprecedented freedom and discretionary time—both of which may facilitate the authentic self. Eccentricities are expected and tolerated; old age is a credible excuse for violations of many social norms. Indeed, Neugarten, Havighurst, and Tobin (1968) pointed out 30 years ago that older people develop a non-normative approach to life. Both scenarios are possible, of course. Some older people may find authenticity more easily pursued in late life, while others find it more difficult. Or there may be intraindividual changes in authenticity during the last segment of life. At any rate, late life would appear to be a strategic site for exploring issues of authenticity—as it has proven to be for many questions about the self.

Obviously, my case for the importance of the authentic self rests on theoretical grounds, rather than empirical evidence. Research is badly needed on sense of authenticity. And this research runs the gamut from the "epidemiology of authenticity" (e.g., how it is distributed across subgroups, characteristics associated with varying levels of commitment to it, the extent to which it varies across social situations) to the antecedents of investments in authenticity to the social and personal consequences of commitment to authenticity. Moreover, attention should be paid to the costs associated with concealing the authentic self, as well as those that result from revealing it. It is my belief that authenticity is an important component of the self and that firm commitments to it allow one to transcend the changing landscape of objective conditions. Commitment to the authentic self may or may not make one invulnerable, but my guess is that it is a major mechanism by which self-enhancement occurs.

The Spiritual Self

Religious or spiritual senses of self also have the potential to enable individuals to transcend their social environments and foster positive views of the self. One of the hallmarks of religious institutions is that they view the self from a different perspective than other sectors of society. Clearly, there are vast differences in the views of the human self across religious traditions. Some traditions view the human race as inherently sinful and weak, and depict life as a battleground in which religious faith is tested by a series of temptations. Other traditions see humans as the beloved children of a kind and loving God who wants to ease their burdens and shower them with blessings. Many traditions—probably most—fall somewhere between these two extremes. Despite wide variations in specific beliefs, there are at least two common themes across religious traditions. First, an essential component of the self lies outside the secular world. Second, the non-secular self is the most important and most authentic self.

Some scholars have paid attention to the implications of religion for the self and/or quality of life, broadly defined. Jung (1933), for example, placed considerable emphasis on the role of religion in the individuation process that he believed characterized the adult life course. Major figures in the early years of psychology, such as James (1902) and Allport (1954), carefully delineated the varieties of religious experience and their implications for personality. And although there is an active field of psychology and religion, most of its efforts focus on the role that religion plays in coping, 12-step programs designed to control addictions, and the relationships between religious practices or beliefs and personality. Within sociology, religious institutions are viewed primarily as structures supporting the status quo, as sources of social support outside the family, and as antecedents of secular beliefs and behavior. Sociologists have documented robust and positive relationships between religious participation and subjective well-being, but explanations for those relationships are primitive and incomplete.

Religion as a source of self-perceptions has been virtually ignored, however. And yet cogent arguments can be made for viewing religious beliefs and commitments as important contributors to self-perceptions. Social and behavioral scientists agree that one of the functions of religion is to provide individuals with a coherent world view, with a cognitive system for understanding the world, the meaning of life, and one's place in the grand design of the universe. To the extent that one's religious beliefs fulfill that function, it is likely that they also affect one's sense of self. In part, religious views may impact directly on self-evaluations. The belief that man is born with original sin, as compared to the belief that one is a beloved child of God, for example, might affect one's general sense of self-worth. Similarly, whether one's religious beliefs focus on "faith in action" via using one's talents to improve the world—or, alternatively, emphasize the notion that the proper role of man is to place his faith in a divine power and passively accept the results of that faith—may play a role in one's sense of self-efficacy.

It is also possible, however, that religion can affect one's sense of self in a broader, richer sense. It is possible that religious or spiritual beliefs provide individuals with a sense of the "sacred self." What is the nature of the sacred self? In terms of the content of the sacred self, the possibilities are infinite, although one would expect religious-based self-perceptions to exhibit predictable denomination-based patterns to some degree. And, of course, not everyone is likely to have a sacred self—even among individuals who actively participate in religious institutions, not everyone's belief structures will include assumptions about the self in relation to God or a higher power.

Although the content of religious self-perceptions will vary widely, it seems to me that the sacred self will share certain properties across individuals. For example, the sacred self would be likely to focus on issues other than achievements in the secular world. In addition, the sacred self would seem to be ageless and timeless in a sense that more secular forms of self-perceptions are not. This doesn't imply that the sacred self is unchangeable, but rather that its dynamics are less likely to rest on the external conditions of life and/or the approval of others. Precisely because the sacred self rests on non-material, non-secular concerns, it may provide a way to transcend secular life, to add a sense of perspective that can buffer the onslaught of discordant messages that one constantly receives in the secular world. For example, a colleague of mine once told me that the sacred and secular worlds emphasize very different time perspectives: that the secular world emphasizes the past and the future, whereas the sacred world focuses on the present and the eternal. He also indicated that he often shifted his perspective to the time frames of the sacred world as a way of putting pressures and problems in perspective.

To my knowledge, there has been very little attention paid to the concept of the sacred self. An exception to that conclusion is the work of Ellen Idler (1995)—and she confesses that she stumbled on the sacred self in her efforts to understand coping with and adjustment to disabling illnesses. In the quantitative component of her study, she was surprised at the relatively high ratings of self-rated health reported by her sample, which was restricted to persons with significant health problems. In the qualitative component of the study, she asked her respondents to explain their health ratings and to talk about how they coped with their illnesses. Religious coping was reported by 62% of her respondents; a figure that is in line with that reported in other studies (e.g., Koenig, Siegler, Meador, & George, 1990; Pargament, 1997). But the reports of these respondents suggested that more was going on than simply using religion as a coping mechanism. The vivid and candid accounts of these persons who were disabled in the secular world suggested a view of the self that transcended their physical limitations, that promoted subjective well-being, and that often translated into reports of excellent health, despite objective evidence to the contrary. One of the respondents she describes was a man with post-polio syndrome (Idler, 1995, p. 686). After 14 surgeries, he was able to walk, but only by using leg braces and two canes. Nonetheless, this man described his health as excellent. Not all of Idler's respondents volunteered religious or spiritual connections to their illnesses and a few blamed God for either allowing them to become ill or for failing to answer their prayers for recovery. A significant proportion of her respondents, however, embodied their religious views in a way that simply is not captured by the term "religious coping." Idler described this as the non-material, religion-based self; I prefer the simpler label of the sacred self.

One study obviously cannot tell us much about the sacred self; but it can illustrate the potential utility of its systematic study. And, although I have never studied the sacred self, I have repeatedly had research participants talk to me about the myriad of ways that religion provides structure and meaning to their lives—not all of them, of course, but a large proportion talk about the importance of religion in their lives, even when that isn't the topic of inquiry. Along with authenticity, I believe that the sacred self merits study.

Is there really an invulnerable self? I do not know. But I believe that there are senses of self, which we have barely glimpsed as scientists, that do not rest upon external conditions, that can flourish despite environmental and personal limitations, and that can both protect and enhance the self when other components of the self cannot do so. These are the components of the self that have nothing to fear from social comparisons, that don't rest on more conventional definitions of "the good life." Compared to other components of the self, they are more ageless, timeless, and, as Idler notes, non-material. I hypothesize that the authentic self and the sacred self are two of these components of the self-system.

FINAL COMMENTS

The questions to be addressed in this chapter were: What do we know about the self and quality of life? And what do we need to know? We know, in general terms, that there are expectable links between self-perceptions and self-evaluations, on the one hand, and judgments about the quality of life, on the other hand. This is hardly surprising. As I stated at the beginning of the chapter, it is hard to believe that one's life is all right if one's self isn't essentially all right also. It is much easier to imagine people with solid perceptions of self-worth and competence, but who are unhappy with their life circumstances, than it is to imagine people who are satisfied with their lives, yet lack positive self-regard. There is certainly much more to be learned about the links between the self and quality of life, even within the rather standard approaches that have characterized the field.

We also know that people are typically quite adept at protecting the self. If possible, we select our environments, select our social networks, and use a myriad of cognitive strategies to sustain reasonable levels of self-worth and self-efficacy. Not everyone is successful in developing or sustaining a solid sense of self-worth, of course, but the normative pattern is one of considerable success, despite the vicissitudes of human existence.

We also know that there is no evidence that older people are any worse off than their younger peers with regard to the structure and levels of frequently-studied components of the self, such as self-esteem and self-efficacy—despite considerable theoretical speculation that the conditions of late life would tend to undermine feelings of self-worth. Moreover, older adults generally protect the self in successful and, sometimes, creative ways.

But we also know that there is a lot that we don't know. I am especially impressed by the extent to which self-enhancement has been ignored in research to date. Individuals have options beyond protecting and defending the psychological status quo. They have the potential to pursue self-enhancement and personal growth, although it is possible that such pursuits place them at risk of social disapproval. I also think that we have focused too much attention on the external world. The self is ultimately internal, despite the fact that it is often affected by external circumstances. At this point in history, individuals have considerable choice in the standards they use as a basis of self-evaluation. I am convinced that some individuals use standards beyond those typically studied in research on the self. I recommend sense of authenticity and the sacred self as two promising avenues for understanding non-external sources of the self, and hypothesize that use of such sources increases enhancement of the self and, ultimately, quality of life.

Finally, I encourage all of us to take a long, hard look at our beliefs about old age. So many of our theories and research rest on assumptions that the normal course of late life is one of loss of internal and external resources, as a time when the very foundations of our identities are battered and frequently fall away. I don't view late life in those terms. I don't think that I am a Pollyanna; I think that most of us have exaggerated views of what humans need to thrive, and that we have yet to appropriately disentangle the effects of disease from those of aging. It may be these negative, stereotypic images of old age that keep our attention on issues such as protecting the self rather than enhancing the self, on coping with problems rather than achieving personal growth, and on accumulating the material rather than nurturing the non-material. If we want to do justice to the human spirit and human lives, we must vigilantly look for the unexpected, for exceptions to general patterns, and with eyes that are informed by what is already known and yet are eager to expand the scope of their vision.

REFERENCES

Allport, G. W. (1954). *The nature of prejudice.* Cambridge, MA: Addison-Wesley.

Andrews, F. M., & Withey, S. B. (1976). *Social indicators of well-being.* New York: Plenum.

Atchley, R. C. (1976). *The sociology of retirement.* New York: Halstead.

Bandura, A. (1977). Toward a unifying theory of behavioral change. *Psychological Review, 84,* 191–215.

Bandura, A., & Jourdan, F. J. (1991). Self-regulatory mechanisms governing the impact of social comparison on complex decision-making. *Journal of Personality and Social Psychology, 60,* 941–951.

Bengtson, V. L., Reedy, M. N., & Gordon, C. (1985). Aging and self-conceptions: Personality processes and social contexts. In J. E. Birren & K. W. Schaie (Eds.), *Handbook of the psychology of aging* (2nd ed., pp. 544–593). New York: Van Nostrand Reinhold.

Burke, P. J. (1991). Identity processes and social stress. *American Sociological Review, 56,* 836–849.

Burke, P. J., & Reitzes, D. C. (1981). The link between identity and role performance. *Social Psychology Quarterly, 44,* 83–92.

Campbell, A., Converse, P. E., & Rodgers, W. L. (1976). *The quality of American life.* New York: Russell Sage Foundation.

Cantril, H. (1965). *The pattern of human concerns.* New Brunswick, NJ: Rutgers University Press.

Carp, F. M., & Carp, A. (1982). Test of a model of domain satisfactions and well-being: Equity considerations. *Research on Aging, 4,* 503–522.

Chudacoff, H. P. (1989). *How old are you? Age consciousness in American culture.* Princeton, NJ: Princeton University Press.

Clark, M., & Anderson, B. G. (1967). *Culture and aging: An anthropological study of older Americans.* Springfield, IL: Charles C. Thomas.

Demo, D. H. (1992). The self-concept over time: Research issues and directions. *Annual Review of Sociology, 18,* 203–226.

Elwell, F., & Maltbie-Crannell, A. D. (1981). The impact of role loss upon coping resources and life satisfaction of the elderly. *Journal of Gerontology, 36,* 223–222.

Ensel, W. M. (1991). "Important" life events and depression among older adults: The role of psychological and social resources. *Journal of Aging and Health, 3,* 546–566.

Erikson, E. H. (1959). Identity and the life cycle. *Psychological Issues, 1,* 1–71.

Essex, M. J., & Klein, M. H. (1989). The importance of self-concept and coping responses in explaining physical health status and depression among older women. *Journal of Aging and Health, 1,* 327–348.

Felson, R. B. (1985). Reflected appraisal and the development of the self. *Social Psychology Quarterly, 48,* 116–126.

Ferraro, K. F. (1985). The effect of widowhood on the health status of older persons. *International Journal of Aging and Human Development, 21,* 9–25.

Fiske, M. (1980). Changing hierarchies of commitment in adulthood. In N. J. Smelser & E. H. Erikson (Eds.), *Themes of love and work in adulthood* (pp. 238–264). Cambridge, MA: Harvard University Press.

Gatz, M., Siegler, I. C., George, L. K., & Tyler, F. B. (1986). Attributional components of locus of control: Cross-sectional and longitudinal analyses. In M. M. Baltes & P. B. Baltes (Eds.), *The psychology of control and aging* (pp. 237–264). Hillsdale, NJ: Erlbaum.

Gecas, V. (1982). The self-concept. *Annual Review of Sociology, 8,* 1–33.

Gecas, V. (1989). The social psychology of self-efficacy. *Annual Review of Sociology, 15,* 291–316.

Gecas, V., & Burke, P. J. (1995). Self and identity. In K. S. Cook, G. A. Fine, & J. S. House (Eds.), *Sociological perspectives on social psychology* (pp. 41–67). Boston: Allyn and Bacon.

Gecas, V., & Seff, M. A. (1990). Social class and self-esteem: Psychological centrality, compensation, and relative effects of work and home. *Social Psychology Quarterly, 53,* 165–173.

George, L. K. (1981). Subjective well-being: Conceptual and methodological issues. *Annual Review of Gerontology and Geriatrics, 3,* 345–384.

George, L. K. (1985). Socialization to old age: A path analytic model. In E. Palmore, J. Nowlin, E. W. Busse, I. C. Siegler, & G. L. Maddox (Eds.), *Normal aging III* (pp. 326–335). Durham, NC: Duke University Press.

George, L. K. (1990). Social structure, social processes, and social-psychological states. In R. H. Binstock & L. K. George (Eds.), *Handbook of aging and the social sciences* (3rd ed., pp. 186–204). San Diego: Academic Press.

George, L. K. (1995). Self-esteem. In G. L. Maddox (Ed.), *Encyclopedia of aging* (2nd ed., pp. 812–814). New York: Springer Publishing Company.

Gergen, K. J. (1991). *The saturated self.* New York: Basic Books.

Goffman, E. (1959). *The presentation of self in everyday life.* New York: Doubleday.

Goffman, E. (1967). *Interaction ritual.* New York: Doubleday.

Goldberg, E. G., & Comstock, G. W. (1980). Epidemiology of life events: Frequency in general populations. *American Journal of Epidemiology, 111,* 736–752.

Gould, R. L. (1978). *Transformations: Growth and change in adult life.* London: Simon & Schuster.

Gubrium, J. F. (1975). *Living and dying at Murray Manor.* New York: St. Martin's Press.

Gubrium, J. F., & Lynott, R. J. (1985). Alzheimer's disease as biographical work. In W. A. Peterson & J. Quadagno (Eds.), *Social bonds in later life* (pp. 349–368). Beverly Hills, CA: Sage.

Gurin, P., & Brim, O. G., Jr. (1984). Change in self in adulthood: The example of sense of control. In P. B. Baltes & O. G. Brim, Jr. (Eds.),

Life-span development and behavior (vol. 6, pp. 281–334). New York: Academic Press.

Gurin, G., Veroff, J., & Feld, S. (1960). *Americans view their mental health.* New York: Basic Books.

Heidrich, S. M., & Ryff, C. D. (1993). Physical and mental health in later life: The self-system as mediator. *Psychology and Aging, 8,* 327–338.

Higgins, E. T. (1987). Self-discrepancy: A theory relating to self and affect. *Psychological Review, 94,* 319–340.

Hochschild, A. R. (1973). *The unexpected community.* Berkeley: University of California Press.

Holahan, C. J., & Moos, R. H. (1991). Life stressors, personal and social resources, and depression: A 4-year structural model. *Journal of Abnormal Psychology, 100,* 31–38.

Holahan, C. K., Holahan, C. J., & Belk, S. S. (1984). Adjustment to aging: The role of life stress, hassles, and self-efficacy. *Health Psychology, 3,* 315–328.

Hughes, D. C., Blazer, D. G., & George, L. K. (1988). Age differences in life events: A multivariate controlled analysis. *International Journal of Aging and Human Development, 27,* 207–220.

Ichiyama, M. A. (1993). A longitudinal analysis of the reflected appraisal process in small group interaction. *Social Psychology Quarterly, 56,* 87–99.

Idler, E. L. (1995). Religion, health, and nonphysical senses of health. *Social Forces, 74,* 683–704.

James, W. (1902). *The varieties of religious experience: A study in human nature.* New York: Modern Library.

Jung, C. G. (1933). *Modern man in search of a soul.* New York: Harcourt.

Koenig, H. G., Siegler, I. C., Meador, K. G., & George, L. K. (1990). Religious coping and personality in later life. *International Journal of Geriatric Psychiatry, 5,* 123–131.

Krause, N. (1986). Social support, stress, and well-being among older adults. *Journal of Gerontology, 41,* 512–519.

Kuypers, J. A., & Bengtson, V. L. (1973). Social breakdown and competence. *Human Development, 16,* 181–201.

Lachman, M. E. (1984). Personal efficacy in middle and old age: Differential and normative patterns of change. In G. H. Elder, Jr. (Ed.), *Life course dynamics: 1968 to the 1980's* (pp. 188–216). New York: Academic Press.

Lasch, C. (1984). *The minimal self: Psychic survival in troubled times.* New York: W. W. Norton.

Lerner, R., & Busch-Rossnagel, N. A. (1981). Individuals as producers of their development: Conceptual and empirical bases. In R. Lerner & N. A. Busch-Rossnagel (Eds.), *Individuals as producers of their development: A life-span perspective* (pp. 1–36). New York: Academic Press.

Liang, J., & Fairchild, T. (1979). Relative deprivation and perception of financial adequacy among the aged. *Journal of Gerontology, 34,* 746–759.

Markus, H., & Nurius, P. (1986). Possible selves: The interface between motivation and the self-concept. In K. Yardley & T. Honess (Eds.), *Self and identity: Psychosocial perspectives* (pp. 213–232). New York: Wiley.

Markus, H., & Wurf, E. (1987). The dynamic self-concept. *Annual Review of Psychology, 38,* 299–337.

Matthews, S. H. (1979). *The social world of older women.* Beverly Hills, CA: Sage.

McGuire, W. J. (1984). Search for the self: Going beyond self-esteem and the reactive self. In R. A. Zucker, J. Arnoff, & A. I. Rabin (Eds.), *Personality and the prediction of behavior* (pp. 73–120). New York: Academic Press.

Mehlman, R. C., & Snyder, C. R. (1985). Excuse the theory: A test of the self-protective role of attributions. *Journal of Personality and Social Psychology, 49,* 994–1001.

Mirowsky, J. (1995). Age and the sense of control. *Social Psychology Quarterly, 58,* 31–43.

Mutran, E., & Reitzes, D. C. (1981). Retirement, identity, and well-being: Realignment of role relationships. *Journal of Gerontology, 36,* 134–143.

Neugarten, B. L., Havighurst, R. J., & Tobin, S. S. (1968). Personality patterns of aging. In B. L. Neugarten (Ed.), *Middle age and aging* (pp. 212–273). Chicago: University of Chicago Press.

Norris, F. H., & Murrell, S. A. (1987). Older adult family stress and adaptation before and after bereavement. *Journal of Gerontology, 42,* 606–612.

Palmore, E. B., Fillenbaum, G. G., & George, L. K. (1984). Consequences of retirement. *Journal of Gerontology, 39,* 109–116.

Pargament, K. I. (1997). *The psychology of religion and coping.* New York: Guilford Press.

Pearlin, L. I., Lieberman, M. A., Menaghan, E. G., & Mullan, J. T. (1981). The stress process. *Journal of Health and Social Behavior, 22,* 337–356.

Rhodewalt, F. C., Morf, C., Hazlett, S., & Fairfield, M. (1991). Self-handicapping: The role of discounting and augmentation in the preservation of self-esteem. *Journal of Personality and Social Psychology, 61,* 122–131.

Rodgers, W. L. (1982). Trends in reported happiness within demographically defined subgroups: 1957–1978. *Social Forces, 60,* 826–842.

Rosenberg, M. (1979). *Conceiving the self.* New York: Basic Books.

Rosow, I. (1967). *Social integration of the aged.* New York: Free Press.

Rosow, I. (1985). Status and role change through the life cycle. In R. H. Binstock & E. Shanas (Eds.), *Handbook of aging and the social sciences* (2nd ed., pp. 62–93). New York: Van Nostrand Reinhold.

Ryff, C. (1989). Happiness is everything, or is it? Explorations on the meaning of psychological well-being. *Journal of Personality and Social Psychology, 57,* 1069–1081.

Ryff, C. (1995). Psychological well-being in adult life. *Current Directions in Psychological Science, 4,* 99–104.

Ryff, C. D., & Essex, M. J. (1992). The interpretation of life experience and well-being: The sample case of relocation. *Psychology and Aging, 7,* 507–517.

Ryff, C. D., & Keyes, C. L. M. (1995). The structure of psychological well-being revisited. *Journal of Personality and Social Psychology, 69,* 719–727.

Ryff, C. D., & Singer, B. (1998). The contours of positive human health. *Psychological Inquiry, 9,* 1–28.

Ryff, C. D., & Singer, B. H. (1996). Psychological well-being: Meaning, measurement, and implications for psychotherapy research. *Psychotherapy and Psychosomatics, 65,* 14–23.

Schwalbe, M. L. (1986). *The psychological consequences of natural and alienated labor.* Albany, NY: State University of New York Press.

Seligman, M. E. P. (1975). *Helplessness: On depression, development, and death.* San Francisco: Freeman.

Staples, C. L., Schwalbe, M. L., & Gecas, V. (1984). Social class, occupational conditions, and efficacy-based self-esteem. *Sociological Perspectives, 27,* 85–109.

Stryker, S. (1987). Identity theory: Developments and extensions. In K. Yardley & T. Honess (Eds.), *Self and society: Psychosocial perspectives* (pp. 89–103). New York: Wiley.

Swann, W. B., Jr. (1990). To be adored or to be known? The interplay of self-enhancement and self-verification. In E. T. Higgins & R. M. Sorrentino (Eds.), *Handbook of motivation and cognition* (pp. 408–450). New York: Guilford Press.

Swann, W. B., Jr., Griffin, J. J., Predmore, S. C., & Gaines, B. (1987). The cognitive-affective crossfire: When self-consistency confronts self-enhancement. *Journal of Personality and Social Psychology, 52,* 881–889.

Swann, W. B., Jr., Pelham, B. W., & Krull, D. S. (1989). Agreeable fancy or disagreeable truth? Reconciling self-enhancement and self-verification. *Journal of Personality and Social Psychology, 57,* 782–791.

Thoits, P. A. (1994). Stressors and problem-solving: The individual as psychological activist. *Journal of Health and Social Behavior, 35,* 143–160.

Turner, R. J. (1981). Experienced social support as a contingency in emotional well-being. *Journal of Health and Social Behavior, 22,* 357–367.

Ward, R. A., La Gory, M., & Sherman, S. M. (1988). *The environment for aging.* Tuscaloosa: University of Alabama Press.

Weigert, A. J. (1991). *Mixed emotions: Certain steps toward understanding ambivalence.* Albany, NY: State University of New York Press.

Wheaton, B. (1985). Models for the stress-buffering functions of coping resources. *Journal of Health and Social Behavior, 26,* 352–364.

Whitbourne, S. K., & Powers, C. B. (1994). Older women's constructs of their lives: A quantitative and qualitative exploration. *International Journal of Aging and Human Development, 38,* 293–306.

Wood, J. V. (1989). Theory and research concerning social comparison of personal attributes. *Psychological Bulletin, 106,* 231–248.

Zurcher, L. A., Jr. (1977). *The mutable self.* Beverly Hills, CA: Sage.

Commentary

Identity and Well-Being
in Later Adulthood

Susan Krauss Whitbourne

L iving up to her reputation as a foremost theorist and researcher on sociological approaches to the aging self, George (this volume) has provided a comprehensive and insightful review of the literature on well-being and self-conceptions in later adulthood. Her proposal of the "spiritual self" is an intriguing one and contributes an important perspective to the current views of the self and adaptation, many of which present the self as a passive responder to experiences.

As George notes, the literature she reviews on subjective well-being does present limitations. Simply feeling "good" about one's life does not necessarily imply a positive state of mental health, as it is also important to consider whether an individual has a sense of purpose and meaning in life. Subjective well-being is relatively easy to measure, but this is perhaps a limitation as well, because the measures of this construct tend to be so simple that they fail to capture the depth and complexity of people's feelings about life. Positive mental health offers an alternative approach that has advantages in that it is more objectively based, but this strength is also its weakness; the individual's own evaluation of life quality is not taken into account. Clinical ratings of mental health may provide an indication of how successfully others view the individual's adjustment, but they are conducted from outside the perspective of the individual.

Other approaches to assessing psychological well-being are not discussed by George, but add important components to the mix. One of these approaches has taken on renewed interest within the current personality and aging literature (Labouvie-Vief & Diehl, 1999). This approach takes into account the quality of the functioning of the "ego," the structure within personality assumed to organize the individual's conscious actions and interpretations of experiences. Researchers working within the perspective of ego psychology have proposed that the quality of the ego's defense mechanisms, or ways of adapting to negative emotions and experience, be used as indicators of psychological health (Vaillant, 1993).

Another important area that would be useful to consider is that of stress and coping. Through coping processes, individuals manage to reduce stress through cognitive (emotion-focused) or behavioral (problem-focused) means (Lazarus & Folkman, 1984). According to this view, and as elaborated in a larger model on emotions in general (Lazarus, 1991), the individual's psychological well-being is a function of the way the individual appraises situations. If a situation is perceived as threatening, this will trigger an appraisal of the situation as stressful; the appraisal of a situation as a challenge stimulates a more positive emotional response. Coping processes then are employed to reduce levels of appraised stress, and vary in effectiveness depending on their appropriateness for the situation. This stress appraisal model was developed in part on community middle-aged samples and has been applied over the past two decades to a wide range of studies on adaptation in the later years of adulthood (Aldwin, Sutton, Chiara, & Spiro, 1996).

The individual's self-attributions of emotions, a topic that is gaining increasing recognition in the field of personality development in adulthood and old age, would also be of relevance to the measurement of subjective well-being (Magai & McFadden, 1996; Markus, Kitayama, & VandenBos, 1996). The positive feelings of joy, elation, and excitement add a zestful element to both subjective and objective evaluations of psychological well-being. A final component to consider adding to the mixture is self-esteem (Whitbourne & Collins, 1998). Although George regards self-esteem as an antecedent of well-being, I would regard self-esteem as a component of overall adjustment. The positive evaluation of the self is an excellent indication of how favorably the individual has resolved potential discrepancies or discontinuities between self-conceptions and the information derived from interchanges with the environment.

The recommendation offered by George to solving, or at least addressing, the dilemma of measuring positive outcomes of self-constructions is to combine subjectively based measures, such as well-being, with objectively based measures, such as positive mental health. Although this approach would help to broaden the theoretical underpinnings of the concept, unfortunately, survey researchers do not have available to them the luxury of providing in-depth assessments of either component of well-being. Large-scale studies sacrifice comprehensiveness for the sake of simplicity of assessment. A good example is provided in Keyes and Ryff's (1999) study of well-being, in which a scale developed on a regional sample was shortened for use in a nationally representative sample. Presumably, the larger study involved more constraints on instrument length. What had been a 120-item measure of the components of well-being in local samples became an 18-item scale when administered in the larger national study. Unfortunately, the results based on these three scales were radically different from those using the more extensive measurement instrument. There is no way of knowing the extent to which the nature of the scales contributed to the disparate pictures of well-being these scales provided regarding the years of adulthood.

These problems aside for the moment, it is now appropriate to turn to George's discussion of the self in relation to well-being. As I have already mentioned, I regard self-esteem to be a component of well-being, rather than being an antecedent. To me, the self and well-being are interwoven entities, and although George makes this point later in her chapter, I think the attempt to determine causal order is somewhat misguided. I do agree, however, with the main thrust of George's paper and what I regard as its greatest contribution: identifying the motivational force of the self and its ability to enhance personal growth. Her suggestion that the self can creatively direct and channel the individual's interchanges with the environment provides a much-needed contrast to some approaches in the psychology and aging field, which regard aging as a matter of coming to terms with loss. For example, theories that focus on the effects of aging on personal control (Brandtstaedter & Greve, 1994; Heckhausen, 1997), although useful in many ways, tend to emphasize that aging individuals must relinquish self-control in a battle with time that they are destined ultimately to lose. These models stem from the approach advocated by those working from the perspective of Baltes emphasizing "selective optimization with compensation" (Baltes & Baltes, 1990). Older adults are limited in their abilities to succeed at important life tasks, and they must therefore decide where to direct their energy and attention.

Not all theories of aging and control portray the older individual as giving in to a loss of the ability to shape experiences (Lachman & Weaver, 1998). However, perhaps the strongest articulation of this position is to be found in Erikson's study of the "vitally involved" elders whose self-determination allowed them to overcome physical, cognitive, and sensory losses (Erikson, Erikson, & Kivnick, 1986). This interview study provided examples of individuals in advanced old age, some with serious health limitations, who managed to accomplish their desired goals undeterred by lack of physical strength or sensory capacity. Similarly, studies of aging and creativity give ample examples of older adults who contribute productively through their works of art, music, and writing until well into their 90s (Simonton, 1998). The findings of these studies seem directly relevant to the emphasis in George's paper on the creativity of the aging self.

The theoretical approach that I have developed postulates a cyclical relationship between the self, or identity, and experiences (Whitbourne, 1996). Identity is theorized to emerge late in adolescence as the collection of self-attributes the individual possesses regarding physical, cognitive, personality, intimate relationships, career or work role, and involvement in the larger social world. For the normal, healthy adult, the content of identity takes a positive self-referential form of "I am loving, competent, and good." Similar to the model of Baumeister (1996, 1997), this identity model proposes that individuals maintain this positive self-view by altering or distorting their life experiences so that they are consistent with this view, even when those experiences have negative implications for identity.

As in Piaget's theory, the identity process of assimilation is theorized to be the mechanism through which experiences are interpreted in a manner consistent with identity. For example, if identity assimilation were being applied to the experience of being fired from one's job for incompetence, the individual would interpret the blow to identity not as a reflection of incompetence, but as a reflection of the employer's unfair attitudes or practices. Although identity assimilation can operate effectively in many situations, there are some experiences that are so discrepant with identity that they cannot be assimilated. It is at this point that identity accommodation takes over. Individuals will then change their identities in response to the new information about the self, and this will be accompanied by a lowering of self-esteem. If a person is continually fired from one job after another, eventually some recognition will have to take place that the individual lacks some crucial quality needed for success in the workplace.

Returning to George's identification of creative aspects of the self, it is possible that she would refer to the identity assimilation process as one of warding off threats to the self, and therefore as reactive rather than active. However, identity assimilation may be regarded as having more creative potential than might be implied by its straightforward definition as the fitting in of experiences to an existing self-structure. Through identity assimilation, individuals can rise above the possible constraints placed on their lives by the aging process and construct views of the self that transcend these potential limitations. They can invent and re-invent the self so that it gains in the ability to incorporate the challenges presented by physical, cognitive, and sensory losses.

One older individual I encountered in a context outside of my professional activities brought this point home to me very dramatically. This was an 80-year-old woman who was an avid craftswoman, and whose primary avocation was needlepoint. She proudly showed me her photograph album full of numerous creations, all of which involved very tiny stitches. At the time, she was not wearing eyeglasses, and insisted that she did not wear eyeglasses while working on her needlepoint. This seemed quite amazing, given what is known about presbyopia and its effects on near vision. However, this woman clearly did not wish to pursue my questions in which I tried to establish how such a feat was possible. I will never know whether she wore eyeglasses or not, but from the standpoint of her identity, it appeared that she preferred to regard herself as a person not needing any kind of age-related prosthesis.

As in Piaget's model, the identity process model also assumes that ideal or healthy adaptation involves a balance between identity assimilation and identity accommodation. Individuals may use identity assimilation as the preferred mode, or first response to an experience, but accommodation may eventually become necessary. Eventually, a readjustment would optimally occur in which the individual manages to construct a revised identity and then apply this new view of the self to subsequent experiences.

The physical changes involved in the aging process present a major challenge to identity because they bring about widespread threats to feelings of competence. However, through the use of identity assimilation, older adults manage to avoid suffering significant blows to their self-esteem (Whitbourne & Collins, 1998). In what we refer to as the "Identity Assimilation Effect," older adults maintain high levels of self-esteem through increased use of identity assimilation. Individuals who engage in identity accommodation, in which they become preoccupied with the problems created by the aging process and begin to think of themselves as "old" (perhaps prematurely), experience low levels of self-esteem and are at higher risk for depression. The Identity Assimilation Effect appears to be specific to the areas of physical and cognitive changes. In terms of identity processes as they apply more generally to life changes and experiences, the optimal state appears to be one of balance or equilibrium between identity assimilation and accommodation. In an investigation of the Identity and Experiences Scale, which assesses general process of assimilation, accommodation, and balance, we are finding more positive associations between balance and self-esteem (Sneed & Whitbourne, 1999).

Given the potential risks of identity assimilation in the area of physical functioning, such as ignoring the warning signs of cardiovascular limitations, the increase in identity assimilation in older adults could be problematic. However, we are exploring the possibility that older adults manage to make behavioral changes ("micro-accommodations") to support their use of identity assimilation at the "macro" level (Skultety, Whitbourne, & Collins, 1999). Such a process would be similar to what Heckhausen has suggested occurs in the realm of primary and secondary control. According to Heckhausen (1997), older adults engage in secondary control processes (changing their perceptions of their goals) in order to maintain their sense of primary control (maintaining control over the environment).

In the case of identity processes, the micro-macro postulate would propose that individuals make accommodations in their behavior, such as taking health precautions, to support their views of themselves as competent and active. The micro-accommodation would consist of the recognition that changes in exercise patterns or diet need to be made to counteract the effect of aging on cardiovascular functioning, body fat, and mobility. Individuals would then make those alterations in behavior, but not process them at the deeper level in terms of thinking of their implications in terms of their getting older. These proposed micro-accommodations serve a protective function as well. Were they not to make those behavioral changes, aging individuals would face experiences that are significantly discrepant with their identities as competent and healthy, because they would suffer heightened risk of serious illness or disability.

One possible limitation of the micro-macro variant of identity process theory is that it can be difficult to know whether a particular behavior serves the purpose of assimilation or accommodation. An individual engaging in exercise may be doing so to serve the function of assimilation (to "stay young") or the function of a micro-accommodation (to adapt to the aging process). Currently, research is underway using a semistructured interview to provide ratings of assimilation and accommodation at the level of such protective and compensatory behaviors.

The inclusion of identity accommodation provides another important addition to conceptions of the self in adulthood. Theories of the self that involve the extension of the self into goals and life plans (Cantor, 1994; Emmons, 1996), describe the impact of the self on the environment and the individual's experiences. Indeed, this is not a specific component of the identity process model, but as in the self-schema model of Markus, it is an implicit assumption that individuals project the desires and interests of identity onto actions taken in the environment (Markus & Nurius, 1986). However, very few theorists discuss the adaptation of an individual's identity or self-conceptions in response to information obtained from interchanges with the environment. The ability to make appropriate shifts in identity when events include sufficient data necessitating such a shift appears to be an essential component of adaptation and well-being in adulthood. Even though the process of identity accommodation may be a painful one, there will ultimately be benefits to well-being of emerging from such interchanges as "sadder but wiser."

The viewpoint presented by George is a crucial one for researchers in the area of self and identity to maintain and apply. Although this discussion has focused on intrapsychic aspects of identity and its relationship to experiences, it is also obviously of key importance to examine identity in relationship to social structural factors. Personality, health, and social structure interact in complex ways (Adler et al., 1994), and when looking at self-conceptions, the "reality" of the external world must not be ignored. For example, individuals who lack the educational and financial background will be either unaware of or unable to take advantage of the kinds of "micro" accommodations needed to maintain favorable physical functioning in later life.

Nevertheless, like the keen-sighted needlepointer discussed earlier, many older individuals are able to maintain, through creative processes, their positive view of the self and outlook on their experiences. Resources that they have developed through years of adaptation, including resources contained within the "spiritual self" as described by George, allow them to reach old age with a healthy sense of who they are and a favorable view of what their lives have meant. In this regard, it is important for the researchers to remember that the older adults who are in our research are the ones who have survived past the many challenges and threats to life that exist all through adulthood. Perhaps, to some extent, their survival reflects what we may think of as the creative self.

REFERENCES

Adler, N. E., Boyce, T., Chesney, M. A., Cohen, S., Folkman, S., Kahn, R. L., & Syme, S. L. (1994). Socioeconomic status and health: The challenge of the gradient. *American Psychologist, 49,* 15–24.

Aldwin, C. M., Sutton, K. J., Chiara, G., & Spiro, A. R. (1996). Age differences in stress, coping, and appraisal: Findings from the Normative Aging Study. *Journal of Gerontology. Series B: Psychological and Social Sciences, 51,* P179–88.

Baltes, P. B., & Baltes, M. M. (1990). Psychological perspectives on successful aging: A model of selective optimization with compensation. In P. B.

Baltes & M. M. Baltes (Eds.), *Successful aging: Perspectives from the behavioral sciences* (pp. 1–34). New York: Cambridge University Press.

Baumeister, R. F. (1996). Self-regulation and ego threat: Motivated cognition, self deception, and destructive goal setting. In P. M. Gollwitzer & J. A. Bargh (Eds.), *The psychology of action: Linking cognition and motivation to behavior* (pp. 27–47). New York: Guilford Press.

Baumeister, R. F. (1997). Identity, self-concept, and self-esteem: The self lost and found. In R. Hogan, J. A. Johnson, & S. R. Briggs (Eds.), *Handbook of personality psychology* (pp. 681–710). San Diego, CA: Academic Press.

Brandtstaedter, J., & Greve, W. (1994). The aging self: Stabilizing and protective processes. *Developmental Review, 14,* 52–80.

Cantor, N. (1994). Life task problem solving: Situational affordances and personal needs. *Personality and Social Psychology Bulletin, 20,* 235–243.

Emmons, R. A. (1996). Striving and feeling: Personal goals and subjective well-being. In P. M. Gollwitzer & J. A. Bargh (Eds.), *The psychology of action: Linking cognition and motivation to behavior* (pp. 313–337). New York: Guilford Press.

Erikson, E. H., Erikson, J. M., & Kivnick, H. Q. (1986). *Vital involvement in old age.* New York: W. W. Norton.

Heckhausen, J. (1997). Developmental regulation across adulthood: Primary and secondary control of age-related challenges. *Developmental Psychology, 33,* 176–187.

Keyes, C. L. M., & Ryff, C. D. (1999). Psychological well-being in midlife. In S. L. Willis & J. D. Reid (Eds.), *Life in the middle: Psychological and social development in middle age* (pp. 161–180). San Diego: Academic Press.

Labouvie-Vief, G., & Diehl, M. (1999). Self and personality development. In J. C. Cavanaugh & S. K. Whitbourne (Eds.), *Gerontology: An interdisciplinary perspective* (pp. 238–268). New York: Oxford University Press.

Lachman, M. E., & Weaver, S. L. (1998). Sociodemographic variations in the sense of control by domain: Findings from the MacArthur studies of midlife. *Psychology and Aging, 13,* 553–562.

Lazarus, R. S. (1991). *Emotion and adaptation.* New York: Oxford University Press.

Lazarus, R. S., & Folkman, S. (1984). *Stress, appraisal, and coping.* New York: Springer.

Magai, C., & McFadden, S. H. (Eds.). (1996). *Handbook of emotion, adult development, and aging.* San Diego, CA: Academic Press.

Markus, H., Kitayama, S., & VandenBos, G. R. (1996). The mutual interactions of culture and emotion. *Psychiatric Services, 47,* 225–226.

Markus, H., & Nurius, P. (1986). Possible selves. *American Psychologist, 41,* 954–969.

Simonton, D. K. (1998). Career paths and creative lives: A theoretical perspective on late-life potential. In C. Adams-Price (Ed.), *Creativity and successful aging: Theoretical and empirical approaches* (pp. 3–18). New York: Springer Publishing Company.

Skultety, K., Whitbourne, S. K., & Collins, K. J. (1999, August). *Relationship between identity and exercise in middle-aged men and women.* Paper presented at 107th Annual Convention of the American Psychological Association, Boston, MA.

Sneed, J., & Whitbourne, S. K. (1999, August). *A measure of assessing identity processing styles in older adults.* Paper presented at symposium, "Stability and Change in Adult Personality and Psychopathology," 107th Annual Convention of the American Psychological Association, Boston, MA.

Vaillant, G. E. (1993). *The wisdom of the ego.* Cambridge, MA: Harvard University Press.

Whitbourne, S. K. (1996). *The aging individual: Physical and psychological perspectives.* New York: Springer.

Whitbourne, S. K., & Collins, K. J. (1998). Identity and physical changes in later adulthood: Theoretical and clinical implications. *Psychotherapy, 35,* 519–530.

Commentary

Deconstructing Self and Well-Being in Later Life

Jaber F. Gubrium

L inda George's chapter, "Well-Being and Sense of Self: What We Know and What We Need to Know" (this volume), provides a specific analytic context for considering the issues raised. The chapter, of course, is limited to a discussion of the sense of self in later life and the commonly related themes associated with well-being. The context is familiar, one that orients to well-being and sense of self as "variables" in the lives of those concerned. Variables, as we know, are subjected mostly to measurement, and that will be my point of departure in considering how the issues as presented construct a particular sense of the experience in question. My aim is to deconstruct the presentation to make visible how this analytic context works to form its very own "sense of self" and "well-being" for older people.

My comments are divided into two parts: (1) a discussion of measurement as it relates to the contemporary self, with implications for George's position; and (2) a consideration of the narrative circumstantiality of the self. I will illustrate with narrative material some of the ways that the two primary variables with which George's chapter is concerned do not as much anchor "what we know and what we need to know" about these topics, as they are leading constructions of the particular analytic context used to conceptualize them. Change that context, and another world is revealed for evaluating what we know and what we need to know about well-being and the sense of self.

Before I begin, it is important to note that in the particular analytic context in which George works, the chapter is a thoughtful summary of the research literature on the relationship between *measures* of quality of life, on the one hand, and *measures* of subjective well-being, psychological well-being, and positive mental health, on the other. The coverage and critical appraisal are informative, and provide the reader with considerable food for thought about how this *measurement* literature conceptualizes the linkages between the categories of self and well-being ("the good life"), which George claims as having lengthy historical resonances. I emphasize the terms "measures" and "measurement" because, as I'll try to explain shortly, these are significant means by which the self and the quality of life are realized, that is, made real, in today's world (see Rose, 1988, 1990, 1996).

MEASUREMENT AND THE CONTEMPORARY SELF

George starts her chapter by pointing out that the idea of "the 'good life' has intrigued scholars for more than 2,000 years" and that "the dictum to 'Know thyself' originated in ancient Greece." This statement raised several questions for me that relate to the historical resonances of subjectivity, on the one hand, and the measurement of self and quality of life, on the other. I will only briefly deal with the issue of historical resonances, because this is not the immediate focus of my research. I am not an historian, and don't claim to have read original source material on the self and the good life from ancient Greece. In any case, I would imagine that these phrases—"the good life" and the maxim to "Know thyself"—are familiar to most of us as being linked with the ancients and that will be my point of departure.

Yes, the Greeks, notably Plato and Aristotle, discussed and debated these matters. The question is, while we now might take up the same terms in reference to our selves and the quality of our own lives, were the Greeks speaking about, or living out, the same experiences we do today? Should we proceed to trace our interest in selves and the qualities of our lives to the ancients, or even to more than a hundred or so years ago? In other words, while the terms—"self" and "the good life"—appear to be identical across history, can we assume that the meanings they were assigned then were the same as those we assign to them today? A difference in semantic context can make for a considerable distinction in what the terms are figured to be about, which couldn't readily justify a historical linkage between them.

Michel Foucault, who was until his death the leading contemporary commentator on subjectivity, if not primarily the self, cast considerable doubt on such linkages, the kind of linkages that supports George's assumption of historical continuity in the relevance of these issues. While Foucault often was flamboyant in making his points, and he frequently totalized his assertions, his spectacular illustrations bring into bold relief the historical disjunctions of subjectivity.

One immediately pertinent illustration is presented in the opening pages of his book *Discipline and Punish* (Foucault, 1977). It centers on the regicide Damiens's torture and death in Paris in 1757. A comparison of the subject of this form of punishment, where the body of the condemned is publicly tortured, with the subject of a much more rehabilitative form of punishment that appears a mere 80 years later in 1837, suggests that radically different subjects were understood to be in place. We sense that as Damiens's body is burned, flayed, drawn, and quartered, few in the crowd that gathered to watch felt sorrow for him. Little or no consideration was given over in related public commentary to what Damiens might have endured. As a subject or "self," Damiens was legally and culturally a mere extension of the crown; he had no personal subjectivity or distinct self to speak of. At the time, it wouldn't have made much sense to be concerned with Damiens as a person with a life of his own, with a self and feelings that one could comment upon in its own right, separate from the regal entity of which he and others were juridically and culturally a part. To be concerned with Damiens's well-being would have been absurd, if not droll. That sort of thing wasn't something anyone wanted, or even needed, to know about. As Foucault might put it, the discursive regime of the times didn't deploy personal selves to practice or contend with, let alone to worry about.

Eighty years later, the condemned, now sequestered and subject to regimens of rehabilitation, are taken to have reformable selves of their own. According to Foucault, this led to the development of all manner of self-constructive technology, including the assessment, if not the measurement, of these new inner entities the condemned now possessed, which, as the story goes, were then subject to manipulation and change. Foucault's famous discussion of the panopticon, in this context, refers to both an actual place of surveillance and a metaphor for what eventually becomes an entire assessment industry—a small part of which George deftly describes. The point is that the relevance of the primary variables with which George is concerned may be rather contemporary, stemming in the French context from the new discursive environment for subjectivity that emerged there in the 19th century.

Fast-forward a few decades, to the landscape of American subjectivity at the turn of the new 20th century and a related debate about *the self* and its relevance in everyday life, which I emphasize because the ordinary selves we all now share were just coming into their own (see Holstein & Gubrium, 2000). This is the subjectivity that George addresses in her chapter. While the historical experience and the cultural context are different from those Foucault considered, we nonetheless hear the likes of William James (1892), George Herbert Mead (1934), even Charles Horton Cooley (1902), working quite concertedly to form the basis for an ordinary self, one strikingly different from the transcendental self of their philosophical forebears. Their collective project is eventually labeled "pragmatism," and it is indeed revolutionary. It is nothing short of an attempt to give birth to a new, now experiential entity that in time would be measured and co-related with other experiential entities, such as the quality of life. It is revolutionary because it is discontinuous with what came before.

In the context of this new subjectivity, it is evident that we all have our own selves. Indeed, James himself forcefully asserts that this includes the likes of the pimp, the whore, the beggar, the cheat, the murderer, the drunkard, the fatuous, the spiritual, the weak in spirit, the socially invulnerable, the child abuser, the wife beater, the thief, and the terrorist, just to name a few (Santayana, 1957). This democratization of the self-concept, as we know, eventually extends subjectivity to the production of the more medicalized selves that arrive on the experiential scene in our own times, such as the codependent, women who love too much, and perhaps even those addicted to sex with cigars.

With the invention and proliferation of the "empirical" self, as James (1892) called it, this ordinary, everyday presence ostensibly located at the center of each and every one of our lives provided us with the opportunity to engage in what came to be called "empirical work." (Never mind that the word "empirical," as the early pragmatists used it, referred to experience in general, and that the term has been incorrectly appropriated by many, if not all, quantitative researchers to designate their focus exclusively.) In time, "empirical" researchers frenetically began to spend huge amounts of time and money to apply, elaborate, and critically assess the invention. If Foucault were here, he might say that there now is as much method in the madness (or positive mental health, as the case might be) of the 20th century, as there was method in the madness of the 18th. In the broad sense of his usage, "method" repeatedly constructs its own subjectivity (see Gubrium & Holstein, 1997).

To return to the question of how far back we should trace concern with the empirical self and a measureable good life, one reasonable answer, then, would be "Not very far." More intriguing to me, however, is the related question of whether what was invented just a short while ago is not an invention still in the making. Are the self and the quality of its life things that we've gotten better at assessing, knowledge of which can be considered in the framework of "what we know and what we need know," as George contends? Or is this very activity—what we know and what we need to know—itself constructing and ramifying these things that we so ardently research?

If the answer to the question is the latter, then strictly speaking we cannot describe, write, or even speak of these matters without hyphens. To be rigorous, George would need to write only about measured-selves, measured-good-lives, measured-global-self-esteem, and so forth. This of course would leave the door open to other hyphenated entities, such as unmeasured- and unmeasurable-subjectivities, constructed-states-of-health, including entire regimes and discourses of their relationship. In the latter context, it would be reasonable to entertain the possibility that not all discourses make it sensible to presume an actual connection between self and well-being, referring to the possibility that in some experiential worlds, to even suggest a link or hyphenation between self-esteem and quality of life would be viewed as ridiculous, if not an abomination (for example, see Demos 1970, 1979).

Actually, I don't have to go back very far in time to illustrate; some of the comments by the older people who responded to my field interviews in the 1970s about their well-being and related sense of self are telling (see Gubrium & Lynott, 1983). For example, one of my very aged respondents once said, in the course of a discussion of her life, that it was kind of stupid (sic) for me to be asking about her thoughts and feelings about herself. I recall her adding, "Why would I ever think about myself or how I feel? You just do what you have to do, don't you?" My youthful scholarly sensibilities were momentarily bruised, but I later moved on to realize that my now much younger respondents have less trouble with such questions. They even dwell on them, especially as self-esteem has become an experiential enterprise to which every one of them contributes (Hewitt, 1998). In that regard, is it possible that we who incite our respondents to articulate aspects of their lives to us along with subjective understandings of the qualities of those lives, on the one side, and they who in turn now readily cooperate with us in this endeavor, on the other, jointly construct and co-relate more selves and qualities for life than ever?

THE NARRATIVE CIRCUMSTANTIALITY OF THE SELF

I now turn to the second part of my comments, which deals with the narrative circumstantiality of the self. Just as George's review of the data shows, my own empirical material conveys strong linkages between how we or others identify who we are, on the one hand, and what the quality of our lives are expected to be, on the other (for example, see Gubrium, 1993).

Following in the footsteps of the early pragmatists, I've been concerned with the "empirical" self, the ordinary, everyday self that presents itself or is presented to us as we go about our lives. My particular focus isn't the measured self, but rather the self referenced in our stories, commentaries, and queries about ourselves and others. This is the self or the selves that we "call out" in each other, or that others "call out" in us, as Mead (1934) was in the habit of putting it. Some of us have taken Mead at his word, and focused on the everyday practices of this calling-out process, as it is publicly expressed in social interaction. (Mead, it should be noted, didn't himself much distinguish between internal and external processes of social interaction. In fact, he called the internal self or mind an "inner conversation.")

If Foucault (1977) suggests that what we refer to as "selves" are historically distinct discursive entities, not subject to quantitative comparison or co-relation with each other, my own work in varied institutional contexts of self construction indicates that this has equally disjoint circumstantial parallels (Gubrium, 1997, 1986, 1992; Gubrium & Holstein, 2000). Much of this work begins with a simple enough premise: That we attend to ourselves and articulate the qualities of experience, among other things, in accordance with the practical circumstances of everyday life.

For example, when we claim at length to know who we really are (the authentic self, perhaps?), it is within particular circumstances that we do so. This might take place in a heart-to-heart gab session about each other over several glasses of beer. It could unfold in an excruciatingly sincere and emotional discussion about "hitting bottom" and discovering the "real me, who ain't worth shit" in an AA group meeting. It might even be expressed in response to a counselor with Rogerian inclinations, who encourages us, in our very own words, to explore and elaborate our core feelings a bit more. Indeed, why shouldn't these circumstances extend to the occasions on which we respond to questionnaire or interview items that ostensibly "tap" into our innermost being, producing the measured-self? Clearly, if the latter circumstance is one among a huge number of others and produces its own self, one would think that there would be a monumental number of selves for us, as researchers, to take into account. Unless, of course, we had good grounds, besides mere convention or tradition, for arguing that measurement occasions aren't really circumstances; that they are separate from social life.

Let's return to George's chapter for a moment. After she presents her review of existing research on well-being and sense of self, she

addresses the question of the balance of research between self-protection, which rests on being vulnerable to the social environment, and
self-enhancement, which is based on being invulnerable to it. In her
view, the balance has weighed in favor of self-protection, and it is
her opinion that this should be redressed. Reading on, it is clear
that George wants to entertain the possibility that people not only
react and respond to the qualities of their lives or estimate them
differently depending on how they respond to themselves, but that
the self, as she puts it, has "the potential to transcend the social
environment." In other words, the self not only protects itself in
reaction to the social onslaught, but has the capacity to develop
beyond it. These selves that would render one invulnerable to the
social environment are what she refers to as the "authentic self" and
the "spiritual self."

Isn't it interesting that these terms borrow from the Romanticist
discourse of social transcendence? This discourse grew to prominence in the 19th century at the very same time that the overration-
alized "machinery" of modern life was perceived to be overwhelming
what Max Weber called the "enchantments" of experience (see
Gerth & Mills, 1958). What's intriguing to me about George's usage
in the context of a discussion of the measured- and co-related-self,
is that, ironically, it seems to conjure up the same sentiments: an
unspoken desire not to confine the self to its measurements and co-
relations. (This is very strange for an "empirical" researcher.) George
soon calls upon Erving Goffman (1959) to support these sentiments,
Goffman alleged to be concerned with the same problem. Referring
to Goffman, George notes further: "He came to the conclusion that
the public self is usually highly non-authentic and that this is a
necessary condition for successful social interaction." In fact, Goffman set aside concern with the authentic self and put his sights
instead on self-presentation, a domain within which issues of authenticity could and do arise.

Returning to my own work, it is evident that in the variety of
institutional sites in which I have collected narrative and ethnographic material, both the authentic and inauthentic self, the invulnerable self, the transcendent self, the spiritual self, and even the
sacred self that by definition ostensibly cannot be spoken, are all
given considerable expression, but within social interaction (Gubrium, 1988; Holstein & Gubrium, 2000). Indeed, related to a point

I will make later, the institutional proliferation of identities in today's world now casts the self out of more interactions than ever. Here, for example, is the self attributed by a social worker in a psychiatric staffing to a 12-year-old boy in residential treatment, the text of which is taken from unpublished fieldnotes (see Buckholdt & Gubrium, 1979):

> I've worked with Ricky for over a year now and, believe me, he's the kind of kid who totally views himself as above it all. He could give a shit about the world around him. Nothing affects him. He's invulnerable. Completely self-contained and impervious. Like he was never socialized. And, boy, do you ever know it when he's around!

In the context of this circumstance, which is a mandated semi-annual psychiatric conference, invulnerability is socially defined—as these things always are—but not in positive terms. The invulnerability in question signifies a lack of sensitivity to the world around one. In the case of an institution that has a considerable investment in behavior modification and prides itself on the healing potential of environmental manipulation, this conjures up a sense of institutional defeat, if not a self that is impervious to change.

Something resembling the sacred self also comes up in my empirical material. Its meanings are also circumstantially mediated. Indeed, I've heard its social rhetoric used to convince others that, to put it in George's words again,

> The sacred self rests on non-material, non-secular concerns [and] may provide a way to transcend secular life, to add a sense of perspective that can buffer the onslaught of discordant messages that one constantly receives in the secular world.

George explains that one of her colleagues actually uses the sacred self to "put pressures and problems in perspective," which I found fascinating, because this is precisely one of the usages that was bandied about in the caregiver support groups I studied (see Gubrium, 1986).

But, significantly, what ostensibly transcends secular life was subject to considerable secular differentiation. Indeed, it was in the very throes of quite secular discussions that the working meaning of the sacred was actually assigned, as shown in the following extracts taken from unpublished fieldnotes of social interaction in Alzheimer's disease caregiver support groups (see Gubrium, 1986). On one occasion, for example, in the course of an emotional exchange between the participants in one of the groups studied, an obviously distressed, middle-aged daughter explained as she wept:

> Mother [*who has Alzheimer's disease (AD) and lives with her*] has gone downhill very fast in the last few weeks. Every day, she loses just a little bit more of her old self. She's becoming [*another participant cuts in, "an empty shell"*]. Yes, an empty shell. [*Quietly weeps and then composes herself*] If, deep down, I wasn't a religious person, I don't know what I'd do. [*Elaborates, then weeps*] This much I can say, I thank God that I have Him in my heart or this ordeal would certainly be the end of me.

At that point, one of the facilitators jumped in and recast the meaning of the daughter's religiosity and the divine inner self she clung to. Ever so gently, the facilitator explained, while comforting the weeping woman:

> That's okay, Helen. [*Hands her a few more tissues*] We know how you feel. Honestly, most of us feel it every day. It hurts to see someone you love decline like that, to the point they don't even know who you are. [*Elaborates*] But, you know, there's another side to it, too, and believe me I'm not questioning how much that Guy up there [*points to heaven*] helps out. But, deep down, you might not actually be facing up to the facts, that Mother is not likely to ever get better, like we talked about in Chapter [*meeting*] last week. [*Elaborates*] It can be a kind of denial that what you're really feeling, deep down, is the agony of letting go, not the importance of hanging on. Think about it, okay? Maybe the real you, Helen, is that woman in there who's very vulnerable, but who wants to finally be free of this and won't admit it to yourself. [*Elaborates*] We've all been there. We know the story.

Helen didn't object to the explanation. Indeed, at the end of the meeting, she was heard joining in and elaborating on the possible self the facilitator had suggested to her, noting in particular that her well-being actually might be improved by a different sense of what was going on deep down in her experience. We can imagine that perhaps she was telling us in her own way that the recognizable discourse of an alternative subjectivity—one not as romanticized—

might be more useful to her. Now, I don't mean to suggest that Helen jumped in with both feet and reconceptualized her inner life at that very moment. But she did begin to interpret her feelings, her recent caregiving experience, and her mother's condition in terms of an alternative conception of whom she was in relation to her mother. The issue she faced was the possibility that what she now was was a person who really should be thinking about what she was doing to herself by hanging on, not the religious woman who could stand above it all. Helen was being given the opportunity to tell a different kind of story about herself, which, upon elaboration, could serve to narrate a rather different self in the circumstance (cf., Gubrium & Holstein, 1998).

The support groups varied along the following lines. Some shared distinctive understandings of the self at stake in the AD caregiving experience, often embedded in stage models of "what you, yourself, go through in this thing," as it was sometimes put. Other groups were less crystallized in such understandings, the selves articulated in them largely developing with the flow of biographical details and integral social comparisons. In these groups, a participant's knowledge of herself could be revealed to her from the self commented upon in another participant's story, communicating to us the intertextuality of subjectivity. In the course of discussing how one felt about one's situation or oneself, it was not uncommon in these groups to hear another participant respond: "Yeah, that's me to a T," or the opposite, as the case could be.

The self, of course, is not a mere product of circumstance, but is diversely and distinctively constructed in different ways from one circumstance to another. Relatedly, the circumstances of daily life are not unique; there's considerable overlap in their descriptive resources, the result of expanding and overlapping discourses. These days, with the rapid proliferation of developmental thinking, medicalized discourses for experience, and 12-step conceptualizations of recovery—just to name a few from the vast array of resources for self construction—even the deepest layers of the self are reproduced circumstantially in terms of what is descriptively available. Indeed, as William James (1892) foresaw, we hold many selves, as different from each other as their local articulations, and yet as similar as the discursive resources that inform them.

The lesson here is that we shouldn't forget how deeply implicated the social is in human experience. As the title of Charles Horton Cooley's (1902) book *Human Nature and the Social Order* implies, our very natures are articulated in the diverse designations of social order. In the context of self and well-being, I take Cooley to mean that selves and the good life are not just affected by, but are part and parcel, *of* distinct social orders. There is no way out, Cooley would say, no way to be invulnerable to the discourses we share, which designate the structure of our very being. It is important that we occasionally recall this now quite old lesson, and figure that well-being and the sense of self are not simply "there" for our perusal and assessment, but that, in practice, the overall manner of our perusal and assessment itself is an integral part, not just a procedural facilitator, of "what we know and what we need to know."

CONCLUSIONS

In conclusion, let me briefly describe a different approach to the important questions raised in George's chapter (see Gubrium & Holstein, 1997). Let us assume that self and well-being are not variables that describe the variability in particular aspects of experience, but instead are social forms and categories we use to represent who and what we are. We do exist figuratively within a world of variables, but we also make use of that world as we go about our everyday lives. This radically shifts our perspective. To the extent we can speak of "variables," they are now things that our respondents actively apply on their own, part of the way they organize their experience. In this context, we, as social researchers, can hardly manipulate the "variables" independently if we are to be objective; that's up to our respondents. It's what they say and do in the distinct circumstances of their lives, where the "variables" are brought up for consideration, that matters.

This suggests that we turn to usage, to the ways in which the "variables" George discusses enter into talk and social interaction. In particular, we turn to what is available for doing so in individual circumstances, and to how what is available gets articulated and communicated to represent experience. As far as the *whats* are concerned, it turns us, for example, to the received stories of denying selves we hear repeated in some caregiver support groups, which are used to represent the unacknowledged self we "really are, underneath it all." This formulates narratives of a deep self not fully controlled by the subject in question. It turns us, too, to the contrasting usage of other support groups, whose received narratives call on different "variables" to construct other stories—such as narratives of resilience, not of denial or authenticity—in representing the self and well-being of their members.

Taken together, this serves to reveal the substantive circumstantiality of these "variables," the extent to which each of them can become distinctly different things—or *whats*—in the local experience of those concerned, disallowing measurement. Measurement assumes object constancy; whatever is being measured and, equally important, compared between measures, requires a continuous object across measurement episodes. The circumstantiality of "variables" abrogates constancy, as from one measurement episode to another, an ostensibly constant object becomes different entities in practice. The deeply authentic self of one circumstance, for example, may readily change into the mere surface manifestation of "denial" in another, changing in kind, not just degree, the meaning of the "variable" in question. To proceed to measure under the circumstances could, unbeknownst to the researcher, readily lead to the proverbial comparison of apples and oranges. In general, circumstantiality works against measurement, calling for an entirely different form of representational regimen, as much of my own work has shown.

The approach also turns us to the *hows* of these matters; it requires us not just to document what is used to represent experience, but how it is used. For example, how do members of a particular caregiver support group use denial to structure and confirm the "real" lack of well-being underlying the conscious experience of a member? How do members apply concepts of social transcendence to represent their social invulnerability? How do they apply other concepts to do likewise, or to represent entirely different senses of their social relationships? Such *how* questions point us directly to the actively constructive side of talk and social interaction.

In today's world, diverse organizations, large and small, increasingly specify our identities and represent our well-being. We can hardly keep in mind who and what we are without running into this or that group or institution's preferred discourse for our identities.

Self and well-being are embedded in myriad discourses and distributed in a broad landscape of possibilities, harkening to a postmodern world. In this empirical context, lest we inadvertently resurrect and confirm a socially saturated self (cf. Gergen, 1991), the *what* and *how* questions must be entertained in relation to institutional life, within the purview of the many going concerns in which we construct, communicate, and thereby understand our lives (Holstein & Gubrium, 2000). This postmodern context takes self-construction far away from the relatively narrow confines of the measured representation of experience.

REFERENCES

Buckholdt, D. R., & Gubrium, J. F. (1979). *Caretakers: Treating emotionally disturbed children.* Beverly Hills, CA: Sage.
Cooley, C. H. (1902). *Human nature and the social order.* New York: Shocken.
Demos, J. (1970). *The little commonwealth: Family life in Plymouth Colony.* New York: Oxford University Press.
Demos, J. (1979). Images of the American family, then and now. In V. Tufte & B. Myerhoff (Eds.). *Changing images of the family* (pp. 43–60). New Haven, CT: Yale University Press.
Foucault, M. (1977). *Discipline and punish.* New York: Vintage.
Gergen, K. (1991). *The saturated self.* New York: Basic.
Gerth, H., & Mills, C. W. (Eds.) (1958). *From Max Weber: Essays in sociology.* New York: Oxford University Press.
Goffman, E. (1959). *The presentation of self in everyday life.* Garden City, NY: Doubleday.
Gubrium, J. F. (1986). *Oldtimers and Alzheimer's: The descriptive organization of senility.* Greenwich, CT: JAI Press.
Gubrium, J. F. (1988). Incommunicables and poetic documentation in the Alzheimer's disease experience. *Semiotica, 72,* 235–253.
Gubrium, J. F. (1992). *Out of control: Family therapy and domestic disorder.* Newbury Park, CA: Sage.
Gubrium, J. F. (1993). *Speaking of life: Horizons of meaning for nursing home residents.* Hawthorne, NY: Aldine de Gruyter.
Gubrium, J. F. (1997). *Living and dying at Murray Manor* (2nd ed.). Charlottesville, VA: University Press of Virginia.
Gubrium, J. F., & Holstein, J. A. (1997). *The new language of qualitative method.* New York: Oxford University Press.

Gubrium, J. F., & Holstein, J. A. (1998). Narrative practice and the coherence of personal stories. *Sociological Quarterly, 39,* 163–187.

Gubrium, J. F., & Holstein, J. A. (Eds.) (2000). *Institutional selves: Troubled identities in a postmodern world.* New York: Oxford University Press.

Gubrium, J. F., & Lynott, R. J. (1983). Rethinking life satisfaction. *Human Organization, 42,* 30–38.

Hewitt, J. P. (1998). *The myth of self esteem.* New York: St. Martin's.

Holstein, J. A., & Gubrium, J. F. (2000). *The self we live by: Narrative identity in a postmodern world.* New York: Oxford University Press.

James, W. (1892). *Psychology.* New York: Harper & Brothers.

Mead, G. H. (1934). *Mind, self, and society.* Chicago: University of Chicago Press.

Rose, N. (1988). Calculable minds and manageable individuals. *History of the Human Sciences, 1,* 179–200.

Rose, N. (1990). *Governing the soul: The shaping of the private self.* London: Routledge.

Rose, N. (1996). *Inventing our selves: Psychology, power, and personhood.* Cambridge: Cambridge University Press.

Santayana, G. (1957). *Winds of doctrine* and *Platonism and the spiritual life.* New York: Harper & Brothers.

CHAPTER 2

Self in the Context
of the Family

Roseann Giarrusso, Du Feng, Merril Silverstein, and Vern L. Bengtson

D o parents matter? Until 1996, this question had seldom been asked in the scientific literature about human development. But Judith Rich Harris has raised it, and in *The Nurture Assumption* (Harris, 1998) she presents a revolutionary answer. Her purpose is "(to) dissuade you of the notion that a child's personality—what used to be called 'character'—is shaped or modified by the child's parents; and second, to give you an alternative view of how the child's personality is shaped"—by interactions with peers and in social settings outside the family (Harris, 1998, *i*). So far, her views have won her an award from the American Psychological Association and a cover story in *Newsweek* (1998).

Harris' argument is that parental influences do not matter, except in terms of genetic predispositions, in contributing to the later behavioral outcomes that reflect personality traits or dispositions. The self, or self-conception, is presumably one of these outcomes, though these terms are curiously absent from her examination. Harris suggests that about 50% of personality differences between individuals—

traits such as friendliness, extroversion, nervousness, openness—are attributable to genes, with the other half attributable to the non-family environment. Her claim is that parental or family environment effects are negligible; that whatever our parents or families do to us, it is overshadowed, in the long run, by what our peers do to us.

This is a radically different view than that accepted by most psychologists and sociologists who study human development. To test Harris' theory requires longitudinal data, and few studies are available by which to examine the long-term effects of parental and other family influences on personality dispositions such as the sense of self. One way of testing whether the effects of families on individual development are immutable—as suggested by Harris' attribution of family influence solely to genetics—is to examine whether dynamic change in family roles and relationships influences the individual's sense of self beyond childhood and into middle and later life.

The purpose of this chapter is to examine long-term effects of family role behaviors on self-esteem, examining 20-year longitudinal data from a study of family relationships and their consequences. First we review theoretical issues in the social psychology of self-esteem and some empirical studies about life-course and family influences. Second, we describe the methods and procedures of our investigation, outlining four specific hypotheses to be tested. Third, we present data analyzing the linkage between family role changes and trajectories of self-esteem for individuals we have followed over 20 years. We then discuss the implications of these findings, concluding with our answer to the questions raised by Harris (1998): "Do parents and families matter?" Yes, families do matter—at least in terms of self-esteem.

SELF-CONCEPTION AND ITS CORRELATES OVER THE LIFE COURSE

Social Psychological Perspectives on the Self

Research on the concept of self is found under a variety of labels, including self-image, self-esteem, self-regard, and self-worth (Wells & Marwell, 1986; Wylie, 1979). Although these terms are not interchangeable, they can be subsumed under the general rubric of self-concept.

Sociologists view the self-concept as the totality of one's attitudes toward the self as an object (Rosenberg, 1979). Like other attitudes, the self-concept is made up of three parts. The cognitive component of the self-concept refers to the way individuals identify themselves in terms of the roles they play or the characteristics that describe them. The evaluative component reflects the extent to which individuals like or dislike this self-defined identity. The conative component refers to individuals' motivations to maintain or change themselves as a result of discrepancies between their real selves and their ideal selves.

While there are three theoretical components to the self-concept, the majority of empirical work to date has focused on self-esteem— the positive or negative evaluation an individual makes regarding the "self" as an object. High self-esteem results when the evaluation is positive; low self-esteem, when the evaluation is negative. Consistent with this body of social psychological literature, our analysis focuses on the evaluative component of the self-concept: self-esteem.

Our concern is the long-term effect of three specific family roles— the spouse role, the parent role, and the child role—on the self-esteem of family members at different stages of the adult life course over a 20-year period. We explore the extent to which long-term change or stability in self-esteem is influenced by changes in role incumbency (the gain and loss of family roles), self-perceived changes in the performance of these family roles, and self-perceived changes in the quality of reflected appraisals received in family role-relationships. We assess these relationships for young, middle, and older adults from the same families from 1971 to 1991.

Our data source is unique, since it is the only long-term study of stability and change in self-esteem in an adult sample over such a long period of time. Further, it is one of the first studies to examine how change in family roles, role performance, and reflected appraisals influences change or stability in the self-esteem of adults.

Longitudinal Perspectives on Self-Esteem

The question of whether family factors result in changes in self-esteem across the life course depends in part on a more general question: Does self-esteem remain stable across the life course, or are there significant variations in individuals' self-esteem over time?

Despite the voluminous research literature on self-esteem, over the last 50 years only a small number of studies have investigated the effect of age on self-esteem (Elliott, 1996; Gove, Ortega, & Style, 1989; McCrae & Costa, 1988; Oates, 1997; for reviews see Bengtson, Reedy, & Gordon, 1985, and Kogan, 1990). Although these studies have produced somewhat contradictory findings as to whether self-esteem changes or remains the same across age groups, they suggest that self-esteem increases from early adolescence through the remainder of the life course.

However, since the majority of the studies used a cross-sectional design in which age and cohort effects were confounded, no definitive conclusions can be drawn. Thus, it is not possible to determine if age differences in self-esteem actually represent changes in self-esteem over time, or whether they represent cohort differences.

Further, among the studies that do examine self-esteem over time, there are no longitudinal studies of stability or change in self-esteem across the adult life course (Demo, 1992). The few longitudinal studies that have been conducted have focused on younger age groups to the exclusion of older age groups, and have followed their respondents for relatively short periods of time (e.g., Elliott, 1996; Oates, 1997). The one exception is the study by Roberts and Bengtson (1996) which followed adolescents over a span of 20 years and found a moderate level of stability in self-esteem for individuals aging across the early stage of the life course.

To adequately study the effects of aging on self-esteem, it is necessary to follow adults across several stages of the life course. Without the inclusion of respondents from all age groups and an examination of the same individuals across a large number of life stages, studies can lead to incomplete findings regarding the pattern and determinants of change in self-esteem across the life course.

Stability or Change in Self-Esteem: Theoretical Perspectives on the Self

The answer to the question of stability in self-esteem across the life cycle depends on the theoretical approach taken. Personality psychology, life-span developmental psychology, and sociological theory each provide a different answer to the question of stability and change in self-esteem (Kogan, 1990)

Personality theorists view self-esteem as a trait—the tendency of individuals to behave consistently across situations. Since personality traits are assumed to be stable once the individual reaches adulthood, trait theorists would predict that self-esteem would also remain stable across the life course.

Life-span developmental psychology grows out of the work of Buhler (1935) and Erikson (1963, 1968, 1982). These theorists share the notion that development, due to its biological foundation, is universal and occurs in a sequence of stages closely corresponding to age. Theories of the stages of adult development suggest that aging is associated with a growing acceptance of self and other (Gove et al., 1989). Thus, based on this perspective, one would predict that self-esteem would progressively increase over the life course.

From a sociological perspective, age-related roles are more important than chronological age or stage of development for shaping individuals' behaviors and attitudes, including self-esteem (Bengtson et al., 1985). Two sociological theories—each based upon the concept of roles—suggest different outcomes regarding long-term stability and change in self-esteem: structural role theory and identity theory.

Structural role theory would predict a curvilinear relationship between age and self-esteem; self-esteem should increase in early adulthood due to role gain, and decrease in late adulthood due to role loss (Rosow, 1974, 1985). Predictions from identity theory are less clear because they depend on individuals' interpretation of the meaning of their roles. Whether self-esteem would increase or decrease with age would depend on whether individuals perceived their roles to be salient to their sense of self and whether they perceived the quality of their performance in those salient roles to be competent (as judged by themselves and significant others—reflected appraisals) (Nuttbrock & Freudiger, 1991; Stryker, 1968, 1980). Thus, according to identity theory, self-esteem would have the potential to increase with age as long as individuals perceived an improvement in role performance and in reflected appraisal over time.

In this chapter we examine self-esteem across the life course within the context of the family from the perspectives of both structural role theory and identity theory. (These theories will be described in more detail below.) We want to assess the linkage between various aspects of family roles and self-esteem over the life course with data from The Longitudinal Study of Generations (LSOG). This data set allows for an examination of both structural role theory—since it contains measures of the loss and gain of several family roles—and identity theory—since it contains measures of individuals' perceptions of the meaning of their family roles. More specifically, this research is directed at studying how changes in family role incumbency, and in the quality of performance of family roles and the reflected appraisals from family members, influence change in self-esteem over 20 years for three generations of family members— grandparents, parents, and children. Since an examination of the grandparent role is beyond the scope of this paper, the grandparent generation is used to provide a second test of hypotheses concerning the parent and spouse roles.

EXAMINING SELF-ESTEEM OVER TIME
IN THE CONTEXT OF FAMILY ROLES

Little research has addressed the extent to which family factors influence the self-esteem of parents (Demo, 1992). Rather, research on the influence of family on self-esteem has largely assumed a unidirectional model of parent-child interaction, i.e., that parents influence children, but that children do not influence parents. This is especially true when considering the effect of adult children on the self-esteem of middle-age or elderly parents; parent-adult child relationships seem to be considered of limited consequence to the self-esteem of aging adults (Lee & Shehan, 1989).

This void in the literature suggests that researchers assume that the determinants of self-esteem in childhood and adolescence are different from those in adulthood, particularly at mid- and later life (Demo, 1992). Yet the influence of family roles on changes in self-esteem over the life course has become increasingly important due to individuals' increased longevity. Parents, spouses, and children will share a longer life together than in years past, thereby creating the possibility that they may have a more dramatic impact on one another (Bengtson, in press). Taking a life course perspective (Bengtson & Allen, 1993), we suggest that the contribution of various aspects of family roles to self-esteem is present at each stage of the life cycle.

Hypotheses to be Tested

A central tenet of social psychology is that individuals' thoughts, feelings, and behaviors are influenced by social structure (Gecas & Burke, 1995). Roles—the basic building blocks of social structure—serve to connect the individual to society (Heiss, 1981). However, structural role theory and identity theory define roles and delineate how individuals learn roles in a different way.

According to structural role theory, for each status position an individual occupies in society, there are rights and duties. Roles are the behavioral expectations attached to the status positions (Merton, 1957). Individuals learn these behavioral expectations through the socialization process. If socialization is successful, individuals will conform to those behavioral expectations and will internalize them (George, 1990).

Structural role theory suggests that the occupation of roles is important to self-esteem because each role helps to integrate the individual with society and to provide opportunities for feelings of mastery and social approval. Thus, involvement in multiple roles provides individuals with multiple opportunities for social rewards and feelings of competence and achievement (Adelmann, 1994; Reitzes & Mutran, 1994; Reitzes, Mutran, & Fernandez, 1994, 1996; Reitzes, Mutran, & Verrill, 1995; Thoits, 1983, 1986). The corollary to this proposition is that the loss of roles denies individuals these same opportunities. Further, each role loss is accompanied by the loss of a role relationship—someone with whom one enacts a particular role. Structural role theory is unclear as to whether the loss of role incumbency, or the corresponding loss of one or more role-relationships, would be responsible for a decrease in self-esteem (Merton, 1957).

Throughout the different stages of life, individuals are engaged in the process of role acquisition, role transition, and role loss. Age influences, if not determines, access to and exit from many roles. During early and middle adulthood, individuals acquire and transition into many new roles such as occupational, marital, and parental roles. Therefore, according to structural role theory, individuals should experience high levels of self-esteem during the early and middle stages of the life cycle. However, during late adulthood many individuals experience role loss as they experience retirement, widowhood, empty nest, and declining health. Consequently, these individuals are less integrated with society, and have fewer opportunities for social rewards and feelings of competence and achievement (Rosow, 1974, 1985). Lack of involvement in social roles (or the corresponding loss of role relationships) should lead to low self-esteem toward the end of the life cycle (Adelmann, 1994).

Based on structural role theory, because changes in role incumbency influence the extent to which an individual is integrated within society and the breadth of their opportunities for receiving positive self evaluation, a loss of family roles should be associated with a loss of self-esteem. Similarly, a gain of family roles should be associated with a gain in self-esteem. Thus, changes in family role incumbency, such as the loss of the child role due to the death of parents or loss of the spouse role due to death or divorce of a spouse, should lead to a reduction in self-esteem. Other changes in role incumbency, such as the gaining of a spouse role due to marriage, or the parent role due to the birth of a child, should lead to an increase in self-esteem. We derive two sets of hypotheses from structural role theory:

Hypothesis 1: Loss of a Family Role Will Result in a Reduction in Self-Esteem over Time

H1a: Loss of the child role (due to the death of both parents) will lead to a decrease in the adult child's self-esteem over time.

H1b: Loss of the spouse role (due to widowhood or divorce) will lead to a decrease in self-esteem over time.

Hypothesis 2: Gain of a Family Role Will Result in an Increase in Self-Esteem over Time

H2a: Gain of the spouse role due to marriage (or remarriage) will lead to an increase in self-esteem over time.

H2b: Gain of the parent role due to the birth of a child will lead to an increase in self-esteem over time.

Structural role theorists are concerned with an individual's location in the social structure as a result of their occupation of multiple roles; they are not concerned with individual's interpretation of the meaning of roles to identity. In contrast, identity theorists are concerned with individuals' interpretations of their roles.

Identity theory has its roots in structural symbolic interactionism (Stryker, 1980). Identity theorists view socialization as a more negotiated process, where individuals are active agents of social change and where the symbolic value of roles is more important than the mere occupation of a large number of roles. The identities of individuals are based on the hierarchical ranking of roles based on the salience of those roles to their sense of self.

According to identity theory, if a role is important to an individual's identity, then the individual's subjective evaluation of their performance in that role should have an influence on self-esteem. Similarly, an individual's perceptions of other's evaluations of them in that role, i.e., reflected appraisals, should also influence self-esteem.

Recently researchers have begun to emphasize that self-esteem is multidimensional (Rosenberg, Schooler, Schoenbach, & Rosenberg, 1995). That is, the individuals' competence within different spheres of their life—role identities—contributes differentially to their global self-esteem. The hierarchical rank of role-identities depends on the importance of that role to an individual's sense of self. If a role-identity is ranked high in the individual's hierarchy, then competence in this role will make a greater contribution to the individual's global self-esteem than will other role-identities. However, the possibility should be acknowledged that it may be difficult to obtain measurements of hierarchical rankings of roles that are consistent across time and place; individuals may provide different rankings depending on the context in which measurements are taken, e.g., home versus work.

The notion of identity salience (or psychological centrality) is based on the assumption that identities are roles which are hierarchically ordered. Social roles, such as parent, spouse, and adult child, may be differentially important to the individual. Whether a poor evaluation on any of these roles leads to lower self-esteem depends on whether these identities are salient to the individual, i.e., high in the hierarchical ranking of role-identities (Stryker & Serpe, 1994). If family relationships remain central to the individual throughout the life-course, then the quality of family relationships should influence the individual's self-esteem across all stages of life.

Little research has been directed at finding out the extent to which changes in a specific dimension or sphere of life influences self-esteem. If the family dimension is central to the individual, then changes in this dimension may affect self-esteem, while changes in other less central dimensions of the individual's life may have little impact on self-esteem. Thus, self-esteem may change over time in response to self-perceived changes in the quality of performance of family roles.

Hypothesis 3: Self-Perceived Improvement in the Performance of Family Roles Will Result in an Increase in Self-Esteem over Time

H3a: Self-perceived improvement in the performance of the parent role will lead to an increase in the parent's self-esteem.

H3b: Self-perceived improvement in the performance of the spouse role will lead to an increase in the spouse's self-esteem.

Identity theory is based on the assumption that individuals develop self-esteem through social interaction. By interacting with others, individuals are able to see themselves as others see them. The principle of reflected appraisal, or "looking glass" self (Cooley, 1968; Mead, 1956), suggests that individuals' self-concepts are based on other's evaluations of them. More recent research suggests that individuals' perceptions of others' appraisals, rather than the actual appraisal, is a more important determinant of self-esteem (Gecas & Burke, 1995).

The family is the first source of social interaction encountered by the individual and is thus the first social institution to shape the self-esteem of the individual. Many studies have shown that positive reflected appraisals by parents lead to high levels of self-esteem in children and adolescents (for reviews see Barber & Rollins, 1990; Gecas & Seff, 1990; Peterson & Rollins, 1987). As children age, their self-esteem is influenced by their interaction with other groups of individuals, such as their teachers, peers, fellow workers, and by newly developing family relationships.

The extent to which parents' reflected appraisals of their children continue to influence the self-esteem of children and adolescents once they acquire these new role relationships in adulthood has largely gone unexplored. One exception is the research by Roberts and Bengtson (1993, 1996). They found that, although parent-child relationships increasingly have less of an effect on children's psychological well-being as they assume the work, spouse, and parent roles, the influence of parents on the self-esteem of teenage children persists over several decades. We seek to extend this finding to the parent generations. From a life-course perspective, we propose that parents derive the same benefits from the reflected appraisals of their children as children derive from the reflected appraisals of their parents.

Parent-child affection is a positive reflected appraisal of a parent toward a child and of a child toward a parent. Similarly, marital affection is a positive reflected appraisal of a spouse toward his or her partner. Based on identity theory, positive reflected appraisals from adult children to middle-age or elderly parents as measured by the perception of mutual affection should yield high levels of self-esteem for the individual. Further, positive reflected appraisals from middle-age or elderly parents to adult children should also yield an increase in self-esteem.

Hypothesis 4: Self-Perceived Improvement in the Reflected Appraisals from Family Members Will Result in an Increase in Self-Esteem over Time

H4a: Self-perceived improvement in the reflected appraisals parents receive from their adult child will lead to an increase in the parent's self-esteem.

H4b: Self-perceived improvement in the reflected appraisals spouses receive from their partners will lead to an increase in the spouse's self-esteem.

H4c: Self-perceived improvement in the reflected appraisals adult children receive from their parent(s) will lead to an increase in the adult children's self-esteem.

METHODS

Sample

The present study is based on data from the USC Longitudinal Study of Generations (LSOG). The LSOG is a study of grandparents (G1), parents (G2), and children (G3) from over 300 three-generation families. The first wave of data collection began in 1971 (Time-1) with a review of a random selection of male subscribers of a southern California prepaid health maintenance organization. Male subscribers aged 55 or older who had a dependent family member covered under the plan and who also had at least one grandchild 16 or older were eligible for inclusion. Self-report questionnaires were mailed to the respondents, their spouse, and their descendants. This procedure was repeated in subsequent waves of data collection in 1985 (Time-2), 1988 (Time-3), 1991 (Time-4), 1994 (Time-5), and 1997 (Time-6). The response rates for each wave of data collection was approximately 70%; the longitudinal response rates are considerably lower (approximately 50%) largely as a result of attrition due to death of the G1s.

The analysis discussed in this chapter is based on longitudinal data from the 1971 (T1) and 1991 (T4) waves of data collection, since these were the only years that contained all the variables of interest. Table 2.1 presents the cross-sectional and longitudinal samples by generation for 1971 and 1991.

The stability and change in self-esteem from 1971 to 1991 for the grandparent, parent, and child generations were examined in relation to: (1) gain and/or loss of the family roles of parent, spouse, and child; (2) self-perceived improvements in the performance of two of these family roles: parent and spouse; and (3) self-perceived improvements in the reflected appraisals from family members. The current study sample includes 89 G1, 342 G2, and 339 G3 respondents who provided information on self-esteem and relevant family role variables in 1971 and 1991.

Measures

Self-Esteem

Self-esteem is measured with eight items selected from the Rosenberg Self-esteem Scale (Rosenberg, 1979) that were common to the first

TABLE 2.1   Cross-sectional and Longitudinal Samples (1971 and 1991)

	Cross-sectional Sample				Longitudinal Sample	
	Time-1 1971		Time-4 1991		Time-1 and Time-4 1971 and 1991	
	N	Mean Age	*N*	Mean Age	*N*	Mean Age
G1 (Grandparents)	516	67	137	83	89	82
G2 (Parents)	701	44	495	63	342	63
G3 (Young Adult Grandchildren)	827	20	697	39	339	39

and the fourth wave of the study. These included positive statements such as "I feel that I am a person of worth, at least on an equal basis as others," and negative ones such as "All in all, I am inclined to feel that I am a failure." Respondents were asked to rate their agreement with each statement from 1 (strongly disagree) to 4 (strongly agree). Items were recoded when necessary so that high scores indicate high self-esteem. Exploratory factor analysis of these eight items for the full sample, and by generation, supported a one-factor solution. The scale score was computed by averaging responses on all the completed items. The reliability (Cronbach's alpha) of the scale, based on the T1/T4 longitudinal sample is .81 for both 1971 and 1991.

Role Loss and Role Gain

In 1971 and 1991, respondents reported incumbency in each family role—adult child, spouse, parent. Preliminary analysis of the longitudinal sample shows that different generations have different patterns of role change between the two time points. Hence, each generation was categorized into subgroups according to the pattern of changes in their family roles. Of the G1s who were married with children in 1971, 46 lost their spouse role by 1991 (more than 95% due to widowhood). Another group of G1s ($n = 43$) maintained their spouse role from 1971 to 1991. No G1s in this longitudinal study sample lost the parent role over this period of time. Of the G2s who had all three family roles in 1971, 40 respondents lost their spouse role by 1991 (95% due to divorce), and 302 respondents maintained their spouse role from 1971 to 1991; 191 respondents lost their child role by 1991, due to the death of their parents, and 138 respondents maintained their child role since they had at least one parent still living. No G2s in this study sample lost their parent role over this period of time.

Among the G3s, three patterns were found for changes in the spouse role: 50 respondents were unmarried in 1971 and remained unmarried in 1991 (i.e., continued not to have the spouse role), 75 respondents were married at both times of measurement ("Maintained Spouse Role"), and 195 respondents were unmarried at T1 but married at T4 ("Gained the Spouse Role"). Two dummy variables were created (one indicating "Maintained Spouse Role," the other "Gained Spouse Role"), in order to distinguish these three groups. Another 19 G3s were married in 1971, but lost the spouse role by 1991. However, these G3s were not included in further analysis due to the small sample size. Similarly, three patterns were found for changes in the parent role of the G3s: 56 respondents were childless in 1971 and 1991 (i.e., continued not to have the parent role), 61 respondents were parents at both times ("Maintained Parent Role"), and 221 respondents were childless in 1971 but had become parents by 1991 ("Gained Parent Role"). Again, two dummy variables indicating "Maintained Parent Role" and "Gained Parent Role" were created.

Self-Perceived Quality of Family Role-Performance

In addition to reporting their incumbency in each family role in 1971 and 1991, respondents also rated their performance on two different family roles: spouse and parent. These were single-item measures of role performance including statements such as "Compared with most people I know, I am a good parent," and "Compared with most people I know, I am a good husband (or wife)." Respondents rated their agreement with these items on a 4-point scale (1 = strongly disagree, 4 = strongly agree).

Self-Perceived Quality of Reflected Appraisals

Parent-child affection (and child-parent affection) is considered a positive reflected appraisal from parent to child (or from child to parent). Each was assessed with the five-item Affectual Solidarity Scale (Mangen, Bengtson, & Landry, 1988) in 1971 and 1991. A scale score was computed as the mean of responses to five survey questions about communication, getting along, closeness, and understanding between respondents and their study-children and/or study-parents. Subjects answered these questions on a six-point scale (1 = not at all; 6 = very much/a great deal). A factor analysis of the Affectual Solidarity items supports a single-factor solution. The α reliability for solidarity for the study-child is .91 for 1971 and .92 for 1991, and the α for solidarity for the study-parents (averaging the items measuring solidarity for mother and for father whenever applicable) is .93 for 1971 and .92 for 1991.

The self-perceived reflected appraisals of spouses, or marital affection, was measured with a five-item, five-point (1 = hardly ever; 5 = almost always) scale (Gilford & Bengtson, 1979) in 1971 and 1991, including items such as "You laugh together," and "You have a good time together." Factor analysis of the five items supports a one-factor solution. The scale score was computed by averaging the completed items. Cronbach's α based on the current sample is .85 for 1971 and .87 for 1991.

Sociodemographic Characteristics

In 1971, measures were also included on respondents' background characteristics, such as age and education. Highest achieved educational level was measured on an 8-point scale (1 = grade school, 8 = postgraduate degrees). In 1991, respondents reported total household income for the past year (measured with 12 income intervals from 1 = less than $10,000 to 12 = $110,000 or more) and rated their own physical health on a 4-point scale (1 = excellent, 4 = poor). These background variables are included as covariates in the current study. The sample was predominantly White, thus, ethnicity is not included as a covariate. The characteristics of each generation are summarized in Table 2.2.

TABLE 2.2   Socio-demographic Characteristics of the Grandparent, Parent, and Child Generations in 1971 and 1991

	n	1971 Age	1971 Education	1991 Household Income	1991 Health
		Mean (*SD*)	Mean (*SD*)	Mean (*SD*)	Mean (*SD*)
G1 (Grandparents)	89	62.4 (4.8)	3.9 (1.5)	2.8 (1.8)	2.1 (0.8)
G2 (Parents)	342	43.7 (5.0)	4.9 (1.4)	5.8 (3.2)	1.9 (0.7)
G3 (Young Adult Grandchildren)	339	19.3 (2.7)	4.3 (1.1)	6.4 (3.0)	1.9 (.07)

RESULTS: THE INFLUENCE OF FAMILY ROLE CHANGES ON SELF-ESTEEM OVER 20 YEARS OF ADULTHOOD

Descriptive Results: Stability and Change in Self-Esteem over Time

Before we report tests of the major hypotheses, we examine some descriptive patterns in our data—whether self-esteem increases in our sample over time, and how much stability over time is shown by aggregate self-esteem scores. We also need to assess the assumption that heterogeneity exists among respondents in the amount of change they demonstrate in self-esteem over the 20-year period in order to examine factors influencing the direction and magnitude of change.

The mean level stability and correlational stability of self-esteem scores for each generation are presented in Table 2.3. Results suggest that the mean self-esteem scores increase significantly for each generation over the 20-year period, and that the magnitude of the increase is similar across generations. The bivariate correlations between 1971 and 1991 self-esteem are moderate and significant for all three generations. The correlations tend to be higher for the older generations than for G3s, indicating more intra-individual discontinuity in self-esteem for the youngest generation. The level of these coefficients suggests stability in most respondents' standing in terms of self-esteem scores from 1971 to 1991, though self-esteem may have in-

TABLE 2.3   Mean Levels of Self-Esteem, and Bivariate Correlations Between Self-Esteem Scores, in 1971 and 1991

	n	1971 Self-Esteem	1991 Self-Esteem	Correlation between Self-Esteem in 1971 and 1991	
	n	Mean (SD)	Mean (SD)	t	r
G1 (Grandparents)	89	3.31 (.53)	3.47 (.49)	2.65**	.44**
G2 (Parents)	342	3.40 (.51)	3.62 (.39)	8.54**	.41**
G3 (Young Adult Grandchildren)	339	3.20 (.54)	3.50 (.51)	8.85**	.31**

*$p < .05$
**$p < .01$

creased for some individuals and decreased for others. Taken as a whole, these findings justify analyses examining correlates of change in self-esteem over the 20-year period.

We use multiple regression in the following analyses to investigate the effects of change in family roles, family role performance, and the quality of reflected appraisals from family members on change in self-esteem between 1971 and 1991. We also examine the effects of role gains, role losses, changes in the performance of existing/ remaining roles, and changes in affection with others in the family. The predictors include 1971 self-esteem and background variables (respondents' age, education, household income, and self-rated health). By controlling for 1971 self-esteem, these regression models predict residualized change in self-esteem over 20 years.

By virtue of their different location along the course of life, not every generation has all measures available for analysis. For example, the G1s can not gain the parent role over the 20 year time period since they were an average age of 67 when the study began. Similarly, the G3s are unlikely to lose the child role as a result of the death of both parents, since their parents were an average age of 44 in 1971. Therefore, different patterns of role gains and role losses for the three generations allow for the test of different hypotheses. Further, even though it may have been possible for individuals within a generation to experience certain role changes, there was often an inadequate number to analyze. Table 2.4 indicates which generation was used to test each hypothesis.

For the G1s, we examine the effects of losing the spouse role (H1b), improvement in the performance of the parent role (H3a), and increases in the quality of the parent-child reflected appraisals

TABLE 2.4 Generations Used to Test Each Hypothesis

	Generation		
Hypotheses	G1 Grandparents	G2 Parents	G3 Children
H1: Loss of a family role will result in a reduction in self-esteem over time			
H1a Loss of child role		X	
H1b Loss of spouse role	X		
H2: Gain of a family role will result in an increase in self-esteem over time			
H2a Gain spouse role			X
H2b Gain parent role			X
H3: Self-perceived improvement in the performance of family roles will result in an increase in self-esteem over time			
H3a Parent role	X	X	
H3b Spouse role		X	
H4: Self-perceived improvement in the reflected appraisals from family members will result in an increase in self-esteem over time			
H4a Child to parent	X	X	
H4b Spouse to spouse		X	
H4c Parent to child			X

(H4a) on changes in self-esteem from 1971 to 1991. For the G2s, we assess the effects of losing the child role (H1a), improvement in the performance of the parent (H3a) and spouse (H3b) roles, and increases in parent-child (H4a) and marital (H4b) reflected appraisals. For the G3s, two multiple regressions are performed: one analyzing the effect of gaining the spouse role (H2a), the other analyzing the effect of gaining the parent role (H2b). In each of these equations, the effect of an increase in child-parent affection (H4c) is also examined. (Note that two separate equations are necessary in order to have enough G3 respondents in each grouping variable: those who gained or lost the spouse or parent roles.)

Grandparent Generation: Effects of Change in Spouse and Parent Roles on Self-Esteem

Table 2.5 reports the regression equation for G1s; the results indicate partial support for the hypotheses. Hypothesis 1b predicts that loss

TABLE 2.5   G1 Grandparent Generation ($N = 88$): Regression of Residualized Change in Self-Esteem on Changes in Roles, Role Performance, and Reflected Appraisals (1971–1991)

Predictors	β
Change in Role Variables (1971–1991)	
H1b: Lost Spouse Role	.19
H3a: Improvement in Performance of Parent Role	.35**
H4a: Increase in Quality of Parent-Child Reflected Appraisals	.07
Baseline Measures (1971)	
Self-Esteem	.27*
Performance of Parent Role	.36**
Quality of Parent-Child Reflected Appraisals	.13
Sociodemographic Characteristics (Controls)	
Age	−.22*
Health	−.25**
Household Income	.14
Education	−.02
R²	.41**

**p < .01
*p < .05

of the spouse role leads to a decrease in self-esteem across time. This hypothesis is not supported for the G1s: the equation shows that losing the spouse role does not appear to significantly affect change in G1's self-esteem. Hypothesis 3a is that a self-perceived improvement in the performance of the parent role results in an increase in self-esteem. This hypothesis is supported for the G1s: a self-perceived improvement in the performance of the parent role from 1971 to 1991 is associated with an increase in G1's self-esteem over this period of time. Hypothesis 4a suggests that a self-perceived increase in the quality of parent-child reflected appraisals leads to an increase in self-esteem from 1971 to 1991. This hypothesis is not supported for the G1s: an increase in parent-child affection is not associated with an increase in self-esteem over time.

Parent Generation: Effects of Change in Child, Spouse, and Parent Roles on Self-Esteem

Table 2.6 shows the regression equation for the G2s; the results indicate only partial support for the hypotheses. Since the number of analyzable G2s who lost the spouse role is less than 20, we drop these respondents from the analysis and examine only those G2 respondents who did have a spouse at both time periods. Hypothesis 1a predicts that the loss of the child role leads to a decrease in self-esteem over time. This is not supported for the G2s: losing the child role through the death of their parents does not affect G2's self-esteem. Hypothesis 3a predicts that improvement in the performance of the parent role leads to an increase in self-esteem. This is also not supported for this generation: a self-perceived improvement in the performance of the parent role is not associated with an increase in self-esteem. Hypothesis 3b, that improvement in the performance of the spouse role leads to an increase in self-esteem, is supported by data in Table 2.6. Hypothesis 4a and 4b suggest that self-perceived increases in the quality of parent-child and martial reflected apprais-als are associated with an increase in self-esteem. Both hypotheses are supported for G2s: increases in the quality of both of these role relationships—with adult children and with spouses—leads to an increase in self-esteem from 1971 to 1991.

TABLE 2.6   G2 Parent Generation ($N = 288$): Regression of Residualized Change in Self-Esteem on Changes in Roles, Role Performance, and Reflected Appraisals (1971–1991)

Predictors	β
Change in Role Variables (1971–1991)	
H1a: Lost Child Role	.03
H3a: Improvement in Performance of Parent Role	.12
H3b: Improvement in Performance of Spouse Role	.31**
H4a: Increase in Quality of Parent-Child Reflected Appraisals	.14**
H4b: Increase in Quality of Spousal Reflected Appraisals	.15**
Baseline Measures (1971)	
Self-Esteem	.29**
Performance of Parent Role	−.04
Performance of Spouse Role	.29**
Quality of Parent-Child Reflected Appraisals	.14*
Quality of Spousal Reflected Appraisals	.07
Sociodemographic Characteristics (Controls)	
Age	−.08
Health	−.18**
Household Income	.06
Education	.05
R^2	.38**

$^{**}p < .01$
$^{*}p < .05$

Grandchild Generation: Effects of Changes in Spouse, Parent, and Child Roles on Self-Esteem

Two multiple regression equations are estimated for the G3 sample and presented in Table 2.7, with one equation testing the effect of gaining/maintaining the spouse role, the other the parent role. Hypothesis 2a predicts that gaining the spouse role leads to an increase in self-esteem. Results of the first equation in Table 2.7 indicate that this hypothesis is supported for the G3s. It is important to note that there are no gender differences (analyses not shown): marriage significantly increases self-esteem relative to the "no spouse" group for both males and females. Hypothesis 2b suggests that gaining the parent role leads to an increase in G3's self-esteem.

TABLE 2.7　Grandchild Generation ($N = 323$): Regression of Residualized Change in Self-Esteem on Changes in Roles, Role Performance, and Reflected Appraisals (1971–1991)

Predictors	Maintained/ Gained Spouse Role β	Maintained/ Gained Parent Role β
Change in Role Variables (1971–1991)		
H2a: Maintained Spouse Role	.14	–
H2a: Gained Spouse	.24**	–
H2b: Maintained Parent Role	–	.07
H2b: Gained Parent Role	–	.09
H4c: Increase in Quality of Child-Parent Reflected Appraisals	.10	.14*
Baseline Measures (1971)		
Self-Esteem	.20**	.23**
Child-Parent Reflected Appraisals	.07	.07
Sociodemographic Characteristics (Controls)		
Age	.02	–.03
Health	–.28**	–.27**
Household Income	.10	.15**
Education	–.03	–.02
R^2	.20**	.23**

** $p < .01$
* $p < .05$

The second equation in Table 2.7 indicates this hypothesis is not supported for the G3s: gaining the parent role does not have a significant effect on the change in G3's self-esteem. Hypothesis 4c predicts that self-perceived increases in the quality of child-parent reflected appraisals is associated with an increase in self-esteem. This is supported, at least in the second equation, when change in parental status is included: an increase in affection for parents leads to a significant increase in G3's self-esteem.

Alternative Hypotheses

Since only one of the role change variables across all the generations is significant in predicting residualized change in self-esteem, an alternative hypothesis is that our lack of findings may be due to compensation among different family roles. That is, it is possible that those who lose an important family role may compensate for the loss by investing more in their remaining family roles, or that the salience of an existing family role might diminish when they gain a new family role. For instance, a G1 who loses his/her spouse may become closer to his/her children emotionally, and thereby perceive an increase in parent-child reflected appraisals. The positive effect of a better relationship with children may cancel the negative effect of loss of a spouse on one's self-esteem. A G3 who becomes a new parent may be so involved in parenting that the relationship with his/her parents and spouse may diminish in salience and therefore have less of an impact on self-esteem. To examine these possibilities, we test a series of interaction terms between role change variables and variables indicating self-perceived change in role performance or reflected appraisals from family members over the period (results not shown). None of the interaction terms are significant, providing little evidence for a compensatory mechanism between role domains.

DISCUSSION

The purpose of the study reported in this chapter was to examine the long-term effect of changes in family roles—the spouse role, the parent role, and the child role—on changes in the self-esteem of adult family members at different stages of the life cycle over a 20-year period. We examined gain and loss of family roles, self-perceived change in the performance of those roles, and self-perceived change in the quality of reflected appraisals from family members for young, middle, and older adults from the same families from 1971 to 1991. We argued that certain family effects on self-esteem that have been demonstrated in the literature for children and adolescents should also hold true for aging adults. We presented four hypotheses for analysis, and summarized the results in Table 2.8.

Before discussing each hypothesis in turn below, we first comment on the whether there was sufficient change in self-esteem across adult stages of life to warrant an examination of the correlates of change.

All three generations showed a significant increase in self-esteem from 1971 to 1991 in terms of descriptive patterns on aggregate

TABLE 2.8   Summary of Support for Each Hypothesis

	Generation		
Hypotheses	G1 Grandparents	G2 Parents	G3 Children
H1: Loss of a family role will result in a reduction in self-esteem over time			
H1a Loss of child role		not supported	
H1b Loss of spouse role	not supported		
H2: Gain of a family role will result in an increase in self-esteem over time			
H2a Gain spouse role			supported
H2b Gain parent role			supported
H3: Self-perceived improvement in the performance of family roles will result in an increase in self-esteem over time			
H3a Parent role	supported	supported	
H3b Spouse role		supported	
H4: Self-perceived improvement in the reflected appraisals from family members will result in an increase in self-esteem over time			
H4a Child to parent	supported	supported	
H4b Spouse to spouse		supported	
H4c Parent to child			supported

change in self-esteem over two decades of the study. Also, the two older generations revealed more correlational stability over the 20-year period than did the youngest generation; this suggests that self-esteem is more malleable from early adulthood to mid-life than it is from middle age to late old age—a conclusion similar to that drawn from Kogan's (1990) 6-year review of the studies examining stability and change in a variety of personality dispositions. Thus, the malleability of self-esteem justifies examination of the correlates of change in self-esteem across the life course, even for the oldest old.

Consequences of Family Role Losses

The first hypothesis was that family role loss would lead to a decrease in self-esteem across 20 years of time. This hypothesis was not supported by our longitudinal data. Neither the loss of the child role nor loss of the spouse role (or the corresponding loss of the parent-child or spouse-spouse role relationship) resulted in a decrease in self-esteem for the grandparent or parent generation. (Too few of those in the child generation experienced role loss to allow for an analysis of this question for these young adults.)

Umberson and Chen (1994) found that not all adult children who experienced the death of a parent showed a decline in physical or psychological functioning; in fact, some actually showed an improvement in functioning. Those who had a neutral or positive reaction to the loss of their child role (due to the death of a parent) were those who had a prior negative relationship with their parent. These findings suggest that in predicting change in self-esteem across the life course, it may be more important to consider the quality of the role relationship which was lost than the actual loss of role incumbency.

Consistent with this line of reasoning is Wheaton's (1990) work on the importance of taking role histories into account when making predictions about the outcomes of certain life events, such as the loss of roles. When role transitions are preceded by stressful conditions, the impact of these life events on psychological well-being is reduced. Structural role theorists need to acknowledge the importance of studying the social circumstances leading up to role transitions. Only then can researchers predict whether the role loss will be stressful or not and thereby effect a long-term reduction in self-esteem.

Thus, the study of role loss is incomplete without consideration of the literatures on stress, life events, and identity theory. Life events and stress often involve either role loss or role gains. However, life events do not always result in psychological distress. What matters is whether the role in question is salient to the individual's identity, i.e., ranks high in the hierarchical ranking of roles (Burke, 1991; Thoits, 1991). If the role loss or gain is of the type that threatens identity, only then does it result in stress. Although one possible mechanism for reducing stress is the devaluation of highly salient roles, recent research suggests that older adults do not use this mechanism (Krause, 1999). Thus, the merger of identity theory and stress and life events research provides a better explanation of the results than does structural role theory.

For example, stress research reveals that because these two losses (death of parent and spouse) are normative for each generation as they move into older years, they have less power to disrupt aspects of the self-concept than if they occurred in the younger generation. Further, stress research has shown that normative losses caused by death do not permanently alter psychological states when followed by an appropriate bereavement period (George, 1996). Thus, this loss in later life does not appear to permanently alter individuals' self-esteem. However, these null findings may not be attributable merely to the resilience of older bereaved individuals, but rather to the fact that they had several decades to adapt to their loss.

There was a 20-year interval between the two waves (1971 and 1991) of measurement. Therefore, it is unknown when the loss of roles occurred. For some, it may have been as long as 20 years ago; for others, the role loss may have occurred as recent as 20 days ago. Structural role theory does not address the importance of timing in role loss. Additional analyses using the LSOG data (not reported) employed a crude measure of "time elapsed since the loss occurred." There was no indication that the relationship between role loss and self-esteem was mediated by the amount of time elapsed since the role was lost, but more refined measurements may uncover such a relationship. However, our limited findings point to the need for structural role theorists to take into account the effects of timing.

Structural role theorists should also take into account other findings from the research on stress and life events: Although the negative impact of the death of a spouse has been found to affect both men and women, life events result in a negative effect on psychological well-being only when they are "unexpected or unscheduled" (Pearlin & Skaff, 1996). However, even expected or scheduled role losses can result in secondary stressors, which may have greater negative effect on psychological well-being than the primary stressor (Pearlin & Skaff, 1998). For example, Umberson, Wortman, and Kessler (1992) found that widowhood results in different secondary stressors for men and women: widowhood brings financial strain for women, whereas it brings household management problems for men. Further, the loss of the child role (due to the death of a parent) is associated with increased marital conflict (Umberson, 1995).

Consequences of Family Role Gains

The second hypothesis was that role gain would lead to a increase in self-esteem from 1971 to 1991. This hypothesis was supported for the child generation for gaining the spouse role, but not for gaining the parent role. It should be noted that these results do not obscure gender differences: no main effects for gender nor interactions with gender were found for the effect of either type of role gain (spouse or parent) on self-esteem across 20 years (analyses not shown).

Thus, members of both genders within the youngest generation appear to benefit from marriage, as structural role theory would predict. Gaining the spouse role is a normative event in this age group and may improve self-esteem by indicating successful negotiation of the marriage market. This finding is consistent with those of two other longitudinal studies, which have found support for the beneficial effects of marriage on young adults. Horwitz et al. (1996) found that both men and women who gain the spousal role demonstrate added psychological well-being as a result. Further, Elliott (1996) found that for women, marriage specifically raises self-esteem.

The lack of findings regarding the beneficial effect of gaining the parent role on self-esteem is consistent with two other longitudinal studies. Elliott (1996) found that gaining the mother role actually led to a decline in self-esteem over a 7-year period for young adult women. Oates (1997), on the other hand, merely found no relationship between assuming the parent role and self-esteem for either men or women.

The reason that gaining the parent role does not improve self-esteem may be linked to the age of the children when the measurement was taken. If by 1991, members of the child generation were parents to teenage children (in contrast to parents of younger children), it could be that the parent role provided them with less opportunities for positive self-evaluation due to possible conflict between the generations at this time. This issue should be addressed in future research.

As with role loss, research on role gain would also be better served by including concepts from the life events and stress literatures. Structural role theory can not explain why one type of role gain leads to an increase in self-esteem while another does not. Gaining the parent role may not increase self-esteem because it leads to secondary stressors, such as decreased marital satisfaction and increased work load. These secondary stressors may overpower any advantages of role gain.

Consequences of Change in Role Performance

The third hypothesis predicted that a self-perceived increase in role performance would lead to an increase in self-esteem across time. This hypothesis was supported for both the parent role and the spouse role.

Improved performance as a parent among the G1s, and improved performance as a spouse among the G2s, leads to having relatively better self-esteem over 20 years. This would be what would be predicted by identity theory. Thus, respondents who perceive that they are increasingly successful in meeting the demands of family roles benefit from the sense of competence that comes from developing better relationship skills. Thus, family roles are salient enough to individuals' identities that improved performance of these roles contributes a significant amount to their long-term self-esteem. These findings are consistent with a series of studies which found a positive relationship between performance as a parent or a spouse and self-esteem (Reitzes et al., 1994, 1995, 1996).

In contrast to structural role theory, identity theory highlights the importance of taking symbolic meanings into account. These findings reveal the usefulness of considering individuals' subjective self-evaluations in examining how self-perceptions of improved role performance in family roles correspond to long-term change in self-esteem.

Finally, these results also have practical implications for parent-child and spousal relationships. Poor performance of family roles early in the family life course does not translate into permanent reductions in self-esteem. If individuals improve their performance of family roles, their self-esteem will increase accordingly.

Consequences of Change in the Quality of Reflected Appraisals from Family Members

The fourth hypothesis stated that a self-perceived increase in the quality of reflected appraisals from family members would result in an increase in self-esteem across time. Our longitudinal data supported this hypothesis for the child role, the parent role, and the spouse role. Adult children who perceived an increase in the quality of the reflected appraisals from their parents over this same time period showed an increase in self-esteem. The finding for adult children is consistent with cross-sectional findings of a relationship between positive parental reflected appraisals (from either fathers or mothers) and high self-esteem among young adults (Amato, 1994).

Middle-age parents who perceived an increase in the quality of reflected appraisals from their adult children over 20 years also showed an increase in self-esteem. The finding that middle-aged parents also receive the benefits of positive reflected appraisals from their adult children supports the notion of reciprocal effects between parents and children. As Umberson (1992) has argued, parents and adult children alike are influenced by positive intergenerational relationships across the life course. Thus, the positive effect of having positive reflected appraisals from parents that has been demonstrated in the literature for children and adolescents (e.g., Clark & Barber, 1994; Felson & Zielinski, 1989; Robertson & Simons, 1989) extends to aging parents with their adult children.

Spouses who perceived an increase in the quality of their spouse's reflected appraisals for them from 1971 to 1991 also displayed an increase in self-esteem across time. This finding is consistent with the cross-sectional study by Lee and Shehan (1989) who found a positive relationship between marital quality (i.e., positive spousal reflected appraisal) and self-esteem for both older men and older women. They conclude that this is true because the marital relationship is seen as more voluntary than other kin relationships; therefore, it has a greater influence on self-esteem.

Identity theory adds to the explanation of how self-esteem changes across the life course beyond the explanation provided by structural role theory, because it takes into account the salience of roles to a person's sense of self. Family roles appear to be highly salient to individuals at every stage in the life cycle, since the relationship between self-perceived improvement in reflected appraisals from family members was associated with improvements in self-esteem across 20 years for grandparents, parents, and adult children.

Suggestions for Future Research

Why do role gains, and self-perceived improvements in the quality of both role performance and reflected appraisals from family members, influence self-esteem? The merger of identity theory with concepts from stress and life events research (Burke, 1991; Thoits, 1991) suggest that we can only answer these questions if we take into account individuals' perceptions of the meanings of roles and of the social context in which these roles are lost, gained, or enacted. Simply knowing what roles are lost or gained does not provide an adequate explanation of the results.

Why did role loss not lead to a decrease in self-esteem? The merger of identity theory with research on stress and life events suggest several possible reasons. First, older adults may have acquired other new roles that weren't measured, such as the grandparent role. The gain of other roles may have offset the role loss measured in this study. Second, if the individual lost the child role or the spouse role as a result of the death of their parent or spouse, the circumstances leading up to that death may have been more stressful than the death itself. If the death of their loved one was preceded by a long and drawn-out illness, the actual passing of the loved one may have been considered a relief. Or if the loss of a spouse was preceded by a tumultuous marital relationship, the divorce may have been less stressful than the marriage. Third, with the loss of certain family roles, the centrality of other family or nonfamily roles may have changed. Roles that may have been less central or peripheral, such as the sibling role, may become more salient, taking the place of the lost role. However, other analyses (not reported here) suggest that, while this may be true for family roles not measured in this study, it was not true for the family roles of adult child, spouse, or parent roles.

Gerontologists in particular have taken an interest in understanding how successful aging is mediated through self-esteem. Researchers are beginning to find that self-esteem may be an important factor in determining health behaviors, coping strategies, self-efficacy, and well-being in old age. The extent to which early, contemporaneous, and dynamic aspects of family roles influence self-esteem over the life-course and into later life should be followed in future research.

CONCLUSIONS

We began this chapter by asking: Do parents—and families—matter? Do they influence personality dispositions, such as self-esteem? In *The Nurture Assumption,* one of the most highly publicized books in recent decades about developmental psychology, Harris (1998) asserts that they do not. Instead, she argues, genetic factors and peer socialization experiences are far more predictive of personality outcomes than are family influences. This is a revolutionary hypothesis; never mind that the data she draws her conclusions from are secondhand, from behavioral geneticists' summary equations or from personal anecdotes of people she interviewed. It is a gripping hypothesis, suggesting that parents and families have relatively little influence on the developmental outcomes of children.

The research results presented in this chapter allow only limited commentary on Harris' hypothesis. We have no behavioral genetics data from our three-generation sample, nor any assessments on the peer influences on our respondents when they were children. Nevertheless, our longitudinal data do provide some important suggestions about the role of family influences on self-esteem for family members as adults and through 20 years of developmental aging. These are:

1. An increase in the affection of middle-aged parents for adolescent children over 20 years improves children's self-esteem as they make the transition from adolescence to young adulthood.

2. The influence of parental affection on the self-esteem of children does not end in early adulthood. An increase in the affection of elderly parents for middle-aged children over 20 years also improves middle-aged children's self-esteem as they make the transition from middle age to late life. Thus, parents influence their children's psychological well-being not only during early stages of adult life but *throughout the life course.*

3.   Finally, parents as well as children benefit from family relations. An increase in the affection of children over 20 years for
their middle-aged parents also results in an increase in middle-aged
parents' self-esteem as they make the transition from middle age to
late life.

ACKNOWLEDGMENTS

This research was supported by National Institute on Aging Grant
#RO1AG07977 to Vern L. Bengtson, Principal Investigator.

REFERENCES

Adelmann, P. K. (1994). Multiple roles and psychological well-being in a
    national sample of older adults. *Journal of Gerontology: Social Sciences,
    49,* S277–S285.
Amato, P. R. (1994). Father-child relations, mother-child relations, and
    offspring psychological well-being in early adulthood. *Journal of Marriage
    and the Family, 56,* 1031–1042.
Barber, B. K., & Rollins, B. C. (1990). *Parent-adolescent relationships.* Lanham,
    MD: University Press of America.
Bengtson, V. L. (in press). Beyond the nuclear family: The increasing
    importance of multigenerational relationships in American society.
    Journal of Marriage and the Family.
Bengtson, V. L., & Allen, K. R. (1993). The life course perspective applied
    to families over time. In P. G. Boss, W. J. Doherty, R. LaRossa, W. R.
    Schuman, & S. K. Steinmetz (Eds.), *Sourcebook of family theories and
    methods: A contextual approach* (pp. 469–498). New York: Plenum.
Bengtson, V. L., Reedy, M., & Gordon, C. (1985). Aging and self-concept:
    Personality processes and social contexts. In J. E. Birren & K. W. Schaie
    (Eds.), *Handbook of the psychology of aging* (2nd ed., pp. 544–593). New
    York: Van Nostrand Reinhold.
Buhler, C. (1935). The curve of life as studied in biographics. *Journal of
    Applied Psychology, 19,* 405–409.
Burke, P. J. (1991). Identity processes and social stress. *American Sociological
    Review, 56,* 836–849.
Clark, J., & Barber, B. L. (1994). Adolescents in postdivorce and always-
    married families: Self-esteem and perceptions of father's interest. *Jour-
    nal of Marriage and the Family, 56,* 608–614.

Cooley, C. H. (1968). The social self: On the meanings of 'I.' In C. Gordon & K. Gergen (Eds.), *The self in social interaction* (pp. 87–92). New York: Wiley.

Demo, D. H. (1992). The self-concept over time: Research issues and directions. *Annual Review of Sociology, 18,* 303–326.

Elliott, M. (1996). Impact of work, family, and welfare receipt on women's self-esteem in young adulthood. *Social Psychology Quarterly, 59,* 80–95.

Erikson, E. (1963). *Childhood and society.* New York: Norton.

Erikson, E. (1968). Generativity and ego integrity. In B. Neugarten (Ed.), *Middle age and aging* (pp. 75–87). Chicago: University of Chicago Press.

Erikson, E. (1982). *The life cycle completed.* New York: Norton.

Felson, R. B., & Zielinski, M. A. (1989). Children's self-esteem and parental support. *Journal of Marriage and the Family, 51,* 727–735.

Gecas, V., & Burke, P. J. (1995). Self and identity. In K. S. Cook, G. A. Fine, & J. S. House (Eds.), *Sociological perspectives on social psychology* (pp. 41–67). Boston: Allyn and Bacon.

Gecas, V., & Seff, M. A. (1990). Families and adolescents: 1980's decade review. *Journal of Marriage and the Family, 52,* 941–958.

George, L. K. (1990). Social structure, social processes, and social-psychological states. In R. Binstock & L. George (Eds.), *Handbook of aging and the social sciences* (3rd ed., pp. 186–204). San Diego, CA: Academic Press.

George, L. K. (1996). Social factors and illness. In R. H. Binstock & L. K. George (Eds.), *Handbook of aging and the social sciences* (4th ed., pp. 229–252). San Diego, CA: Academic Press.

Gilford, R., & Bengtson, V. L. (1979). Marital satisfaction in three generations: Positive and negative dimensions. *Journal of Marriage and the Family, 41,* 387–398.

Gove, W. R., Ortega, S. T., & Style, C. B. (1989). The maturational and role perspectives on aging and self through the adult years: An empirical evaluation. *American Journal of Sociology, 94,* 1117–11145.

Harris, J. R. (1998). *The nurture assumption: Why children turn out the way they do; Parents matter less than you think and peers matter more.* New York: Free Press.

Heiss, J. (1981). Social roles. In M. Rosenberg & R. H. Turner (Eds.), *Social psychology: Sociological perspectives* (pp. 94–129). New York: Basic Books.

Horwitz, A. V., White, H. R., & Howell-White, S. (1996). Becoming married and mental health: A longitudinal study of a cohort of young adults. *Journal of Marriage and the Family, 58,* 895–907.

Kogan, N. (1990). Personality and aging. In J. E. Birren & K. W. Schaie (Eds.), *Handbook of the psychology of aging* (3rd ed., pp. 330–346). San Diego, CA: Academic Press.

Krause, N. (1999). Stress and the devaluation of highly salient roles in late life. *Journal of Gerontology: Social Sciences, 54B,* S99–S108.

Lee, G. R., & Shehan, C. L. (1989). Social relations and the self-esteem of older persons. *Research on Aging, 11,* 427–442.

Mangen, D. J., Bengtson, V. L., & Landry, P. H., Jr. (Eds.) (1988). *The measurement of intergenerational relations.* Beverly Hills, CA: Sage.

McCrae, R. R., & Costa, P. T., Jr. (1988). Age, personality, and the spontaneous self-concept. *Journal of Gerontology: Social Sciences, 43,* S177–S185.

Mead, G. H. (1956). *Mind, self, and society.* Chicago: University of Chicago Press.

Merton, R. K. (1957). The role-set: Problems in sociological theory. *British Journal of Sociology, 8,* 106–120.

Nuttbrock, L., & Freudiger, P. (1991). Identity salience and motherhood: A test of Stryker's theory. *Social Psychology Quarterly, 54,* 146–157.

Oates, G. L. (1997). Self-esteem enhancement through fertility? Socioeconomic prospects, gender, and mutual influence. *American Sociological Review, 62,* 965–973.

Pearlin, L. I., & Skaff, M. M. (1996). Stress and the life course: A paradigmatic alliance. *The Gerontologist, 36,* 239–247.

Pearlin, L. I., & Skaff, M. M. (1998). Perspectives on the family and stress in late life. In J. Lomranz (Ed.), *Handbook of aging and mental health: An integrative approach* (pp. 323–340). New York: Plenum.

Peterson, G. W., & Rollins, B. C. (1987). Parent-child socialization. In M. B. Sussman & S. K. Steinmetz (Eds.), *Handbook of marriage and the family* (pp. 471–507). New York: Plenum.

Reitzes, D. C., & Mutran, E. J. (1994). Multiple roles and identities: Factors influencing self-esteem among middle-aged working men and women. *Social Psychology Quarterly, 57,* 313–325.

Reitzes, D. C., Mutran, E. J., & Fernandez, M. E. (1994). Middle-aged working men and women. *Research on Aging, 16,* 355–374.

Reitzes, D. C., Mutran, E. J., & Fernandez, M. E. (1996). Preretirement influences on postretirement self-esteem. *Journal of Gerontology: Social Sciences, 51B,* S242–S249.

Reitzes, D. C., Mutran, E. J., & Verrill, L. A. (1995). Activities and self-esteem. *Research on Aging, 17,* 260–277.

Roberts, R. E. L., & Bengtson, V. L. (1993). Relationships with parents, self-esteem, and psychological well-being in young adulthood. *Social Psychology Quarterly, 56,* 263–277.

Roberts, R. E. L., & Bengtson, V. L. (1996). Affective ties to parents in early adulthood and self-esteem across 20 years. *Social Psychology Quarterly, 59,* 96–106.

Robertson, J. F., & Simons, R. L. (1989). Family factors, self-esteem, and adolescent depression. *Journal of Marriage and the Family, 51*, 125–138.

Rosenberg, M. (1979). *Conceiving the self.* New York: Basic Books

Rosenberg, M., Schooler, C., Schoenbach, C., & Rosenberg, F. (1995). Global self-esteem and specific self-esteem: Different concepts, different outcomes. *American Sociological Review, 60*, 141–156.

Rosow, I. (1974). *Socialization to old age.* Berkeley, CA: University of California Press.

Rosow, I. (1985). Status and role change through the life cycle. In R. H. Binstock & E. Shanas (Eds.), *Handbook of aging and the social sciences* (2nd ed., pp. 62–93). New York: Van Nostrand-Reinhold.

Stryker, S. (1968). Identity salience and role performance: The relevance of symbolic interaction theory for family research. *Journal of Marriage and the Family, 30*, 558–564.

Stryker, S. (1980). *Symbolic interactionism: A social structural version.* Menlo Park, CA: Benjamin/Cummings.

Stryker, S., & Serpe, R. T. (1994). Identity salience and psychological centrality: Equivalent, overlapping, or complementary concepts? *Social Psychological Quarterly, 57*, 16–35.

Thoits, P. A. (1983). Multiple identities and psychological well-being: A reformulation and test of the social isolation hypothesis. *American Sociological Review, 48*, 174–178.

Thoits, P. A. (1986). Multiple identities: Examining gender and marital status differences in distress. *American Sociological Review, 51*, 259–272.

Thoits, P. A. (1991). On merging identity theory and stress research. *Social Psychology Quarterly, 54*, 101–112.

Umberson, D. (1992). Relationships between adult children and their parents: Psychological consequences for both generations. *Journal of Marriage and the Family, 54*, 664–674.

Umberson, D. (1995). Marriage as support or strain? Marital quality following the death of a parent. *Journal of Marriage and the Family, 57*, 709–723.

Umberson, D., & Chen, M. D. (1994). Effects of a parent's death on adult children: Relationship salience and reaction to loss. *American Sociological Review, 59*, 152–168.

Umberson, D., Wortman, C. B., & Kessler, R. C. (1992). Widowhood and depression: Explaining long-term gender differences in vulnerability. *Journal of Health and Social Behavior, 33*, 10–24.

Wells, L. E., & Marwell, G. (1986). *Self-esteem: Its conceptualization and measurement.* Beverly Hills, CA: Sage.

Wheaton, B. (1990). Life transitions, role histories, and mental health. *American Sociological Review, 55*, 209–223.

Wylie, R. (1979). *The self-concept.* Lincoln: University of Nebraska Press.

Commentary

Role Loss, Personal Loss, and Self-Esteem: Intergenerational Changes and Continuities

Leonard I. Pearlin and Yan Yu

There is no doubt that the study of the life course is both an important and a difficult undertaking. It is important because it can bring into view the changing range of social and experiential conditions that shape the lives of people: what we are, what we have been, and what we are likely to become. It is difficult to study because it is as complex as it is important. It requires an understanding of the historical, material, and social contexts in which people have lived their lives and of the personal dispositions and resources they possessed as they acted, reacted, and interacted within these contexts. Ideally, it also calls for studies that can track individuals over a considerable span of time in order to chart both the relevant changes in their environments and related changes in their personal and social lives. Obviously, we do not yet have the substantive prescience, the methodological sophistication, or the resources to achieve this ideal.

However, there is still much that can be learned from our less-than-perfect inquires into life-course continuities and changes. This has been demonstrated by a few key long-term studies that have catapulted us to a greater awareness and understanding of life-course issues. Among such studies are Elder's (1974) classic analysis of the economic depression of the '30s, its impact on access to opportunity structures, and its effects on the organization and direction of people's life course. The work of Bentgson and his colleagues (e.g., Bengtson & Roberts, 1991), with its focus on attachments across multiple generations of families, stands as another outstanding example. Although the journey into life-course research must be considered to be in its very early stages, we can emphasize that a great deal has already been learned.

PROGRESS AND SOME PROBLEMS OF LIFE-COURSE RESEARCH

One of the salient features of life-course research is the sustained intellectual commitment that is demanded by multi-wave investigations that extend over considerable spans of time. The visions and the devotion to ideas that are required to develop the research and to repeatedly collect and analyze data over several decades are impressive, indeed. Such research depends on the willingness, early in the investigators' careers, to set aside a substantial part of her/his own future life course for the tasks that lie ahead. For over two and one-half decades, Bengtson and his colleagues have epitomized this kind of intellectual commitment through their USC Longitudinal Study of Generations (LSOG).

Although there is much to admire about such efforts, we can also recognize that long-term inquiries into the life course are susceptible to certain kinds of risks. The assessment of change and continuity necessitates repeating the same questions around the same issues. To do otherwise, understandably, limits the comparisons that can be drawn as people move across the life course. However, aspects of the work that might have been quite innovative in earlier years may become outdated by later theoretical and methodological advances. Issues that were of great importance at an earlier intellectual era may fade in their significance, and the ways in which questions had previously been formulated and used to form measures may now be clumsy and inadequate. The dilemma between the need for repetition and the need to take advantage of intellectual progress is built into all long-term studies. The chapter by Giarrusso and her co-authors (chapter 2, this volume) attempt to confront this dilemma, it seems, by testing hypotheses derived from the more current concepts of role structure and role identity. The fit between the concepts, the derived hypotheses, and the data is not entirely congenial. Yet, whatever its limitation, this chapter and the study from which it is drawn focus on issues of fundamental importance to research into aging and the life course. This discussion seeks to identify and expand on some of these issues.

Any study of the life course must necessarily be selective in what it can observe; the swath of continuities and changes that can potentially emerge is so broad that an attempt to chart all of them would be neither wise nor realistic. We need to question, therefore, what kinds of choices represent good bets for illuminating the complex trajectories of people's lives. Ideally, these choices should be guided by theories that direct attention to environmental and experiential forces that enhance, support, or diminish people's physical and mental well-being. In important respects, the analysis by Giarrusso and her colleagues of the LSOG data satisfies this desideratum. First, its focus on the self and self-esteem makes eminently good sense; these are vitally important components of individuals' psychological dispositions that, although tending to be continuous and stable over time, can be sensitive to and fluctuate with changes in their external social, economic, and experiential circumstances. Additionally, self-esteem has repeatedly been shown to be associated with mental and physical health (Pearlin & Schooler, 1978; Rosenberg, 1965); it is difficult to imagine that one can entertain a global disparagement of one's self and still enjoy well-being.

A related feature of the LSOG investigation is its emphasis on family roles and their changes as powerful contexts for the formation and change of self-esteem. If, as there is reason to believe (Krause, 1999), the consequences of self-esteem for well-being vary with the centrality of the roles on which it is based, then family roles must be considered as paramount in their importance. The normative importance of the family to the emotions and thoughts of its members stems in part from the fact that the family typically has a monopoly on access to children over the first months and years of their lives. Beyond the intense bonds that are forged in early life, family roles and relationships are also the most enduring, lasting until people are separated by death. Indeed, because of their enduring presence in the biographies of people, the termination of family relations is likely to have a profound emotional impact. Deceased family members, long after their deaths, may continue to affect survivors and succeeding generations through the memories they leave and through the reenactment of past interactions.

In sum, if life-course research is to stake itself on the development and change of a single aspect of the persona, self-esteem is an excellent bet. And if the research is to focus on a single institutional domain whose conditions influence the development and change of self-esteem, to focus on the family is a similarly good bet. Having made these assertions, however, the identification of the conditions and the mechanisms by which the family may affect self-esteem remains challenging. The following discussions certainly do not address all of the many challenges. Instead, they are largely directed to an explication of the connections between role loss, personal loss, and self-esteem. It will be recognized that in large measure these connections underlie the analysis presented by Giarrusso and her colleagues.

ROLE LOSS AND PERSONAL LOSS

Consider first the matter of objective role loss, and the circumstances under which it is likely to be converted to personal loss. The loss of roles, of course, accelerates as one traverses the life course. If early adulthood is considered the period in which there is a relatively rapid acquisition of roles, late life can be viewed as one in which there is an increased pace of exits from established roles. Some of these exits are closely associated with the normative unfolding of family and occupational life cycles, what we have referred to as "scheduled transitions" (Pearlin, 1980). The last-born leaving home, retirement, and "timely" widowhood are examples of such transitions. It can be noted that in addition to their own transitions, people may be indirectly affected by the transitions of others with whom they are in interaction. These have been called non-egocentric transitional events (Aldwin, 1990). Salient among these are the deaths of friends and relatives and the concomitant constriction of social networks. In contrast to scheduled transitions are many potential unscheduled transitions, involving both one's self and members of one's network. Divorce, losing a job because of plant closing or downsizing, a disabling injury or illness, and accidental and "premature" death are among examples of unscheduled transitions involving role loss.

One more distinction needs to be made, this one entailing a difference between voluntary and involuntary role loss, a difference that overlaps with, but is not identical to, the distinction between scheduled and unscheduled role loss. Take as an example a situation in which there is a mandatory retirement at age 65. Two people may reach this scheduled retirement age together, but for one it is a long-awaited opportunity to be seized while for the other it is an involuntary, forced departure from a cherished job.

Each type of transition described above is likely to have a different personal impact. Thus, it is clear that unscheduled events have more negative effects than those that are scheduled and built into people's expectations as they contemplate the future (Pearlin, 1980). Similarly, and understandably, transitions that are voluntary are more benign in their effects than those that are involuntary. Finally, transitional events experienced by others to whom we are close tend to be less potent than those experienced directly by ourselves, particularly for men (Kessler & McLeod, 1984). The essential point to be drawn from these kinds of differences is that the transition out of a role doesn't necessarily result in a sense of loss. Put it in another way: *Role loss cannot be equated with personal loss.* Personal loss, the sense that a person has been separated from a quintessential part of her/himself, may certainly result from separation from role incumbency, but exiting a role does not always, or even frequently, have this consequence. Furthermore, transitions involving role exit do not necessarily affect self-esteem. Many exits will be experienced as irrelevant to the estimate of self-worth or, quite the reverse, might contribute to one's sense of recognized achievement.

What needs to be done, then, is to ask what kinds of role losses are likely to be converted into personal loss and, in turn, diminish self-esteem. We have already suggested part of the answer to this query: personal loss is most likely to be experienced when role loss is unscheduled, placing it outside individuals' normative expectations and leaving little or no opportunity for anticipatory preparation; involuntary, leaving individuals with the feeling that they are the unwilling objects of circumstances beyond the range of their control; and one's own role loss, which usually cuts more directly into people's lives than do the exits of significant others.

In each instance, circumstances either undermine what people want, and/or leave them unprepared for what they cannot control. The ungoverned separation from a role one desires, we submit, leaves one more vulnerable to feeling of personal loss. To the extent that former roles were linked to feelings of self-worth, their relinquishment leaves people susceptible to a lessened self-esteem. We further submit that the more important or salient the role to those who must yield them under these conditions, the greater will be the sense of personal loss and the threats to self-esteem. Although for most people, family roles are of paramount importance, much of the gain and loss of these roles are typically scheduled and without lasting negative effects. For this reason, it would be surprising if there were a relationship between the loss of most family roles and the loss of self-esteem.

The conditions outlined above are not the only or even most important circumstances determining whether or not people will experience personal loss as a result of transitional losses. The quality of the roles that are exited, as well as that of the new roles or statuses into which people may be entering also needs to be drawn into consideration. In looking back at exited roles, it is also useful to ask what personal loss entails: what is lost when there is personal loss.

THE DIMENSIONS OF PERSONAL LOSS

When we consider loss in its psychological sense, we usually assume that an important part of the self is being torn away as a result of an untoward event, often an event entailing the involuntary loss of an important role or person. The loss of a spouse through death, for example, may involve separation from one who had been become part of one's very self-identity. Something within ourselves dies with the loved one; to the extent that one's identity is based on a relationship that no longer exists, we have lost that part of our selves. By itself, a loss of this sort can leave one bereft; we grieve not only for the deceased person, but also for that part of ourselves that has been taken from us. But the loss of self and of identity are not necessarily the only losses triggered by the fact that one ceases being a wife or husband. Death and the cessation of the marital role might also leave the survivor with a host of attendant losses (Pearlin & Mullan, 1992). One's economic resources might be reduced, for example; or former friends and associates of the deceased person may withdraw, reducing the scope of one's social network and opportunities for leisure. A uniquely shared past also disappears with the loss of the role; there may be no one else with whom the survivor can reminisce about a particular vacation, the first weeks of a child's life, private jokes, or secret delights. Similarly, a shared future and the plans for it are necessarily lost to eternity.

Finally, the loss of a loved one can diminish a critically important sense of *mattering*, which we know leads to heightened depressive affect (Pearlin & LeBlanc, in press). Mattering is a two-edged construct: it is formed by the knowledge that one's own welfare is of concern to a significant other and also by one's knowledge that s/he is contributing to the well-being of a significant other. The relevance of mattering to self-esteem is immediately evident when we imagine the rather barren existence of being a person of no importance to another, or having no other whose well being makes a difference to us. Of course, the loss of mattering is usually not this stark or complete. We matter at different levels, and in different ways, to those with whom we have different social relations; as a result, the loss may be confined to the way in which we had mattered in the context of a particular role set.

The foregoing discussions, then, are intended to emphasize two points. First, it cannot be assumed that role loss necessarily produces personal loss, for this conversion is more likely to occur under some conditions than under others. Next, the scope and substance of personal loss and its consequences for self-esteem may vary widely. Moreover, it is useful to look at loss across time, for personal losses do not always remain as losses. We briefly consider this matter.

THE REVERSIBILITY AND COMPENSABILITY OF LOSS

We acknowledge, of course, that it is possible for the loss of a role to lead immediately to personal loss and, perhaps, to the depletion of self-esteem. Moreover, there are losses that may eternally remain losses; the loss of a uniquely shared past noted above represents such a loss. However, we have observed (Pearlin & Mullan, 1992) that there may be other losses that over time are restored, partially or wholly. Still using our example of the cessation of marriage, the loss of the deceased spouse can be considered to be an eternal, unalterable loss. Nevertheless, the former spouse can be, and frequently is, replaced by another, in effect recapturing the role and reversing at least some of the personal losses that had followed the earlier role loss. Thus, a prior loss of intimacy, of social and leisure life, of finances, and of a sense of mattering may all be reversed with the reacquisition of the role. With these reversals, a restoration of any reduced self-esteem might also be expected.

The timing of role losses and the stage of the life course at which they occur may regulate, to some extent, the responses to these losses. Specifically, we can speculate as to whether opportunities for the reversal of lost roles decrease as people traverse the life course. Whether it is the loss of marriage or of other losses, such as involuntary separation from a paid job, time and opportunity may both serve to limit the reversal of role loss among people in the upper regions of the age structure. The issue to be recognized here is that one's location in the life course may shape the meaning of the loss and, at the same time, constrain efforts to reverse the loss.

This is not the case with the second mechanism through which people seek to reduce the impact of loss: that involving what we think of as compensatory activities. These represent new activities and relationships in which individuals become engaged. The new activities and relationships are not necessarily identical to those that have been lost, but function to fill the gaps that have been left by those that have been lost. This kind of compensatory adjustment to loss, which has been identified as a marker of successful aging (Baltes & Baltes, 1990), is very evident among past caregivers to friends or relatives who have died (Aneshensel, Pearlin, Mullan, Zarit, & Whitlatch, 1995). Not uncommonly, such people become involved in voluntary community organizations that advocate for the needs of people who suffer the same diseases or impairments as the deceased individual for whom they had cared. Among many examples that can be drawn are the Alzheimer Association chapters and AIDS walks. Participation in these activities of these kinds of organizations may help to reframe the meaning of loss, to stimulate a sense of personal gain and enrichment, and to give a boost to self-esteem.

Embedded in the above discussion is an implication that needs to be underscored: *it cannot be assumed that personal loss invariably leads to a lowered self-esteem or to other negative outcomes.* First, in the course of reversing or compensating for loss, one may gain a level of self-esteem that exceeds earlier feelings of self-worth. To the extent that individuals are able to discover, test, and savor their previously unrecognized abilities, tastes, and desires, they may also enjoy corresponding increments to self-esteem. Such increments may be further advanced if the lost role was not benign and rewarding but, instead, was noxious and punishing. Consider, for example, the death of a spouse who was tyrannical and repressive. The loss of the spouse, however painful in the short run, may produce long-term benefits for the survivor. New relationships and activities can provide opportunities for the reappraisal of the self that is more positive than previously possible. Similar observations can be made with regard to roles of which one was an unwilling incumbent. The loss of a role that the individuals did not want, as in the case of a hated job or conflictful marriage, will have consequences far different from those found with the loss of prized and rewarding roles that were a part of positive self-identification.

On the other hand, just as we are cautioning that role loss does not necessarily result in personal loss, nor personal loss in the loss of self-esteem, we may raise a flag warning that role gain does not always lead to personal gain and the elevation of self-esteem. Becoming a grandparent may be an expansive and prideful experience, but if it involves a single mother who returns to her parental home with her newborn, the chances are excellent that grandparenthood will stimulate feelings other than personal gain and pride. More likely, the grandparents will castigate herself/himself for having failed their errant daughter. By itself, the knowledge that one has become an incumbent of a role does not inform us on what the person might be gaining, no more than knowledge of the yielding of a role informs us by itself on what may be lost.

SOCIAL STRUCTURE, ROLE LOSS, AND PERSONAL LOSS

If one wishes to study role transitions and their consequences, there is probably no richer a domain on which to focus attention than the multigenerational family. Not only does each generation experience its own gains and losses of roles, but the gains and losses of one generation might constitute the transitions of another. Thus, the firstborn of an adult child not only moves one immediately into parenthood but, at the same time, creates a grandparental and even great-grandparental roles in the preceding generations of the family. In cases where role transitions are not automatic, the role gains or losses of one generation may produce *personal* gains or losses in another. The child who has acquired a high-paying job after finishing college may leave the parent filled with a prideful sense of accomplishment, the same son who is later fired and deeply in debt can leave the parent feeling deflated and embarrassed. However, as we have repeatedly emphasized, the meanings and consequences of role transitions, whether our own or those of close family members, depends on many conditions. A major part of the research task is to identify those conditions. Among those that unequivocally must be taken into consideration are the status characteristics of people that signal their placement in surrounding social systems. We refer in particular to gender, economic class, and race and ethnicity.

To gauge their significance accurately, these kinds of characteristics cannot be regarded only as statistical controls, as in the Giarrusso analysis. They also need to be examined as independent conditions influencing the timing and consequences of transitions. Although there has been little study of the potential linkages of these statuses to role transitions, loss, and self-esteem, it is possible to speculate with confidence on the nature of some of these linkages. Take gender, for example. It is known that women and men are not at equal risk for certain role losses. A notable case in point is the great likelihood that women will survive their husbands. Since much of our social and economic life is organized around marriage and the family, furthermore, women are more likely than men to experience the personal losses, including the loss of economic resources, that may follow from the loss of the spouse. Economic limitations, especially when combined with advanced age, may serve to constrain opportunities to reverse or compensate for what has been lost. Piecing together our somewhat fragmented knowledge, we can posit that the death of a spouse will have more severe consequences for self-esteem among poor widows than among rich widowers. While we can offer only hypothetical snippets in the absence of systematic empirical inquiry, we can assert that any study of the connections between role losses and self-esteem must take into account variations that are likely to be associated with people's social and economic status characteristics.

CONCLUSIONS

In focusing on role loss and its consequences, this discussion has bypassed some of the issues addressed by Giarrusso and her colleagues. Among these issues is the substantial influence on self-esteem of the affection of family members for each other. As Rosenberg (1965) demonstrated decades ago, the interest and respect of parents is a vital influence on the self-esteem of their children. We would assume that the same qualities among generational peers would have similar effects. What are less clearly understood, although they are an inexorable accompaniment of movement across the life course, are the gains and losses of major institutional roles and their consequences. Indeed, it is the fact that role gains and losses are inherently and universally built into the aging process that helps to make our lack of knowledge about them even more striking. Among the substantive issues considered by Giarrusso, we regard role transitions and their consequences to be both most interesting and most challenging. The role losses that can be observed in the context of the multigenerational family were not found to affect self-esteem, nor, from our perspective, should it be expected that such effects would be observed. This is not to say that such losses are irrelevant to the self; it is, rather, to assert that potential consequences of role loss to the self will appear only under certain conditions. Among such conditions, we suggest, are the circumstances under which the loss occurred. In this regard, there is reason to believe that it is primarily the unanticipated, undesired, and involuntary transitions out of one's salient roles that are most likely to reach into self-conceptions and self-esteem. However, the loss of a role itself, regardless of the circumstances leading up to it, may not fully account for changes in the self. In addition, it is useful to consider proliferated losses that can result from role loss. Included among such *personal* losses may be the following: financial status, shared memories of the past and plans for the future, social network attachments, intimacy, and a sense of mattering. The scope and intensity of these kinds of ancillary loss are probably capable of regulating the effects of the initial role loss on the self.

The matter of loss, furthermore, cannot be fully understood if we confine our observations of its effects to a period immediately following the loss. By extending these observations, we are in a stronger position to detect recovery from loss, something that might come into view only after the lapse of considerable time. By tracking people across time following loss, it may be discovered that earlier effects of loss on self are no longer in evidence as a result of people's replacement of or compensation for role loss and its ancillary losses.

Finally, and emphatically, all of the conditions that impact on the self can and are likely to vary with people's positions in larger social systems. These need to be taken into account at every step of our inquiries.

ACKNOWLEDGMENTS

This paper was supported by Merit Award MH 42122 to Leonard I. Pearlin.

REFERENCES

Aldwin, C. M. (1990). The elders life stress inventory: Egocentric and non-egocentric stress. In M. A. Stevens, S. E. Hopfall, J. N. Crawther, & D. L. Tennenbaum (Eds.), *Stress and coping in later-life families* (pp. 49–69). New York: Hemisphere.

Aneshensel, C. S., Pearlin, L. I., Mullan, J. T., Zarit, S. H., & Whitlatch, C. J. (1995). *Profiles in caregiving: The unexpected career.* San Diego, CA: Academic Press.

Baltes, P. B., & Baltes, M. M. (1990). Psychological perspectives on successful aging: The model of selective optimization and compensation. In P. B. Baltes & M. M. Baltes (Eds.), *Successful aging: Perspectives for the social sciences* (pp. 1–34). Cambridge, England: Cambridge University Press.

Bengtson, V. L., & Roberts, R. E. L. (1991). Intergenerational solidarity in aging families: An example of formal theory construction. *Journal of Marriage and the Family, 53,* 856–870.

Elder, G. H., Jr. (1974). *Children of the great depression.* Chicago: University of Chicago Press.

Kessler, R. C., & McLeod, J. D. (1984). Sex differences in vulnerability to undesirable life events. *American Sociological Review, 49,* 620–631.

Krause, N. (1999). Stress and the devaluation of highly salient roles in late life. *Journal of Gerontology: Social Sciences, 54B*(2), S99–S108.

Pearlin, L. I. (1980). Life strains and psychological distress among adults. In N. J. Smelser & E. H. Erickson (Eds.), *Themes of work and love in adulthood* (pp 174–192). Cambridge, MA: Harvard University Press.

Pearlin, L. I., & Mullan, J. T. (1992). Loss and stress in aging. In M. L. Wykle, E. Kahana, & J. Kowal (Eds.), *Stress and health among the elderly* (pp. 117–132). New York: Springer Publishing Company.

Pearlin, L. I., & Schooler, C. (1978). The structure of coping. *Journal of Health and Social Behavior, 19,* 2–21.

Pearlin, L. I., & LeBlanc, A. J. (In press). Bereavement and the loss of mattering. In T. J. Owens, S. Stryker, & N. Goodman (Eds.), *Extending self-esteem theory and research: Sociological and psychological currents.* New York: Cambridge University Press.

Rosenberg, M. (1965). *Society and adolescent self-image.* Princeton, NJ: Princeton University Press.

Commentary

Family Selves

Sarah H. Matthews

My comments focus on conceptual issues raised in the chapter (this volume) by Giarrusso, Du Feng, Silverstein, and Bengtson, "Self in the Context of the Family," and in particular on their equating of the family self with roles. My approach is that of a qualitative researcher. An overly simple distinction between qualitative and survey research methods is that the latter focuses more on reliability while the former tends to pay more attention to validity. All research findings, of course, even when they are strictly phenomenological, are abstractions, images of a world that is there. Emphasis on validity focuses attention on how well images of families created by research findings match the reality of family life. I begin my comments inside the family to argue that the family self cannot be captured adequately by the concept of role. In keeping with the theme of the volume, I then argue briefly that the backdrop be acknowledged of social/historical arrangements that set the stage on which family members negotiate their selves and relationships.

THE FAMILY CONTEXT

One of Judith Harris' points (1995) is that inside the family and outside the family are two different contexts, each with its own sets of rules. As a result, how a child behaves within the family may be very different from how she or he behaves away from the family:

> Western societies demand very different behaviors in the home and outside the home; for example, displays of emotion that are acceptable in the home are unacceptable outside of it. Children in contemporary urbanized societies go back and forth between their privatized homes and the world outside the home—two environments that seldom overlap. They must learn what is expected of them in each environment. (Harris, 1995, pp. 462–463)

Following Harris' logic, self-esteem is not global, but context-specific. That is, a child may have high self-esteem at school and among age peers, but low self-esteem at home. Similarly, an adult may have high self-esteem on the job and think positively of him or herself in that role, and simultaneously have low self-esteem as a family member. As Peter Berger (1963) wrote in *Invitation to Sociology,* it is one thing when a man's boss tells him that he is worthless, but quite another when his wife tells him that he is.

To incorporate this variation, measures of self-esteem would need to be context-specific. This would argue against Rosenberg's conceptualization (1979) of the self-concept as the "totality of one's attitudes toward the self as an object" because self-esteem is assumed to vary from one context to another. When examining self in the context of the family, statements in Rosenberg's scale might be modified to read, for example, "All in all, I am inclined to feel that I am a failure as a family member," or "I feel that I am a person of worth, at least on an equal basis as others in my family." Whose opinion matters most will vary not only from individual to individual, but also from one culture and historical period to another. The absence of support for hypotheses tested in "Self in the Context of the Family" may stem from a measure of self-esteem that is global, rather than contextual.

Unlike self-esteem, "role performance" is not conceptualized in the chapter by Giarrusso, et al. (chapter 2, this volume) as global but, instead, is tied to specific roles. Respondents were asked to assess each role separately by rating themselves on such statements as, "Compared to most people I know I am a good parent." Significantly, the statements instruct respondents to compare themselves not with other family members, but with others who occupy the role. Again, following Harris' argument, if inside the family and outside the family are different contexts, then the standard against which someone judges his or her role performance as a family member would not be the behavior of strangers, acquaintances, or friends who occupy the same role, but the behavior of other family members. The same argument can be made for reflected appraisals: It is those members of that special group of people who share a history and a projected future and constitute a family whose appraisals are important.

An additional concern is that asking respondents to evaluate their performance role by role obscures the interdependence of these roles. Most adults are members of both a family of orientation and a family of procreation. Evaluation of performance in a particular family role occurs within this set of relationships. A man, for example, may see himself as a good husband, a poor son to his mother, a good son to his father, a poor brother to his sister, a good brother to his brother, a good father to his older son, and a poor father to his younger son. He may regard himself as a poor son to his mother because his energy goes into being a good husband, or he may be forced to choose which parent to support because they do not agree with one another. His performance in each relationship affects his assessment of his self in the family. The degree of complementarity among these roles, not the number occupied, affects assessments of the self, although fewer roles may reduce the likelihood of role conflict.

To illustrate these two points—that self is context-specific and that a family self is a set of specific, interdependent relationships that cannot be separated into independent roles without sacrificing validity—I cite a recent letter to Dear Abby. I treat it as a "case study" to serve as a reminder of the complexity of the self in family life that, as social scientists, we attempt to capture in the research findings we create.

Dear Abby: I need your advice. My mother wants to live with me. I'm 56. She's 78. My household now includes my husband, my unmarried daughter and her son, who is 6 years old.

My mother is in great condition. Her main problem is that she's a hypochondriac and is lonely. She would be miserable living with us, but I can't convince her. She wants to sell her condo, help us buy a bigger home and move in. I have countered that if she ever becomes ill and unable to take care of herself, we could buy a duplex. Abby, I cannot live with my mother and I don't want to live with her. She wants her own room in the same house, no duplex. I can't even describe the dread this is causing me.

I do not like her. If she were not my mother, I couldn't even be friends with her; I would avoid her. She's extremely self-centered, controlling, over-critical and rude, with an opinion on everything. She's been married and divorced many times, and she has no friends. She turns every conversation on any topic back to herself.

Mother knows that I do not want her to live with us, but she's pushing. She knows that I hate it when she drops in on me unannounced early in the morning but she does it anyway, saying, "I know this drives you crazy, but . . . "

If my daughter or I plan to meet Mother at a restaurant for a noon lunch, she shows up at the house at 10 a.m. to wait for us.

When Mother eats with us at home every week, she samples the food and makes comments like she's the food critic for the *New York Times*.

I could write pages about her annoying habits. What can I do, Abby? Please help me. *Stressed Daughter in Florida*

Dear Stressed Daughter: If you want my support, you have it. Do not allow yourself to be pushed into residency with your mother and don't feel guilty about it. Your mother may want to be a bigger part of your lives, but it could harm your marriage if you bow to her demands. Stand firm and enlist your husband to present a united front. (*Cleveland Plain Dealer*, Oct. 2, 1998. As seen in a Dear Abby column by Abigail Van Buren. ©1998 Universal Press Syndicate. Reprinted with permission. All rights reserved.)

The immediate concern of "Stressed Daughter" is that her role performance as a daughter is poor. Because she is providing a home for her unmarried daughter and grandchild, she may feel that her role performance as mother and grandmother is adequate, although she may blame herself for her daughter's failed marriage or out-of-wedlock birth. She makes only passing reference to her role as a wife, that is, to the husband whom Abby suggests is a key player. She also makes no mention of brothers or sisters. Given that her mother gave birth to her at the age of 22 and has been married numerous times, Stressed Daughter may have at least one half-sibling not mentioned in her account. Although she focuses on only one of her family roles, clearly her role performance as a daughter is contingent on her other family relationships.

This daughter's plight also illustrates the other dilemma encountered in assessing role performance: Self in the context of *which* family? Most people have two families—one into which they were born, and one that they create when they have children. In the first, they are children and siblings (unless they are only children). In the second, they are parents and tied through their children to their children's other parent (and her or his family, their in-laws). The challenge of "Stressed Daughter in Florida" is to find a way simultaneously to feel good about herself as a mother, a grandmother, and a wife, as well as a daughter. Note that there is no indication in her letter that her husband is her daughter's father.

This "case" also draws attention to another important issue that is lost when the concept of individual role is used. The tie between two role partners is not necessarily symmetrical. I am curious to hear the mother's side of the story. How does she justify her "role performance"? My guess is that the mother does not see herself as a "hypochondriac," or as unreasonably critical or demanding of her daughter. Improvement or deterioration in performance of a particular role over time depends very much on the role partner's performance. Nydegger's and Mittness' research (1996) on middle-aged fathers, for example, demonstrates the degree to which fathers' positive self-appraisals depend on whether their children have been "successfully" launched. Adults are not required to consult members of their childhood families when their relationships change. A daughter's decision to marry or to divorce, for example, is hers to make. Nevertheless, she and her parents must then negotiate what effect the change in her marital status will have on their relationship as role partners. An example that is less obvious is that when one child provides a particular service to a needy elderly parent, her or his sibling is precluded from doing so, a circumstance that may affect their respective feelings about their family selves (Matthews & Heidorn, 1998; Sprey, 1991).

Including a member of three generations in each family in the University of Southern California Longitudinal Study of Generations makes it possible to examine the degree to which role partners agree in their assessments of their relationship, and to explore what the causes and consequences of various levels of agreement might be. Rather than treating the respondents as if they were independent of one another, shifting to the dyad or triad as the unit of analysis might yield more "realistic" hypotheses; that is, ones that are more in line with the complexity of family life and relationships (see, for example, Keith, 1995; Silverstein & Bengtson, 1997).

An alternate approach is to use the family as the unit of analysis. This involves constructing typologies (Marshall, Matthews, & Rosenthal, 1993), a technique used well by Johnson (1988) to illuminate how family members responded to a divorce in the middle generation (see also Mangen & McChesney, 1988). Every family has its own culture. This does not mean that family members necessarily agree on what their culture is or should be. "Normative solidarity," the degree which family members agree on the appropriate levels of affectional, functional, and consensual solidarity (Mangen, Bengtson, & Landry, 1988), varies among families.

SOCIETAL IMPACTS ON FAMILY RELATIONSHIPS

In this section, two issues that focus on the societal context in which families operate are identified and briefly discussed. First, what are important aspects of a society that influence families, how their members feel about themselves and one another, and how they evaluate their own and other members' performance? Second, the data analyzed for the chapter written by Giarrusso et al. (chapter 2, this volume) were collected 20 years apart, in 1971 and 1991. Is the family the same institution at these two points? In focusing in these two issues, the intention is to raise rather than to answer questions.

Social Arrangements

Families by definition comprise at least two generations. Therefore, societal arrangements including social policies that differentially affect members of each generation have an impact on what members expect of one another. Mogey (1991, p. 52) argues that between generations "amity operates in families":

> Goods and services, money and love, flow from those who control these resources to those who have need of them. . . . This self-regulat-

ing behavior is continuous between members of different generations and remains an important and essential form of social behavior in all modern societies.

Economic and cultural resources are unlikely to be distributed equally among generations in a family. Formal and informal societal arrangements, not only the physical dependency of children and other family members, affect which generations "control resources" and which "need them."

The societal distribution of income, for example, is related to age and, therefore, affects intergenerational relationships. This was clear in the early 1970s when the balance of resources among generations in families in the United States was altered: The number of households that included old parents declined as a result of increases in Social Security and welfare or SSI benefits. As another example of how the economic distribution of resources affects intergenerational relationships, length of participation in the labor market and wages are positively correlated in American society by design, so that those who are young are likely to make less money than their seniors. As a consequence of this social arrangement, parents in their fifties and sixties often have more money than their children in their twenties, thirties, and forties. This probably accounts in part for the fact that "Stressed Daughter," like other parents her age, is sharing her home with her daughter and grandson.

The distribution of noneconomic or cultural resources also varies across generations. More difficult to recognize because they are less tangible, their content and distribution nevertheless are consequential. Currently in American society, for example, sons and daughters, brothers and sisters, husbands and wives, find it increasingly difficult to justify differential participation in family life based on gender. The rules that were taken-for-granted by older family members no longer apply without question to younger ones. Other cultural resources are more formal. The family is a group in which members' responsibilities to one another are specified in laws. But laws are not static. Those that once directed adult children to provide for their old parents, for example, are no longer on the books. As another example, the ease with which parents are able to abandon minor children has changed in the last decade. Not only do laws prohibit it, but DNA testing has made enforcing those laws possible.

Societal impacts on the aging self in the context of the family, then, can be seen in social arrangements that lead to a distribution of resources, both economic and cultural, among different generations and within generations in families. "Those who control resources" and "those who need them" (Mogey, 1991) are not simply the result of individual decisions but depend very much on "societal aspects."

Change in the Institution of the Family

Chapter 2, "Self in the Context of the Family," relies on data collected at 20-year intervals from members of three generations. The effects of historical change seem important to consider. Gillis (1997, p. 4) writes, "It comes as a considerable surprise to most people that our cherished family traditions are of relatively recent origins, few older than the mid-nineteenth century." We tend to think of the ideal family as unchanging when, in fact, the meaning and significance to self of family membership varies across time. Family itself may mean different things to different generations, particularly in times of rapid social change, because they are members of different age cohorts:

> The character of everyday family life is gradually changing: people used to be able to rely upon well-functioning rules and models, but now an ever greater number of decisions are having to be taken. More and more things must be negotiated, planned, personally brought about. And not least in importance is the way in which questions of resource distribution, of fairness between members of the family, have come to the fore. Which burdens should be allocated to whom? Who should bear which costs? Which claims have priority? Whose wishes have to wait? (Beck-Gernsheim, 1998, p. 59)

The answers to these questions may vary by age cohort and, therefore, by generation within families. A parent and a child may judge as adequate or better their respective role performance, but the criteria they use may be very different.

CONCLUSIONS

This chapter questions the wisdom of equating family self with roles. The concept of role has the unintended effect of focusing attention on individuals rather than on family relationships. One advantage of qualitative research is that it does not depend on statistics, that almost invariably lead to using the individual as the unit of analysis. Even when individuals are the focal point in qualitative research, it is possible—although not easy—to keep in mind that each family member is tied to specific others, and that evaluations of self and role performance are made in light of those relationships (Matthews, 1991). Rating role performance or evaluating the self in the context of the family, then, cannot be done role by role. Instead, the family self is a product of and is evaluated in relation to all other members of the family.

The institution of the family is often assumed to be a constant, but family ties are very much affected by the societal context, both with respect to the likely distribution of resources among generations and the actual meaning and expectations attached to particular ties within families. Using the same questions to collect data about the meaning of family membership from the same people at a 20-year interval implicitly asserts that expectations for family ties do not vary through time. Taking into account the broader societal context within which family members forge their ties has the potential to enhance interpretation of data about the self in the context of the family.

REFERENCES

Beck-Gernsheim, E. (1998). On the way to a post-familial family: From a community of need to elective affinities. *Theory Culture and Society, 15,* 53–70.

Berger, P. (1963). *Invitation to sociology.* Garden City, NY: Anchor.

Gillis, J. R. (1997). *A world of their own making: Myth, ritual and the quest for family values.* Cambridge, MA: Harvard University Press.

Harris, J. R. (1995). Where is the child's environment? A group socialization theory of development. *Psychological Review, 102,* 458–489.

Johnson, C. L. (1988). *Ex familia.* New Brunswick, NJ: Rutgers University Press.

Keith, C. (1995). Family caregiving systems: Models, resources, and values. *Journal of Marriage and the Family, 57,* 179–189.

Mangen, D. J., Bengtson, V. L., & Landry, P. H., Jr. (1988). *Measurement of intergenerational relations.* Newbury Park, CA: Sage.

Mangen, D. J., & McChesney, K. Y. (1988). Intergenerational cohesion: A comparison and linear and nonlinear analytical approaches. In D. J. Mangen, V. L. Bengtson, & P. H. Landry, Jr. (Eds.), *Measurement of intergenerational relations* (pp. 208–221). Newbury Park, CA: Sage.

Marshall, V. W., Matthews, S. H., & Rosenthal, C. J. (1993). The elusiveness of family life: A challenge for the sociology of aging. *Annual Review of Gerontology and Geriatrics, 13,* 39–72.

Matthews, S. H. (1991). The use of qualitative methods in research on older families. *Canadian Journal on Aging, 12,* 157–165.

Matthews, S. H., & Heidorn, J. (1998). Meeting filial responsibilities in brothers-only sibling groups. *Journal of Gerontology, 53B,* 278–288.

Mogey, J. (1991). Families: Intergenerational and generational connections—conceptual approaches to kinship and culture. In S. P. Pfeifer & M. B. Sussman (Eds.), *Families: Intergenerational and generational connections* (pp. 47–64). New York: Haworth.

Nydegger, C. N., & Mitteness, L. S. (1996). Midlife: The prime of fathers. In C. D. Ryff & M. M. Seltzer (Eds.), *The parental experience in midlife* (pp. 533–559). Chicago, IL: University of Chicago Press.

Rosenberg, M. (1979). *Conceiving the self.* New York: Basic Books.

Silverstein, M., & Bengtson, V. (1997). Intergenerational solidarity and the structure of adult child-parent relationships in American families. *American Journal of Sociology, 103,* 429–460.

Sprey, J. (1991). Studying adult children and their parents. In S. K. Pfeifer & M. B. Sussman, *Families: Intergenerational and generational connections* (pp. 221–235). New York: The Haworth Press.

CHAPTER 3

Work Status and the Construction of Work-Related Selves

Gerben J. Westerhof and Freya Dittmann-Kohli

Over the last century, institutionalized trajectories have evolved that regulate the course of one's life in chronologically ordered sequences of roles and life phases (Kohli, 1985). Work plays a central role in this institutionalization of the life course: The triad of education, work, and retirement is the central core around which it has taken place. On a societal level, the life course has become an institutional pattern that structures the social relations among persons in Western societies. On an individual level, society provides a standard biography, particularly for men: education, work, and retirement. Adults in our society define and interpret themselves and their lives generally in relation to this standard biography. Work plays an important role in one's subjective theory about aspects of self and life that may impede or facilitate the quest for a meaningful existence (Dittmann-Kohli, 1988, 1990, 1995). In short, work characterizes the structure of social relations among persons in our society, as well as the temporal structure of an individual's life.

OBJECTIVES OF OUR STUDY

In this chapter we combine a sociological perspective on the institutionalization of the life course and a psychological perspective on the construction of meaning of self and life. We explore how societal regulations relate to the patterning of the individual life course and its mental representations at the level of self-constructions. Our empirical study assesses individual biographical perspectives of self and life at the micro level and relates them to societal structures of the life course at the macro level. It utilizes a representative sample of the German population in the second half of life (40–85 years; the German Aging Survey; Dittmann-Kohli, Bode, & Westerhof, 1999; Kohli & Künemund, 1998). In this manner, the chapter presents a particular approach to the interdisciplinary study of societal structures and the aging self.

In the theoretical introduction we describe first in greater detail the structuralization of the life course around work during the second half of life. We discuss some recent historical changes and political debates. This provides the context of the societal regulations and the social representations characterizing the second half of life and work in contemporary Germany. Second, we discuss why it is important to study the dynamic relations between societal structures and aging individuals at the level of self-concepts. Third, we present our theoretical approach to mental representations of self and life. We introduce the concept of the "personal meaning system" and explain how it relates to other theoretical approaches to the study of self-concepts. Fourth, we discuss individual and social processes in the construction of the meaning of self and life. We include life span theories on adaptation to changing life circumstances and cognitive, discursive, and role theories on the self. We use them to understand how mental representations of self and life relate to the institutionalization of the life course.

WORK STATUS AND THE LIFE COURSE

During the second half of life, the major social and cultural constructions of one's societal position in relation to work are: being employed, unemployed, retired, or homemaking. We refer to these different constructions as "work status." In this section, we describe how they are related to the institutionalization of the life course.

In societal laws and regulations that are related to the institutionalization of the life course, the *retiree* is not expected, or is even prohibited, to work. In contrast to the United States, Germany has a mandatory age of retirement (65 years). Under certain conditions, it is possible to retire before 65. Retirement is basically a single transition: it is far less common than in the U.S. to return to a job (Kohli, 1994). Only 7.5% of persons who receive a pension and are younger than 70 years of age are employed; between age 70 and 85 this figure is only 2.9% (Künemund, 1998). Subsequent to the age of retirement, the "normal" situation is to be without a job, both in statistical terms and in terms of social and cultural norms.

Joblessness, by contrast, is not considered to be normal prior to retirement. Individuals without a job are legally defined as "unemployed." Although a Social Security net has been developed for the unemployed, they are expected or even forced to look for a job. Their work status is negatively defined as being *un*employed.

The traditional division of labor between the sexes allows women the position of "homemaker." Even before retirement, being a homemaker is a socially and culturally legitimate position without work for women. The homemakers' biography is a more or less accepted exception of the standard biography for women.

Recent Historical Changes in Societal Structures and Work Status

Recent historical processes have effected changes in the institutionalized life course. The unification process of the former Federal Republic of Germany (FRG) and German Democratic Republic (GDR) resulted in massive changes in the social and temporal structuralization of work. Work was a central part of the ideological regime in the socialist republic, and labor force participation rates were very high for both men and women (Kohli, 1994). After unification, unemployment rates rose in the Western part of Germany (the former FRG) to 10.1% and in the Eastern part (the former GDR) to 16.7% (Statistisches Bundesamt, 1997, p. 91). Unemployment struck women especially hard: they make up about two-thirds of the East

German unemployed (Kohli, 1994). Furthermore, preretirement regulations resulted in a massive exit of older workers. For example, labor force participation rates in the former GDR dropped for 55- to 59-year-old men from 93.7% in 1989 to 47.7% in 1992; for women, from 77.8% to 24.8% (Kohli, 1994). Before unification, it was not uncommon in Eastern Germany to work after retirement, but this is no longer the case today.

Some more gradual transformations of the institutional program of the life course took place in Western Germany. In particular, there is a clear tendency towards early retirement. Nowadays, less than one-third of the male population between 60 and 64 is part of the labor force (compared to about one half in the U.S.; Kohli, 1994). Furthermore, although after the reunification many East German women were excluded from the work force, more and more West German women take part in the work force, also at older ages (Clemens, 1996).

To summarize, recent historical changes in the societal structures of the life course have occurred along regional lines (West and East Germany), age, and gender.

Social Representations of Work and the Life Course

Historical changes in the social construction of the life course are not simply a function of a changing economy. For example, political ideologies also contribute to changes in the institution of the life course (Bijsterveld, 1995). We use the concept of "social representations" to refer to socially shared cognitions which emanate from macro-level systems (Doise, 1993; Moscovici, 1984). Social representations of regulations concerning work and the life course are produced in political discourse and gradually disseminated to the general public.

With regard to retirement, the main political questions are whether pensions are affordable in an aging society, at what age retirement should take place and whether retirement rules should become more flexible. However, there is no discussion of whether retirement should be totally abolished. German public opinion is much more favorable to mandatory retirement than is the American population (Hayes & Vandenheuvel, 1994). Hence, retirement is generally seen as an accepted and legitimate life course transition. By contrast, unemployment is seen as one of the main social problems for. Germany, not only by professional politicians but also by the general public (Noll, 1994). The negative definition of *un*employment is reproduced at the level of social representations. With regard to homemaking, the traditional division of labor between the sexes has been questioned in emancipatory discourse. Acceptance of the role of homemaker is greater in West than in East Germany: even after unification, East Germans are found to have more positive attitudes about the employment of women (Braun & Borg, 1997).

SOCIETAL STRUCTURES, AGING INDIVIDUALS, AND THE SELF

As mentioned above, the institutionalization of the life course provides a frame of reference for individual biographies. We expect that persons in the second half of life take into account the changing societal regulations of the life course in developing and structuring their sense of self. It is important to study the dynamics between societal structures and aging individuals at the level of self-concepts from two theoretical perspectives.

First, from a more sociological perspective, the existing social institutionalization of the life course can only be reproduced when persons recognize it as legitimate and use it in constructing views of themselves and their lives (cf. Bourdieu, 1990; Dannefer & Perlmutter, 1990). By connecting macro levels of societal structures and micro levels of self-systems, a better perspective of the reproduction of societal structures may be obtained than by studying attitudes or public opinion. For example, a majority of the population acknowledges that people should have the freedom to work after age 65. However, only few people have plans to do so, and still fewer actually continue to work (cf. Kohli & Künemund, 1997). Interdisciplinary studies of the relations between societal structures of the life course and individual structures of the self-system are scarce. The existing studies focus on self-esteem: they assess how work status affects self-esteem, or whether self-esteem is a resource in maintaining well-being after retirement or unemployment (Zapf, 1991).

This brings us to the second, psychological perspective. Recent psychological life span theories focus on the different strategies by which individuals contribute to their own successful aging (e.g., Baltes & Baltes, 1990; Brandtstädter & Greve, 1994; Schulz & Heckhausen, 1996). They describe these adaptive strategies mainly as individual processes. The societal structuralization of the life course and the accompanying social representations, however, provide opportunities and limitations to successful aging. Studies have documented that the well-being of retirees and homemakers is less affected by their non-work status than is the well-being of unemployed persons (Diener, 1984; Warr, 1998; Zapf, 1991). Such findings call for an investigation of the dynamics between societal structures and individual adaptation strategies. Although it has been recognized that adaptation processes often imply a reorganization of the self, structural differences or changes in self-systems have not often been studied empirically. To better understand the implications of such structural differences, our theoretical perspective on self-systems is presented below.

PERSONAL MEANING SYSTEMS

Studies on the aging self have mainly focused on personality (Bengtson, Reedy, & Gordon, 1985; Costa & McCrae, 1989; Kogan, 1990) and self-esteem (Bengtson et al., 1985; Demo, 1992). These studies have used a trait-based paradigm that makes it difficult to observe change as people grow older. Most studies have concluded that personality and self-esteem are indeed rather stable across age.

In our conceptualization of the self, we expand the study of the aging self in two ways. First, we examine the content of self-concepts beyond personality traits. Second, we study other ways of giving meaning to oneself besides the evaluations which are the focus in studies on self-esteem. Our broader concept of the self is referred to as "personal meaning system" (Dittmann-Kohli, 1988; 1995; Dittmann-Kohli & Westerhof, 2000).

Meaning Domains

The trait-based paradigm of personality has been criticized from a cognitive perspective. Although studies on personality traits generally use self-reports, they fail to examine the cognitive structures and processes which are the basis of such self-reports. From a cognitive perspective, the main question about self-concepts is how people mentally represent their own person (Kihlstrom & Hastie, 1997). The structures of cognitive self-representations and the processing of self-relevant information have been empirically studied (e.g., Fiske & Taylor, 1991; Kihlstrom & Hastie, 1997; Markus & Wurf, 1987).

Studies of the content of cognitive structures of the self have shown that mental representations of one's personality traits are just one specific aspect of self-concept content. Cross-cultural studies have documented that persons describe themselves more often in terms of personality traits in the United States than in Japan (e.g., Cousins, 1989). In a life-span study, we found that older adults use fewer references to personality traits than younger adults (Dittmann-Kohli, 1995).

Cognitive representations of the self are not restricted to character traits. James (1890/1983) observed already that self-concepts refer not only to the psychological "me," but also to what is considered "mine." Self-concepts may also include how a person relates to her body as well as to her social and material life contexts. Cognitive representations of the self may include a range of different contents, such as psychological and physical attributes, work and other activities, social relations, and material and societal conditions, as well as evaluations of one's personal life in general. We refer to psychological, physical, and contextual aspects that are relevant to the self as "meaning domains" in the personal meaning system (Dittmann-Kohli, 1995; Dittmann-Kohli & Westerhof, 2000). In this chapter, we focus on the meaning domain of work-related selves.

Recent studies of age-related differences in self-concept content suggest that work is less relevant in self-concepts of older than of younger adults (Borozdina & Molchanova, 1996; Byrd & Stacey, 1995; Cross & Markus, 1991; Dittmann-Kohli, 1995; Freund & Smith, 1997). We use the concept of "centrality" to describe such differences in the relevance of a specific meaning domain. Centrality refers to the intensity of psychological activity directed towards a motivational object such as one's personality, one's body, or one's work status. Studies have shown that more central cognitions are "chronically available," i.e., they are easily and automatically retrievable from long-term memory (Higgins, 1990). They are therefore more likely to be used in spontaneous self-descriptions (McClelland, 1980). More central cognitions are also more coherent, more resistant to change, and more strongly related to behavior than less central ones (Petty & Krosnick, 1995; Thomas, 1989; Westerhof, 1994). Furthermore, adaptations in the centrality of self-aspects appear to be relevant in maintaining well-being in response to changing life situations (Kling, Ryff, & Essex, 1997). Similar concepts that have been used in the study of self-concepts are commitment, importance, identity salience, ego involvement, or ego strength (Byrne, 1996; Fiske, 1980; Rosenberg, 1979; Stryker & Serpe, 1994; Thomas, 1989).

Evaluation and Other Psychological Modes

In cognitive studies of the self-concept, the evaluative dimension has been of primary importance. Studies of self-esteem typically ask for positive or negative evaluations of the self in general. Studies in which the self-concept is seen as a multifaceted construct focus on the evaluation of different self-aspects. They assess how evaluations of different facets are combined in making general judgments about the self (Byrne, 1996).

Although these studies clearly point to the importance of distinguishing an evaluative dimension in the personal meaning system, an individual may relate to a specific meaning domain in many more ways. Markus and Nurius (1986) distinguish between "real selves" and "possible selves." The content of "real" and "possible selves" is not restricted to purely psychological attributes. Cross and Markus (1991) reported "possible selves" that are congruent with the meaning domains of the personal meaning system. "Real selves" do not refer to an objective reality. They describe representations of one's past and present self and life that are central to a person. In other words, they refer to what is subjectively experienced as real. "Real selves" not only include evaluations of aspects of the self, but also more neutral psychological modes, such as perceptions and beliefs, and more affective modes, such as attraction or anger. By contrast to "real selves," "possible selves" refer to hypothetical self-states. Psychological modes that are related to "possible selves" include intentions, hopes, wishes, desires, fears, and expectations. "Possible selves" refer to the more dynamic aspects of the self.

To summarize, the personal meaning system can be described as a cognitive structure of the self, consisting of meaning domains that differ in centrality. The more specific meaning of a given domain is established via different psychological modes, such as evaluating, believing, feeling, intending, striving, or fearing.

INDIVIDUAL AND SOCIAL PROCESSES IN THE CONSTRUCTION OF MEANING

We assume that the cognitive schemata of the personal meaning system are used to interpret the stream of sensations and experiences in the course of one's life. Considering psychological assumptions about man as a seeker of meaning and fulfillment in life, the personal meaning system can be thought of as a subjective theory on the various aspects of self and life that may impede or facilitate the quest for meaning and fulfillment. The personal meaning system is also assumed to guide our daily life and our short- and long-term decisions. In line with recent life span theories (Ruth & Coleman, 1996), we see the aging individual as an active participant in his or her own development.

Individual Adaptation to Changing Life Contexts

An individual should adapt his/her personal meaning system in face of biological, psychological, social, or material changes. Otherwise, the personal meaning system would become inadequate for the search for meaning in life. We assume that the personal meaning system at a certain moment in time is the result of a dynamic process of reactive and proactive adaptation to one's life context.

Scholars have identified different strategies of adaptation of the aging self in studies on life span development. For example, Brandtstädter and Greve (1994) distinguish between accommodative and assimilative strategies. In accommodating strategies, persons adjust their self-concepts to fit a changed life context. In assimilative strategies, individuals maintain their self-concepts and try to change their life context in accordance with these. Cognitive theories on mental representations of the self describe cognitive strategies that are used to protect existing structures of the self in face of change. Examples of such strategies are selective attention, self-serving attribution biases, or downward social comparison (Dittmann-Kohli, 1990; Fiske & Taylor, 1991; Kihlstrom & Hastie, 1997; Markus & Wurf, 1987).

In this literature, it has often been pointed out that the impact of changing life contexts is not determined by their "objective" nature. Diener (1984) pointed out that the objective nature of one's life context is less strongly related to well-being than the way one perceives and evaluates oneself and one's life. For example, whereas retirement has long been described as a stressful life event, studies have shown that the impact of retirement on one's mental health depends much on the way one copes with this transition (Fiske, 1980). Consequently, adaptive and cognitive strategies are seen as individual response styles in the face of changing life contexts. They are located within the individual and mainly studied from a perspective of individual differences.

The Social Construction of the Self

Building on the theories of Cooley (1902/1983) and Mead (1934/1962), social constructivists argued that giving meaning to oneself is not just an individual process, but also implies social and cultural processes. Two processes are important in this respect: the construction of meaning in linguistic expressions, and self-identification through societal roles.

"Narrative" and "discursive" psychologists have addressed the question of how the self is given meaning in the course of making up "accounts" (Bruner, 1990; Polkinghorne, 1991; Ruth & Coleman, 1996; Shotter & Gergen, 1989). In their "accounts," people construct a particular version of themselves and the social world they are living in (Potter & Wetherell, 1987). People appropriate and reproduce the meaning structures that are inherent in existing social representations. Moreover, people actively relate themselves to these social representations. They do so through the use of so-called "verbal functors" (Nowakowska, 1973). Verbal functors express the psychological modus by which a person relates to the object mentioned in an "account." Nowakowska (1973) distinguishes "motivational" functors (e.g., intentions, desires, hopes, fears) and "epistemic" functors (e.g., descriptions, beliefs, evaluations). These represent the linguistic expression of "possible selves" and "real selves."

The social constructivist perspective has been criticized for its tendency towards relativism. One way to escape this relativism is to study "accounts" in relation to societal structures (Bourdieu, 1991; Westerhof & Voestermans, 1995). This brings us to the second kind of social processes: self-identification through social roles (McCall, 1987; Stryker, 1991; Thoits & Virshup, 1997). Social roles are derived from one's position in macro-level societal structures. Since social roles structure everyday experiences and interactions between persons, they also structure people's "accounts." Hence, social roles provide a basis for self-identification, for example, through dialogues about one's work status.

THE EMPIRICAL STUDY

Up to this point we have described our theoretical perspective on the macro-level societal structures of the life course and the micro-level individual structures of the personal meaning system. We described their juncture at individual and social processes in the construction of meaning. In our empirical study, we investigate the micro-level structures of the personal meaning system: the centrality of the meaning domain of work as well as specific ways of giving meaning to work in linguistic "accounts" of self and life. We study these aspects in relation to one's actual work status, which is an important indicator of the macro-level societal structure of the life course. We have already mentioned that one's region of residence (West or East Germany), age and gender are closely tied to historical changes in the institutionalized trajectory of the life course. We therefore study the centrality of work by region (West and East Germany), age and gender. The following sections describe the methodology and results of our representative study of 40- to 85-year-old Germans. In the concluding sections, we discuss the results of our study with respect to individual and social processes of meaning construction that represent the "interface" between the societal structures of the life course and the individual structures of the personal meaning system.

Rationale for Methodology

We used a representative sample of the German population in the second half of life (40–85 years) to study the meaning of work-related selves. A sentence completion instrument was used that identified cognitions about "real" and "possible selves": the SELE-instrument (an acronym of the German *SE*lbst and *LE*ben, i.e., self and life; Dittmann-Kohli & Westerhof, 1997). In the absence of appropriate standardized measures for studying the aging self (Byrne, 1996), a qualitative method has the advantage that researchers do not have to predetermine all possible relevant meanings of the self in old age. Since central cognitions are readily activated from long-term memory (Hannover, 1997; Higgins, 1990; Thomas, 1989), sentence completions are assumed to be an expression of such cognitions. Work-related selves will be highly relevant for respondents who spontaneously mention them in reaction to an open-ended instrument that does not explicitly ask for work-related selves.

Qualitative research is also the method of choice in studying meaning construction (Rubinstein, 1992; Westerhof, 1994). Analysis of narratives and texts has often been used in self-concept research from the perspective of social constructivism (Polkinghorne, 1991; Shotter & Gergen, 1989). However, this approach would not be possible via survey methodology. Standardization of sentence stems does make the SELE-instrument suitable for the study of self-related cognitions in large-scale survey research. At the same time, the openness of the sentence completion method enables us to sample those self-related cognitions that respondents consider as most relevant in describing themselves.

Methods

Sample

In the German Aging Survey 4,838 independently living persons between 40 and 85 years were interviewed. The sample consisted of randomly chosen individuals from the population registers of 290 cities in the Federal Republic of Germany. It was stratified by age group (40–54; 55–69; 70–85 years), sex, and residence in the former FRG/GDR. The three age groups were chosen in relation to the transition of retirement. Taking into account this disproportionate sample design, a corresponding weighting procedure was used in the analyses to obtain population estimates. The response rate was 50.3% (Smid, Hess, & Gilberg, 1997). It varied according to age group (40–54y.: 62%; 55–69y.: 56%; 70–85y.: 40%), gender (male: 54%; female: 47%) and region of residence (East: 56%; West: 48%). Besides general refusals, health impairments and illnesses were the major reasons for not participating in the study, in particular, for the older groups. The sentence completions on the SELE-Instrument were coded and analyzed for a subsample of 2,934 respondents.

Procedure

The interview consisted of three parts (Dittmann-Kohli et al., 1997). First, the SELE-sentence completion instrument was presented to the respondents. A face-to-face interview followed which contained questions about living conditions and their subjective evaluation. A paper-and-pencil questionnaire with psychological scales and attitude questions was left behind and collected later by the interviewer (response rate = 83%).

SELE-instrument

The SELE-instrument consists of 28 sentence stems that probe descriptions of real and possible selves (Dittmann-Kohli & Westerhof, 1997). Sentence stems concerning real selves contain characteristics and observations about the self, aging and one's life, for example, abilities, weaknesses, feelings, evaluations, and beliefs. Furthermore, sentence stems ask for descriptions of possible selves, like plans, goals, desires, future expectations, fears, and anxieties. Subjects were asked to finish the sentence stems so as to describe what they considered to be true and important about themselves.

Response Coding

The sentence completions were coded by means of the hierarchical coding scheme which is visualized in Table 3.1. On the first level, the responses were coded on the basis of the meaning domain to which they referred. This could be either work or one of a number of other meaning domains (e.g., psychological self, physical self, social self). On the second level, the combination of sentence stem and sentence completion provided the information about the context in which a person referred to work, e.g., positive or negative

TABLE 3.1 Coding Scheme for SELE-data

1st Level	2nd Level	3rd Level
Work-related selves	Real self positive: present work	Positive evaluations of own achievements and competencies in paid job or other activities defined as work, work as an important value
	Real self positive: no work	Positive evaluations of not working and retirement
	Real self positive: past work	Positive retrospections on own achievements and long work life
	Real self negative: present work	Negative evaluations of lack of achievements and competencies in paid job or other activities defined as work; negative evaluations of uncertain job, work demands, working hours
	Real self negative: no work	Negative evaluations of being without work and of difficulties in finding a job
	Real self negative: past work	Negative retrospections of occupational choices, not working, having worked too much
	Possible self: improvement	Desires and plans for finding a better job or for working less
	Possible self: having a job	Desires and plans for retaining one's job, for finding a (part-time) job; fears of unemployment and of remaining unemployed
	Possible self: retirement	Desires and plans for retirement
Psychological self Physical self Social self Etc.		

Note: Ramifications exist for all meaning domains, such as those shown for work-related selves.

evaluations of past or present work. On the third level of coding, more specific meanings of work were distinguished. These categorize the specific aspects of work that respondents mentioned (e.g., their own achievements, external work conditions). The coding of the answers proved to be reliable (interrater agreement: kappa = .83; see Dittmann-Kohli, Bode, & Westerhof, 1999, for details).

Construction of Variables

Using the first level of coding, a measure of the centrality of work-related selves in the personal meaning system was created for each person: an individual received a score of "1" when he/she mentioned work in at least one of the 28 sentence completions, and a score of "0" when he/she did not mention work at all.

On the basis of the second level of coding, two variables were created: one for real work-related selves and one for possible work-related selves. If a person made no reference at all to real work-related selves in the 28 sentence completions, he/she received the score "real self: not mentioned." If a person referred to a particular real work-related self in at least one of the 28 responses, we assigned a score indicating that particular work-related self ("real self positive: present work," "real self positive: no work," "real self positive: past work," "real self negative: present work," "real self negative: no work," "real self negative: past work"). Some persons referred to more than one of these real work-related selves in their 28 responses: they received the value "real self: more than one category." In a similar way, each person received a score to indicate to which "possible work-related selves" they referred: either the score "possible self: not mentioned," "possible self: improvement," "possible self: having a job," "possible self: retirement" or "possible self: more than one category."

The third level of coding is used to provide a qualitative description of the more specific meaning content that is found to prevail in the groups with different work status.

Based on a question which asked for one's legal work status, four groups were distinguished: employed (more than 30hrs/week; $N = 1168$), unemployed ($N = 123$), homemaker ($N = 371$), and retiree ($N = 793$). Some smaller groups of persons with another work status, like part-time workers, disability pensioners, persons on parental leave, or employed retirees were omitted from the analyses.

Results

Work-Related Selves by Work Status

In order to analyze differences in the centrality of work-related selves, a dichotomous variable was created that indicated whether a respon-

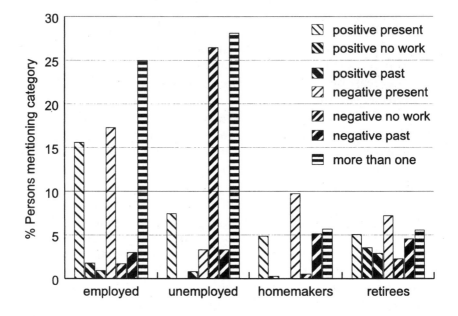

FIGURE 3.1 **Real work-related selves according to work status.**

dent did or did not refer to work in any of the 28 sentence completions. The proportion of persons for whom work was a central concern is lower for retirees (36.8%) and homemakers (41.5%) than for employed persons (83.0%) and unemployed persons (89.4%; $X^2_{(3)} = 561.2$; $p < .001$).

Two variables were created that capture differences in "real" and "possible" work-related selves at the second level of coding. Both variables show large differences according to work status. Figure 3.1 presents the differences in real work-related selves ($X^2_{(21)} = 595,1$; $p < .001$) and Figure 3.2 shows the differences in possible work-related selves ($X^2_{(12)} = 702,3$; $p < .001$). In the following, we describe for each group the scores for real and possible work-related selves that are most often found in comparison to the other groups. For each group we also provide a qualitative description of the sentence completions at the third level of coding. Examples are presented in

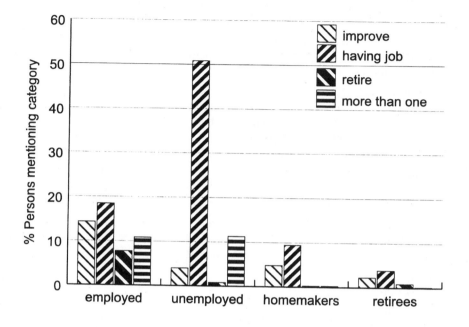

FIGURE 3.2 Possible work-related selves according to work status.

Tables 3.2 to 3.5 and are referred to by numbers in parentheses in the text.

Employed Persons. Most employed persons mention one or more work-related selves. Those who mentioned real work-related selves referred most often to positive or negative aspects of their present work situation. About one quarter of the employed mentioned more than one category. Positive meaning was derived mainly from own competencies and achievements (see Table 3.2; examples 1, 2). Work was also described as an important value (3). Although some employed persons criticized themselves (4), most negative meanings of work were attributed to work conditions and especially to long working hours (5–7). Almost all persons who mentioned more than one category included both a positive and a negative evaluation of present work in their self-descriptions.

TABLE 3.2 Examples of Sentence Completions, Employed

Real self: Present work, positive
(1) I am quite good at . . . working.
(2) I am proud that . . . I am successful in my profession.
(3) Most important for me is . . . work.

Real self: Present work, negative
(4) My weaknesses are . . . underachievement at work.
(5) What's been bothering me recently . . . the insecurity of my job.
(6) I often feel . . . burdened by work.
(7) What's been bothering me recently . . . the great deal of work.

Possible self: Improvement
(8) I plan to . . . change my profession.
(9) Later, when I'm older . . . I would like to reduce my working hours.

Possible self: Having a job
(10) In the next few years . . . I hope to maintain my job.
(11) I am afraid that I . . . might become unemployed.

Possible self: Retirement
(12) I would like to . . . retire.
(13) I plan to . . . work until 63.

TABLE 3.3 Examples of Sentence Completions, Unemployed

Real self: No work, negative
(1) It is difficult for me . . . to be jobless.
(2) It is difficult for me . . . to find a job.

Real self: Present work, positive
(3) Most important for me is . . . to get a job.
(4) I am quite good at . . . working.

Possible self: Having a job
(5) I would like to . . . work again.
(6) I intend to . . . find work.
(7) I am afraid that I . . . will not get work at 50.

TABLE 3.4   Examples of Sentence Completions, Homemakers

Real self: Present work, positive
(1) Most important for me is . . . a secure job.
(2) I am proud that . . . I am still able to do my work.
(3) I feel really good . . . when I work and no one disturbs me.

Real self: Present work, negative
(4) It is difficult for me . . . to do physical work (at present).
(5) What's been bothering me recently is . . . a lot of work.

Real self: Past work, negative
(6) When I look at my past life, I regret that . . . I did not succeed in holding an interesting job outside of the home.

Possible self: Having a job
(7) In the next few years . . . I will try to enter professional life.
(8) I would like to . . . take up a part-time job.

TABLE 3.5   Examples of Sentence Completions, Retirees

Real self: Present work, positive
(1) I am quite good at . . . still arranging my work.

Real self: Present work, negative
(2) My weaknesses are . . . I can't do heavy jobs anymore.

Real self: No work, positive
(3) What I like about getting older . . . that I don't have to work anymore.
(4) I am proud that . . . I am a retired person.

Real self: No work, negative
(5) It is difficult for me . . . that I'm not allowed to work anymore.

Real self: Past work, positive
(6) I am proud that . . . I was successful professionally.

Real self: Past work, negative
(7) When I look at my past life, I regret that . . . I did not become what I wanted to professionally.
(8) When I think about myself . . . I have worked too much in my life.

Possible self: Having a job
(9) I would like to . . . still be in my professional life.

Among the possible selves, the employed expressed concerns for improvement, having a job, and retirement. Some employed mentioned more than one category. In accordance with the negative meanings of one's present work, employed persons wanted to improve their work conditions (8, 9) or were concerned about retaining their job (10, 11). However, possible selves about retirement showed that some persons also wanted to give up their job (12, 13). Among persons who mentioned more than one possible work-related self, a concern for having a job was most often combined with a concern for improvement.

For almost all employed, work is a central concern. Work can provide positive and negative meanings. Describing oneself in positive terms and one's work conditions in negative terms suggests the use of a self-serving attribution bias in construing work-related selves. Furthermore, it can be seen that some employed persons appropriate the existing negative social regulations and representations of unemployment. By contrast, and in agreement with the social regulations and representations of retirement, some employed construe retirement as a positive transition in their "accounts" of self and life.

Unemployed Persons.   Work was a central concern for almost all unemployed. The unemployed typically expressed negative evaluations of not working (Figure 3.1). About one in four persons referred to more than one category of real selves. The unemployed often described problems with their unemployment (see Table 3.3; examples 1, 2). Furthermore, they mentioned work as a value (3) and describe their own potentials in terms of working (4). Most unemployed who mentioned more than one category combined a negative evaluation of not working with a positive evaluation of work at present.

The possible selves of the unemployed are clearly dominated by concerns for having a job in the future: wishes and plans for becoming employed again (5–7) are mentioned by about half of the unemployed.

Only for a few of the unemployed, work is not a central concern. It seems that these persons have adjusted their self-concepts to fit their actual situation. Brandtstädter and Greve (1994) would consider this an "accommodative strategy." For those persons who do mention work in their "accounts" of self and life, it becomes clear that they experience a discrepancy between their current situation and their aspirations. The meaning they attribute to their situation is overwhelmingly negative. Most unemployed maintain their work-related self-concepts and want to change their situation accordingly. This response pattern suggests an "assimilative strategy" (Brandt-städter & Greve, 1994). It is in line with the social representations and regulations with regard to unemployment.

Homemakers. Homemakers did not usually mention work, as we have seen in the analysis of centrality. Whenever they did so, they usually mentioned only one category. The categories of real selves that were sometimes found for this group refer to positive and negative evaluations of present work or to negative evaluations of past work. A few homemakers mentioned work as a value (see Table 3.4; example 1). Some homemakers defined work broadly to include non-paid work, such as homemaking or family care. This involved positive meanings, such as being proud (2) or having specific preferences (3), as well as negative ones, e.g., physically demanding work (4) or too much work to do (5). Negative retrospections concern mostly the choice not to work besides raising a family (6).

Whenever work-related possible selves are mentioned, having a job was the main concern for about 10% of the homemakers. Responses in this category referred to plans to reenter employment (7). Unlike the unemployed, homemakers commonly preferred a part-time job (8).

For a large part of the homemakers, work is not a central concern: they appear to have "accommodated" to their situation as a homemaker. For those who did mention work, it may have positive or negative meanings. Unlike the unemployed, only a few homemakers expressed the desire to work again, and thus gave proof of the use of "assimilative" strategies. By expanding the definition of work, homemakers are able to define themselves as "working," although they do not have a paid job. Some homemakers retrospectively construct the meaning of work in terms of the work trajectories that they did not follow. In general, homemakers were especially concerned about the balance between broadly defined work and paid, part-time employment. The pattern of their answers suggests that they make use of social regulations and representations regarding their position as homemakers. However, some effects of emancipatory social representations are also found at the level of self-concepts.

Retirees. Retirees did not customarily mention work in their self-descriptions. Whenever they did so, they mentioned most often only one single aspect. The pattern of categories about real selves varied widely among the retirees, whereas possible selves were almost never mentioned. Like homemakers, some retirees included positive and negative meanings of other than paid activities as work (see Table 3.5; examples 1, 2). Besides negative evaluations of their situation without work (5), a few positive evaluations were found as well (3, 4). Some positive (6) as well as negative (7, 8) retrospections on their work life were found.

Most of the retirees do not mention work as a central concern: they appear to have "accommodated" to their situation. Since retirement is a normally anticipated event, the present situation might confirm the expectations, or even desires, which the retirees had while they were still working (Fiske, 1980). This would explain why work has lost its salience in their "account." This line of reasoning also holds true for the few persons who attributed a positive meaning to being without a job. These retirees express a pleasant sense of relief that they were able to give up their job (Fiske, 1980). Almost no retirees have a desire to go back to work and use an assimilative strategy to cope with their situation. Like some homemakers, a few retirees use a broader definition of work, and are thus able to continue to see themselves as "working." Through positive and negative retrospections on their past work trajectories, some retirees also create a kind of continuity of their work-related selves. From this pattern, it becomes clear that work is not of central concern for most retirees. Whenever work is a central concern, a wide variety of meanings does exist. Although some of the retirees are negative about their situation, they construe their "accounts" of themselves and their lives by and large in accordance with societal regulations and social representations of retirement.

Centrality of Work by Age, Region, and Gender

Work status was found to be strongly associated to the centrality of work-related selves. Nevertheless, the centrality of work is not identi-

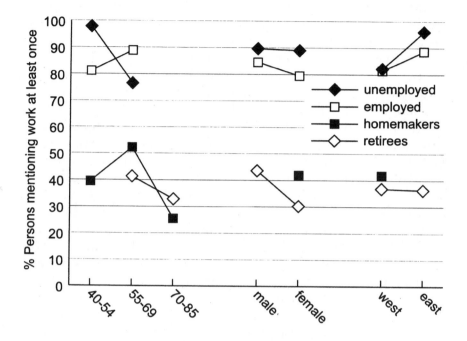

FIGURE 3.3 **Centrality of work according to work status, age group, gender, and region.**

cal for everybody with the same work status. As argued in the introduction, the institutionalization of the life course is changing according to the lines of age, region of residence, and gender. Hence we analyzed the relation between centrality of work and age, region, and gender to explain some of the variation within groups with the same work status.

In a bivariate analysis, it was found that the proportion of persons who mentioned work is lower in older age groups than in younger age groups ($X^2_{(2)} = 310,0$; $p < .001$), for women than for men ($X^2_{(1)} = 99,4$; $p < .001$) and for West Germans than for East Germans ($X^2_{(1)} = 15,7$; $p < .001$).

Differences according to age group, gender, and region were also computed for each of the four groups with different work status. Figure 3.3 clearly suggests an interaction effect between work status on the one hand and age, sex, and region on the other hand. For the employed it was found that a smaller proportion of the 40- to 54-year old mentioned work than of the 55- to 69-year old ($X^2_{(1)}$ = 9,8; $p < .01$). Somewhat more male than female employed mentioned work ($X^2_{(1)}$ = 4,5; $p < .05$) and more East German than West German employed ($X^2_{(1)}$ = 7,2; $p < .01$). For the unemployed it was found that more 40- to 54-year-olds mentioned work than 55- to 69-year old ($X^2_{(1)}$ = 13,9; $p < .001$). Male and female unemployed did not differ ($X^2_{(1)}$ = 0,1; $p < .05$) and East German unemployed mentioned work more often than West German unemployed ($X^2_{(1)}$ = 6,0; $p < .05$). Younger retirees (55- to 69-year-olds) mentioned work more often than older retirees ($X^2_{(1)}$ = 6,0; $p < .05$). Retired men mentioned work more often than retired women ($X^2_{(1)}$ = 15,2; $p < .001$). There were no differences between East and West German retirees ($X^2_{(1)}$ = 0,0; $p < .05$). Among the homemakers, no gender and East-West differences were computed, since virtually all homemakers were West German women (97.6%). Significant differences were found according to age group: the middle group mentioned work more often than did the younger or older group ($X^2_{(2)}$ = 16,4; $p < .001$).

Although the bivariate analysis showed evidence for a linear association between age group and centrality of work, the multivariate analysis showed a more complex interaction between work status and age. Even in the same age groups, work is more central to the unemployed than to homemakers or retirees. For employed persons, homemakers, and retirees, the centrality of work was greatest in the age group around retirement (55–69 years), whereas for the unemployed centrality was lower in this age group than in the younger group. Apparently, people take the social timing of retirement into consideration in their self-construals. These age differences suggest that not simply work status as such, but work status at a specific age, is related to the centrality of work-related selves.

More East than West Germans mentioned work as a central concern. Within groups with the same work status, this only holds for employed and unemployed Germans, but not for retirees. The high rates of unemployment subsequent to the transition to a capitalist economy were experienced as especially harsh and unjust in the former GDR, which had been characterized as a "work-society." Since defining oneself as a homemaker is not considered desirable among East German women, this "escape" from unemployment is almost never used. The historical changes related to the transformation from a socialist into a capitalist economy appear to have influenced, especially, the East German employed and persons unemployed.

With regard to gender differences, work was found to be less central for employed and retired women than for employed and retired men. However, no gender differences were found for the unemployed. Perhaps those (West German) women for whom work is not a central concern used the specific (West German) female career as a homemaker to avoid the negative role of "being unemployed." These findings suggest that, at least in West Germany, the traditional division of labor between the sexes still exists. However, some homemakers desire a better balance between paid and unpaid work. They appear to integrate emancipatory representations in their self-concepts.

DISCUSSION OF THE FINDINGS ON THE PERSONAL MEANING SYSTEM

In our representative study of Germans in the second half of life, people attributed a variety of meanings to work in their "accounts" of self and life. They not only evaluated how well they were doing at work, but they also referred to work in other ways, for instance, by expressing desires, plans, and fears about work and employment. These findings clearly suggest that cognitive representations of the self go beyond personality traits and self-esteem, as we asserted in the introduction. In this section, we discuss our findings in relation to individual and social processes of attributing meaning. In the next section, we comment on the relevance of our findings to theories of successful aging in social contexts.

Meaning Construction as as Individual and Social Process

Individual Processes of Meaning Construction

The different ways of giving meaning to work might be interpreted in terms of individual processes of attributing meaning to work status.

The findings show that individuals with and without work attribute a variety of meanings to their present situation. Some of them are more positive about their situation, whereas others are more negative.

The concepts of adaptive and cognitive strategies could be used to interpret the findings of our study. An example for persons with a job is found in the pattern that suggests a self-serving attribution bias in construing work-related selves: Positive meaning is attributed in particular to one's own competencies and achievements, whereas negative meanings are attributed in particular to work conditions. An example for persons without a job is found in the use of "accommodative" and "assimilative" strategies. For some individuals, work is not of central concern. They might have "accommodated" their self-concepts to fit their actual situation. Other individuals expressed a clear discrepancy between their actual situation and their aspirations. They want to "assimilate" their situation in order to maintain their work-related self-concepts.

Only a longitudinal design can reveal changes and adaptations in the meaning of work-related selves. For example, it remains uncertain in our cross-sectional study whether accommodation has really taken place when work is not of central concern for individuals without a job. It might also be the case that work already was not of central concern when they still had their job. They might also have had a desire to give up their job, like some of the employed persons in our study. Given the fact that work is of central concern for a large majority of employed persons, it may be expected, however, that many unemployed persons, homemakers, or retirees, for whom work is not of central concern, have reorganized their personal meaning system to fit their current circumstances. Furthermore, the specific meaning content that is found among the employed is not shared by the unemployed, homemakers, or retirees. Positive and negative evaluations of not working, or possible selves about employment, would have been developed only since they do not work anymore. It can be concluded that a reorganization of the personal meaning system has taken place, at least on the level of meaning content.

Social Processes of Meaning Construction

In the introduction, it was argued that the attribution of meaning to work is not simply an individual process, but takes place in the context of the social regulations and representations of the life course. Two processes were considered important in this respect: the construction of meaning through language use, and self-identification through societal roles.

In constructing an "account" of themselves and their lives, people used the existing meaning structures that are inherent in social regulations and representations about work and the life course. The negative meaning that employed and unemployed persons attributed to unemployment is clearly in line with the existing negative social definition of *un*employment. Whereas nobody attributed positive meaning to unemployment, it proved possible for employed and retired persons to attribute positive meaning to retirement. This more positive evaluation of retirement at the level of self-concepts corresponds with the more positive social definition of retirement. Homemakers were almost never negative about their situation. However, they were concerned about the balance between employment and their activities as a homemaker. This finding shows that emancipatory social representations are at least partly retrieved in the self-concepts of aging women. It can be concluded that the social representations of work and the life course are not only disseminated on an attitudinal level from the political elites to the general public. People actively relate to these social representations when they account for themselves and their lives.

It was found that the centrality and the specific meaning content of work-related selves differed between groups with a different work status. In other words, each work status corresponds to a particular constellation of the meaning of work. This finding shows that people use their social roles in attributing meaning to themselves and their lives. By incorporating the social structures of work and the life course in our analyses, we were able to show that not every meaning construction is possible. By showing these regularities in social meaning constructions, we could escape the tendency towards relativism of social constructivist theories.

Age, Regional and Gender Differences

Part of the variation within groups with a certain work status could be explained by one's life course position in terms of age, region of residence, and gender. These analyses showed a complex interaction between work status and age. Among employed, homemakers, and retirees, centrality was largest in the group around retirement age, but not for the unemployed. Apparently, people take the social timing of retirement into consideration in their self-construals. Given this complex interaction, it is unlikely that a cohort effect is responsible for the differences. A finding that might be attributed to cohort effects is that work is least central for the oldest age group. However, there appears to be no clear reason why work would be less central for the generation that contributed to the spectacular economical growth of (West) Germany after World War II.

Our findings with regard to West and East Germans show that the historical changes which are related to the transformation from a socialist into a capitalist economy affected the employed and the unemployed. These historical changes, however, seem to affect the retirees much less than those groups, probably because they are legitimately outside the labor force. The finding that almost no East German women had the status of homemaker suggests that this specific aspect of the structuralization of work and the life course in the former socialist republic "survived" the transformation process. Although women increasingly take part in the work force in West Germany, we found that gender differences subsist in respect to the traditional division of labor between the sexes.

The centrality of work within the personal meaning system is not only related to the social and cultural rules and representations of the life course and work status as such, but also to variations according to age, region, and gender. Because these variables only explain part of the individual differences between persons with the same work status, further analyses should include other indicators of societal positions, such as education and occupational status, and more precise descriptions of work status, such as work conditions of the employed, or the trajectories of becoming unemployed, homemaker, or retiree. Individual-level variables, such as control beliefs, coping styles, or health status, might also have an effect on the meaning of work within the personal meaning system.

The Delicate Balance Between Individual and Social Processes in the Construction of Meaning

In this section, we interpreted our findings in terms of individual and social processes of meaning constructions. On the one hand, we could interpret the centrality and meaning content of work-related selves in terms of adaptive and cognitive strategies that people might use in the construction of the meaning of work. There was evidence of individual variation in the use of such strategies. On the other hand, the meaning of work was related to existing social representations of work and the life course, as well as to the societal structuralization of the life course on the basis of work status, age, region of residence, and gender. The latter finding clearly shows that the construction of meaning is not just an individual process. Adaptive and cognitive strategies appear to be used in relation to one's life-course position. They are, however, not completely determined by this. It can be concluded that the construction of meaning is the result of a delicate balance between individual and social processes.

CONCLUSIONS: SOCIETAL STRUCTURES, SELF-STRUCTURES AND SUCCESSFUL AGING

By examining the individual and social processes of meaning construction in relation to the institutionalization of the life course around work, our interdisciplinary study contributed to an understanding of the relation between cognitive structures of the self and structures of our society. Existing social and cultural norms, rules and representations on work and the life course are adopted and integrated into the cognitive structures of the self. People define themselves and adjust their aspirations in relation to what they perceive as possible or impossible for themselves. In this way people contribute to the reproduction of the existing structures (Bourdieu, 1990; Dannefer & Perlmutter, 1990). What people did not say is especially instructive in this respect. Had the unemployed described their situation as positive or had the retirees had plans to go back to work, a potential for change would have been found. Such a potential for change is mainly found in the work-related selves of the employed persons who see their long working hours as problematic or express desires and plans to reduce them. A redistribution of the existing labor between the employed who work too hard and the unemployed who long for a job appears obvious from this perspective.

In our study, people appeared to attribute meaning to work-related selves in a variety of ways. Some persons gave a more positive meaning to their situation, whereas others gave it a more negative meaning. In this sense, there are clear differences in aging successfully in the domain of work. The differences between persons of different work status are interpreted as evidence that successful aging is not just a matter of individual strategies, but also of social opportunities and limitations. Whereas the unemployed attributed almost only negative meaning to being unemployed, the other groups expressed both positive and negative meanings. These findings agree with studies that found the well-being of the unemployed to be much lower than that of employed, homemakers, or retirees (Diener, 1984; Warr, 1998; Zapf, 1991). Our study suggests that such differences in well-being co-occur with differential ways in giving meaning to self and life.

ACKNOWLEDGMENTS

The German Aging Survey was carried out at the Department of Psychogerontology at the University of Nijmegen, the Netherlands and the Research Group on Aging and the Life Course at the Free University of Berlin, Germany. It was sponsored by the Federal Ministry of Family Affairs, Senior Citizens, Women and Youth. Data collection was accomplished by Infas-Sozialforschung, Bonn, Germany.

Gerben J. Westerhof, Freya Dittmann-Kohli, Section of Psychogerontology, University of Nijmegen, the Netherlands.

Correspondence concerning this article should be addressed to Gerben J. Westerhof, Section of Psychogerontology, University of Nijmegen, PO Box 9104, 6500HE Nijmegen, The Netherlands. Email: westerhof@psych.kun.nl.

REFERENCES

Baltes, P. B., & Baltes, M. M. (1990). Psychological perspectives on successful aging: The model of selective optimization with compensation. In P. B. Baltes & M. M. Baltes (Eds.), *Successful aging: Perspectives from the behavioral sciences* (pp. 1–34). New York: Cambridge University Press.

Bengtson, V. L., Reedy, M. N., & Gordon, C. (1985). Aging and self-conceptions: Personality and social contexts. In J. Birren & K. Schaie (Eds.), *Handbook of the psychology of aging* (2nd ed., pp. 544–593). New York: Van Nostrand Reinhold.

Bijsterveld, K. (1995). *Geen kwestie van leeftijd: Verzorgingsstaat, wetenschap en discussies rond ouderen in Nederland, 1945–1982* [Not a matter of age: Welfare state, science and discussion on seniors in the Netherlands, 1945–1982]. Amsterdam: Van Gennep.

Borozdina, L. V., & Molchanova, O. N. (1996). Characteristics of self-esteem in old age. *Journal of Russian and East European Psychology, 34,* 16–41.

Bourdieu, P. (1990). *The logic of practice.* Cambridge, England: Polity Press.

Bourdieu, P. (1991). *Language and symbolic power.* Cambridge, MA: Harvard University Press.

Brandtstädter, J., & Greve, W. (1994). The aging self: Stabilizing and protective processes. *Developmental Review, 14,* 52–80.

Braun, M., & Borg, I. (1997). Einstellungen zur Erwerbstätigkeit der Frau in Ost- und West-Deutschland: Trends, Strukturen und ihre Beziehung zu wirtschaftlichem Pessimismus [Attitudes to female employment in East- and West-Germany: Trends, structures and their relation to economic pessimism]. *ZUMA-Nachrichten, 40,* 21–35.

Bruner, J. (1990). *Acts of meaning.* Cambridge, MA: Harvard University Press.

Byrd, M., & Stacey, B. (1995). Cross-sectional age differences in the self-conceptions of adults. *Psychological Reports, 77,* 540–542.

Byrne, B. M. (1996). *Measuring self-concept across the life-span: Issues and instrumentation.* Washington, DC: American Psychological Association.

Clemens, W. (1996). Ältere Arbeitnehmerinnen: Spätphase der Erwerbstätigkeit und Übergang in den Ruhestand [Older female workers: The last phase of employment and the retirement transition]. *Zeitschrift für Gerontologie und Geriatrie, 29,* 328–333.

Cooley, C. H. (1983). *Human nature and the social order.* New Brunswick, NJ: Transaction Books. (originally published 1902).

Costa, P. T., & McCrae, R. R. (1989). Personality continuity and the changes of adult life. In M. Storandt & G. R. van den Bos (Eds.), *The adult years: Continuity and change* (pp. 41–77). Washington, DC: American Psychological Association.

Cousins, S. D. (1989). Culture and self-perception in Japan and the United States. *Journal of Personality and Social Psychology, 56,* 124–131.

Cross, S., & Markus, H. (1991). Possible selves across the life-span. *Human Development, 34,* 230–255.

Dannefer, D., & Perlmutter, M. (1990). Development as a multidimensional process: Individual and social constituents. *Human Development, 33,* 108–137.

Demo, D. H. (1992). The self-concept over time: Research issues and directions. *Annual Review of Sociology, 18,* 303–326.

Diener, E. (1984). Subjective well-being. *Psychological Bulletin, 95,* 542–575.

Dittmann-Kohli, F. (1988). Sinndimensionen des Lebens im frühen und späten Erwachsenenalter [Dimensions of meaning in life in early and late adulthood]. In H. W. Bierhoff & R. Nienhaus (Eds.), *Beiträge zur Psychogerontologie* (pp. 73–115). Marburg: Universität Marburg.

Dittmann-Kohli, F. (1990).The construction of meaning in old age. *Ageing and Society, 10,* 270–294.

Dittmann-Kohli, F. (1995). *Das persönliche Sinnsystem: Ein Vergleich zwischen frühem und spätem Erwachsenenalter* [The personal meaning system: a comparison between early and late adulthood]. Göttingen: Hogrefe.

Dittmann-Kohli, F., Bode, C., & Westerhof, G. J. (Eds). (1999). *Die zweite Lebenshälfte: Psychologische Perspektiven—Ergebnisse des Alters-Survey, Band 2.* [The second half of life: Psychological perspectives—findings of the German Aging Survey, Vol. 2]. Nijmegen, The Netherlands: University of Nijmegen.

Dittmann-Kohli, F., Kohli, M., Künemund, H., Motel, A., Steinleitner, C., & Westerhof, G. J. (1997). *Lebenszusammenhänge, Selbst- und Lebenskonzeptionen: Erhebungsdesign und Instrumente des Alters-Survey* [Life contexts and conceptions of self and life: Design and instruments of the German Aging Survey]. Berlin: Freie Universität, FALL.

Dittmann-Kohli, F., & Westerhof, G. J. (1997). The SELE-sentence completion questionnaire: A new instrument for the assessment of personal meaning in research on aging. *Anuario de Psicologia, 73,* 7–18.

Dittmann-Kohli, F., & Westerhof, G. J. (2000). The personal meaning system in a life span perspective. In G. Reker & K. Chamberlain (Eds.), *Exploring existential meaning: Optimizing human development across the life span* (pp. 107–123). Thousand Oaks, CA: Sage.

Doise, W. (1993). Debating social representations. In G. M. Breackwell & D. V. Canter (Eds.), *Empirical approaches to social representations* (pp. 157–171). Oxford: Clarendon Press.

Fiske, M. (1980). Tasks and crises of the second half of life: The interrelationship of commitment, coping and adaptation. In J. E. Birren & R. B. Sloane (Eds.), *Handbook of mental health and aging* (pp. 337–373). Englewood Cliffs, NJ: Prentice Hall.

Fiske, S., & Taylor, S. (1991). *Social cognition* (2nd ed.). New York: McGraw-Hill.

Freund, A. M., & Smith, J. (1997). Die Selbstdefinition im hohen Alter [Self-definitions in old age]. *Zeitschrift für Sozialpsychologie, 28,* 44–59.

Hannover, B. (1997). *Das dynamische Selbst: Die Kontextabhängigkeit selbstbezogenen Wissens* [The dynamic self: The contextual dependencies of self-knowledge]. Bern: Verlag Hans Huber.

Hayes, B. C., & Vandenheuvel, A. (1994). Attitudes towards mandatory retirement: An international comparison. *International Journal of Aging and Human Development, 39,* 209–231.

Higgins, E. T. (1990). Personality, social psychology, and person-situation relations: Standards and knowledge activation as a common language. In L. A. Pervin (Ed.), *Handbook of personality* (pp. 301–338). New York: Guilford Press.

James, W. (1983). *The principles of psychology.* Cambridge: Harvard University Press. (Originally published 1890).

Kihlstrom, J. F., & Hastie, R. (1997). Mental representations of persons and personality. In R. Hogan, J. A. Johnson, & S. Briggs (Eds.), *Handbook of personality psychology* (pp. 711–735). San Diego: Academic Press.

Kling, K. C., Ryff, C. D., & Essex, M. J. (1997). Adaptive changes in the self-concept during a life transition. *Personality and Social Psychology Bulletin, 23,* 981–990.

Kogan, N. (1990). Personality and aging. In J. E. Birren & K. W. Schaie (Eds.), *Handbook of the psychology of aging* (3rd ed., pp. 330–346). San Diego: Academic Press.

Kohli, M. (1985). Die Institutionalisierung des Lebenslaufs [The institutionalization of the life course]. *Kölner Zeitschrift für Soziologie und Sozialpsychologie, 37,* 1–29.

Kohli, M. (1994). Work and retirement: A comparative perspective. In M. W. Riley, R. L. Kahn, A. Foner, & K. A. Mack (Eds.), *Age and structural lag: Society's failure to provide meaningful opportunities in work, family, and leisure* (pp. 80–106). New York: Wiley.

Kohli, M., & Künemund, H. (1997). *Nachberufliche Tätigkeitsfelder: Konzepte, Forschungslage, Empirie* [Activities after retirement: Concepts, state of the art and empirical findings]. Stuttgart: Kohlhammer.

Kohli, M., & Künemund, H. (Eds.). (1998). *Die zweite Lebenshälfte: Gesellschaftliche Lage und Partizipation* [The second half of life: Societal positions and participation]. Berlin: Freie Universität, FALL.

Künemund, H. (1998). "Produktive" Tätigkeiten in der zweiten Lebenshälfte [Productive activities in the second half of life]. In M. Kohli & H. Künemund (Eds.), *Die zweite Lebenshälfte: Gesellschaftliche Lage und Partizipation* (pp. 325–375). Berlin: Freie Universität, FALL.

Markus, H., & Nurius, P. (1986). Possible selves. *American Psychologist, 41,* 954–969.

Markus, H., &. Wurf, E. (1987). The dynamic self-concept: A social psychological perspective. *Annual Review of Psychology, 38,* 299–337.

McCall, G. J. (1987). The structure, content and dynamics of self: Continuities in the study of role-identities. In K. Yardley & T. Honess (Eds.), *Self and identity: Psychosocial perspectives* (pp. 133–149). Chichester, England: Wiley and Sons.

McClelland, D. C. (1980). Motive dispositions: The merits of operant and respondant measures. *Review of Personality and Social Psychology, 1*, 10–41.

Mead, G. H. (1962). *Mind, self and society*. Chicago: University Press of Chicago. (Originally published 1934).

Moscovici, S. (1984). The phenomenon of social representations. In R. Farr & S. Moscovici (Eds.), *Social representations* (pp. 3–69). Cambridge: Cambridge University Press.

Noll, H. H. (1994). Steigende Zufriedenheit in Ostdeutschland, sinkende Zufriedenheit in Westdeutschland [Raising life satisfaction in East Germany, decreasing life satisfaction in West Germany]. *Informationsdienst Soziale Indikatoren, 11*, 1–7.

Nowakowska, M. (1973). *Language of motivation and language of actions*. The Hague, The Netherlands: Mouton.

Petty, J. A., & Krosnick, R. E. (1995). *Attitude strength: Antecedents and consequences*. Mahwah, NJ: Lawrence Erlbaum.

Polkinghorne, D. E. (1991). Narrative and self-concept. *Journal of Narrative and Life History, 1*, 135–155.

Potter, J., & Wetherell, M. (1987). *Discourse and social psychology: Beyond attitudes and behaviour*. Beverly Hills: Sage.

Rosenberg, M. (1979). *Conceiving the self*. New York: Basic Books.

Rubinstein, R. L. (1992). Anthropological methods in gerontological research: Entering the realm of meaning. *Journal of Aging Studies, 6*, 57–66.

Ruth, J. A., & Coleman, P. (1996). Personality and aging: Coping and management of the self in later life. In J. E. Birren & K. W. Schaie (Eds.), *Handbook of the psychology of aging* (4th ed., pp. 308–322). San Diego: Academic Press.

Schulz, R., & Heckhausen, J. (1996). A life span model of successful aging. *American Psychologist, 51*, 702–714.

Shotter, J., & Gergen, K. J. (1989). *Texts of identity*. London: Sage.

Smid, M., Hess, D., & Gilberg, R. (1997). *Alterssurvey: Methodenbericht zur Erhebung der ersten Welle* [The German Aging Survey: Methodological report on the first wave]. Bonn: Infas Sozialforschung.

Statistisches Bundesamt. (1997). *Datenreport 7* [Facts and figures 7]. Bonn: Bonn Aktuell.

Stryker, S. (1991). Exploring the relevance of social cognition for the relationship of self and society: Linking the cognitive perspective and identity theory. In J. A. Howard & P. L. Callero (Eds.), *The self-society dynamic: Cognition, emotion, and action* (pp. 19–43). Cambridge: Cambridge University Press.

Stryker, S., & Serpe, R. T. (1994). Identity salience and psychological centrality: Equivalent, overlapping, or complementary concepts? *Social Psychology Quarterly, 57,* 16–35.

Thomas, M. (1989). *Zentralität und Selbstkonzept* [Centrality and self-concept]. Bern: Huber.

Thoits, P. A., & Virshup, L. K. (1997). Me's and we's: Forms and functions of social identities. In R. D. Ashmore & L. Jussim (Eds.), *Self and identity: Fundamental issues* (pp. 106–137). New York: Oxford University Press.

Warr, P. (1998). Age, work and mental health. In K. W. Schaie & C. Schooler (Eds.), *Impact of work on aging adults* (pp. 252–297). New York: Springer Publishing Company.

Westerhof, G. J. (1994). *Statements and stories: Towards a new methodology of attitude research.* Amsterdam: Thesis.

Westerhof, G. J., & Voestermans, P. (1995). Het belang van spreken: De economie van taalhandelingen in het werk van Pierre Bourdieu [The importance of speech: The economy of speech acts in the work of Pierre Bourdieu]. *Psychologie en Maatschappij, 71,* 142–154.

Zapf, D. (1991). Arbeit und Wohlbefinden [Work and well-being]. In A. Abele & P. Becker (Ed.), *Wohlbefinden: Theorie, empirie, diagnostik* (pp. 227–245). Weinheim/München: Juventa.

Commentary

What Goals Motivate Individual Behavior?

Eileen M. Crimmins and Richard A. Easterlin

Over three decades ago, social psychologist Hadley Cantril (1965) asked the following question of a representative sample of respondents in 12 countries scattered across five continents: "All of us want certain things out of life. When you think about what really matters in your life, what are your hopes for the future? In other words, if you imagine your future in the *best* possible light, what would your life look like then, if you are to be happy?" (Cantril, 1965, p. 23, emphasis in original). The responses to this open-ended question provide perhaps the best self-testimony available on what Westerhoff and Dittman-Kohli (this volume) call one's Personal Meaning System. In this brief comment, we use Cantril's data and a Roper survey that asks about perceptions of the good life to complement the interesting results of the Westerhoff and Dittman-Kohli chapter.

There is little in the Westerhoff and Dittman-Kohli chapter with which we seriously disagree. We share their view that behavior is shaped by a personal meaning system, that the personal meaning

system tends to be similar enough among people to permit general-
izations, and that behavior is goal-directed. We also agree that the
personal importance of work declines in the latter part of the life
course. However, we think it is important to differentiate between
work as a goal valued in itself, and work as a means to other goals.
As we shall see, this distinction between work as a means and work
as an end is clear in Cantril's data. We also think it is important to
understand the importance of work relative to other goals in one's
personal meaning system in order to get at the issue of centrality—
what is really motivating behavior. Finally, we believe it is important
to check inferences from point-of-time data against life-course observations. We believe Westerhoff and Dittman-Kohli would agree with
these statements, and hence our comment is best viewed as a supple-
ment to their chapter.

What goals motivate individual behavior? The responses to Cantril's open-ended question at the start of this comment give us a
good idea. The answers range from statements regarding living-
levels, work, and family to broad issues of war and peace, civil liberty,
and social justice. To simplify the responses, Cantril organized them
into nine broad categories (see Appendix A). His classification is of
special help here, because it differentiates between work as a goal
in itself and living-level concerns, where work is a means. Because
the ranking of concerns is quite similar among countries, we have
averaged them here for all 12 countries.

Our first interest is in the relative importance of different goals.
Generally speaking, what matters most to people are the things that
take up the great part of everyday life—making a living, raising a
family, and health (Cantril, 1965, p. 169). Broad political, economic,
and social issues are typically mentioned by less than 10% of the
population. In contrast, in every country, concerns about living level
are most important and, on average, are mentioned by almost 80% of
the population. Next come concerns about family matters (averaging
50% of the population) and health (34%). Concerns about work as
a goal in itself rank about equally with concerns about values and
personal character, being mentioned, on average, by about 20%.

Most people must work to support themselves. Hence, the importance of living-level concerns, such as securing an improved or decent
standard of living for oneself and one's family, necessarily implies
that jobs are important to most people. They are important, however,

as a means to reaching the goal of better living levels, not as an end in themselves. The contrast between living level desires, mentioned by almost four persons out of five, and job desires such as a "good" or "congenial" job, mentioned by one in five, supports the view that the centrality of work is as a means, not an end. The kind of work people do also matters less to them than how they live—their material circumstances.

The variation in concerns by age is shown in Figure 3.4. Living-level and family concerns maintain their dominant position at all ages, although family concerns decrease in the oldest age group, once children are raised and out of the home. At young ages, job concerns are somewhat more important, being mentioned by almost 30% of respondents, and health concerns less, at 24%. Consistent with Westerhoff and Dittman-Kohli's results, job concerns decline with age. Health concerns become correspondingly more im-

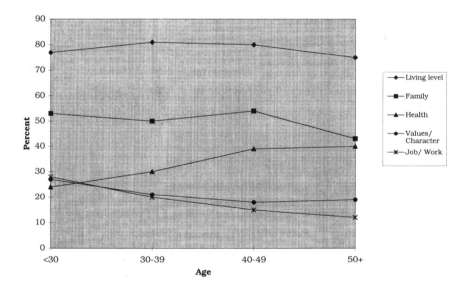

FIGURE 3.4 Percent of population naming specified item as part of what matters in life, by age, around 1960 (average for 12 countries).

Source: Cantril, H. *The pattern of human concerns.* New Brunswick, NJ: Rutgers University Press.

portant—at older compared with younger ages, job concerns drop from third to fifth in rank, and health rises from fifth to third. At no age, however, does reference to job concerns come anywhere near the frequency of living-level concerns. This result is again consistent with the view that, for most people, the importance of work is very largely because it is a means to maintaining or improving living levels, rather than an end in itself.

The oldest age category in Figure 3.4 is 50 and over, the group typically used in Cantril's tabulations. One of the 12 countries included in Cantril's analysis was West Germany, and for West Germany, the oldest group is 60 and over. Hence, it is of interest to note the results because Westerhoff and Dittman-Kohli's chapter is based on German data. Among those 60 and over in West Germany in 1960, 71% cited living-level concerns as important to their well-being, while only 3% mentioned job concerns (Cantril, 1965, p. 408). This is consistent with Westerhoff and Dittman-Kohli's finding about the low importance of work among those at or close to retirement; it is also consistent with the notion of the centrality of living-level concerns throughout the age range.

The responses by age here are for a given point of time. To get a better view of change over the life cycle, we use Roper surveys (Roper-Starch, 1979, 1995) that include questions on "the good life." Such surveys have been taken about every 3 years since 1975 in the United States. In these surveys, the question is as follows:

> We often hear people talk about what they want out of life. Here are a number of different things. [The respondent is handed a card with a list of 24 items.] When you think of the good life—the life you'd like to have, which of the things on this list, if any, are part of that good life as far as you personally are concerned?

We have seen that the concerns typically cited in response to open-ended questions are matters of everyday life—living levels, family circumstances, health, and work. The good life questions are not open-ended, but the list of 24 items presented to respondents overlaps substantially the concerns typically cited, falling mainly into three categories—living levels (a consumer goods group), family concerns, and job circumstances. We have reduced the list to nineteen items. We deleted one item—"a college education for myself"—

because schooling is already completed for almost all respondents. Also, we reduced five queries on specific numbers of children to "one or more children," because the additional detail added little of value.

The items most frequently cited as part of the good life are hardly surprising—a home, a car, a happy marriage, children, and an interesting job (Table 3.6). The most important concern omitted in the good life survey is health. Aside from this, the good life questions largely tap the same set of personal interests as Cantril's questions.

To obtain a view of life-cycle change, we use two surveys, those for 1978 and 1994, and follow several cohorts between these 2 years

TABLE 3.6   Percent of Population Identifying Specified Item as Part of Good Life, 1994

Consumer Goods	Percent
A home you own	90
A car	77
A yard and lawn	63
A color TV set	58
Really nice clothes	48
A second car	46
A vacation home	44
Travel abroad	43
A swimming pool	37
A second color TV set	34
Family	
A happy marriage	77
One or more children	66
A college education for my children	62
Job	
A job that is interesting	63
A job that pays much more than the average	63
A job that contributes to the welfare of society	42
A four-day work week	30
A five-day work week	25
Other	
A lot of money	63
(Number of cases)	(1,943)

Note: Within each category, items are listed by rank.

using demographers' long-established technique of cohort analysis. A birth cohort is a group of individuals born in a given year or period. Thus, the birth cohort of 1935–49 comprises all persons born in those years. The membership of a cohort changes somewhat over the cohort's life cycle as a result of mortality and international migration, but not very greatly. We construct the life-cycle experience of a birth cohort here by linking age data for 2 years. To trace the mid-life cycle change in aspirations of the cohort born between 1935 and 1949, we would ideally link the data of those ages 30–44 in 1979 to that of those ages 45–59 in 1994. Because 1978 rather than 1979 data are available, and we do not have single-year-of-age data, we use the 1978 data for persons 30–44 as an approximation to the ideal. The three cohorts and the ages used to trace the life cycle patterns here are:

Early life cycle: the birth cohort of 1950–64 at ages 18–29 and 30–44.
Mid-life cycle: the birth cohort of 1935–49 at ages 30–44 and 45–59.
Late life cycle: the birth cohort of 1920–34 at ages 45–59 and 60 and over.

The life-course patterns largely confirm those in the point-of-time data. Living-level concerns remain high throughout the life cycle and, if anything, increase (Table 3.7). Family concerns too remain high. They decrease a little in the latter part of the life cycle, but not as much as in the cross-sectional data. The importance of work as a goal declines, especially in the later stages of the life cycle.

These data differ somewhat from Cantril's in suggesting that the importance of work is more like that of living-level and family concerns, at least at the start of the adult life cycle. But we think this gives a misleading impression of work as a *goal* (rather than a means to other goals) that influences behavior. Other data from the Roper survey indicate that less than 40% of respondents actually have an interesting job, and, unlike the other goals, there is no positive progress toward acquiring an interesting job in the course of the life cycle. Our impression is that people either do or do not start out with a fairly permanent job that is interesting, and that this condition changes very little as they progress through the life cycle. In contrast, progress toward living-level and family goals is substantial, suggesting that these are what is motivating behavior.

TABLE 3.7 Principal Sources of the Good Life: Percentage Mentioning Specified Item at Start of Adult Life Cycle and Change During Three Life-Cycle Stages[a]

	Start of life cycle (Percent mentioning)	Change (percentage points)		
		Early life cycle	Mid life cycle	Late life cycle
Living level				
Home	83	+8	+4	+6
Car	74	+2	+4	−1
Family				
Happy marriage[b]	80	n.a.	n.a.	n.a.
One or more children	67	+3	−1	−3
Job				
Interesting job	75	−6	−4	−23

[a]See text for specification of life-cycle stages.
[b]Data for end point of each life-cycle stage are not comparable with those at beginning.

In sum, the two surveys combined confirm that the centrality of work declines with age, and especially at older ages. They also suggest that work is chiefly viewed as a means to other ends, such as better living levels, health, and improved family circumstances. We suggest that while people generally would like to have meaningful and interesting jobs, the majority do not, and are more or less resigned to this. Hence, work as an end in itself does not motivate behavior nearly as much as work as a means to other ends. What is most on people's minds are concerns about living levels, family, and health.

APPENDIX A

Classification of Personal Concerns in Table 3.6

The question asked, together with the parenthetical instructions to interviewers, is:

All of us want certain things out of life. When you think about what really matters in your own life, what are your wishes and hopes for the future? In other words, if you imagine your future in the best possible light, what would your life look like then, if you are to be happy? Take your time in answering; such things aren't easy to put into words.

Permissible Probes: What are your hopes for the future? What would your life have to be like for you to be completely happy? What is missing for you to be happy? [Use also, if necessary, the words "dreams" and "desires."]

Obligatory Probe: Anything else? (Cantril, 1965, p. 23)

The detailed concerns elicited by this question are classified by Cantril (1965, pp. 159–161, 329–338) as follows (the "miscellaneous" category under each head is omitted):

1. LIVING LEVEL

Improved or decent standard of living for self or family; sufficient money to live better or to live decently; freedom from debt; make ends meet; relief from poverty; not suffer want, hunger, etc.

Have *own business;* ability to increase or expand one's business.

Have *own land or own farm.*

Have own *house,* apartment, or garden; or get better ones.

Have *modern conveniences,* such as a car, bathroom, fine or new furniture, fine clothes, large appliances such as washing machine, radio, television, etc.

Have *wealth*—money to do anything I/we wish.

Employment—steady work for self, spouse, or other family member.

Happy old age—long and happy life; peaceful, pleasant, secure old age.

Recreation, travel, leisure time; sports, reading for pleasure, etc.

Social Security, including pensions, annuities, etc.

2. FAMILY

Happy family life—happy marriage; pleasant home; love within family; have a (good) husband or wife; have children.

Relative—concern for spouse, children, parents, or other relatives; be close to them; keep them together or get them together again; help or take care of them; live up to their expectations.
Children—adequate opportunities for them (including education); children themselves do well, be happy, successful.

3. HEALTH

One's own *health*—continued or regained health (physical or mental) for self; strength to enjoy life.
Health of family—continued good health or improved health (physical or mental) for members of family.

4. VALUES/CHARACTER

Emotional stability and maturity—peace of mind, mental health and well-being; sense of humor, understanding of others, etc.; harmonious life.
Be a normal, decent person—leading a quiet life, harming no one.
Self-development or improvement—opportunity for independence of thought and action, for following through with own interests; further study; reading for non-leisure purposes; no "rut."
Acceptance by others—recognition of my status by others; to be liked, respected or loved.
Achieve sense of my own personal worth—self-satisfaction; feeling of accomplishment; lead a purposeful life.
Resolution of one's own religious, spiritual, or ethical problems.
To lead a disciplined life.

5. JOB OR WORK SITUATION

Good job, congenial work for self, spouse, or other family member; independence in choice of occupation; pleasant, interesting job or work situation; chance of advancement.
Success in one's work for self, spouse, or other family member; make a contribution to one's field.

6. SOCIAL VALUES

Social justice—greater equality in the treatment, benefits, and opportunities afforded all elements of the population, irrespective of race, color, class, caste, religion, etc.; integration; fairer distribution of wealth; elimination of discrimination or exploitation.
Future generations—better prospects and opportunities.
Desire to be useful to others; ability and opportunity to serve the people, community, nation, world; or to hold public office.

7. INTERNATIONAL SITUATION AND WORLD

Peace—maintenance of; no war; no threat of war.
Better world—more international cooperation; countries working together; more international understanding and responsibility; relaxation of international tensions; stronger U.N.; world government.

8. POLITICAL

Freedom, including specifically freedom of speech, of religion, of occupation, of movement, etc.

9. STATUS QUO

Maintain status quo (in general); person is happy with things as they are now.

Cantril also questioned respondents on the worst of all possible worlds, and tabulated the answers. Because these responses largely mirror those obtained in the question above, we have based Figure 3.4 on that question only.

REFERENCES

Cantril, H. (1965). *The pattern of human concerns.* New Brunswick, NJ: Rutgers University Press.
Roper-Starch Organization. (1979). *Roper Reports 79-1.* New York: Author.
Roper-Starch Organization. (1995). *Roper Reports 95-1.* New York: Author.

Commentary

Work Status and Identity: Further Consideration of Contextual and Individual Factors

Erika L. Ringseis and James L. Farr

INTRODUCTION

How we conceptualize, define, and explain our self-concept and beliefs may affect our attitudes, behaviors, and performance outcomes. As suggested by Westerhof and Dittman-Kohli (this volume), the examination of individual "personal meaning systems" can yield valuable insight into the complex interaction of individual and social factors that creates our identities and self-concepts. In order to offer a broader examination of Westerhof and Dittman-Kohli's chapter, we begin with a look at some other perspectives on the psychological concept of identity. Then, we highlight some of the important findings of the Westerhof and Dittman-Kohli study, while suggesting potential research links to other areas of interest, especially those within our personal subdiscipline of industrial/organizational psychology.

IDENTITY AND PERSONAL MEANING SYSTEMS

"Identity is the individual's psychological relationship to particular social category systems" (Frable, 1997, p. 139). How we identify and classify ourselves can affect choices and perceptions we make in the world around us. Additionally, identity theory "posits that there are individual differences in the salience of a given role identity for self-identification" (Frone, Russell, & Cooper, 1995, p. 2). Thus, we differ individually in how we define ourselves and in what attributes we consider important to our identity. Frable (1997) notes the complexity of a person's identity. People form identities on the basis of many factors, including gender, race, ethnicity, sex, and class. Frable does not mention age, although age presumably plays a role in the change of our identities over time.

Although previous research has examined the development and maintenance of gender, race, ethnic, and sex identities, little attention has been paid to the role of class and occupational status in identity development (Frable, 1997). One method by which occupational identity could be addressed is through an investigation of employee construal of their employment identities, as initiated by the research of Westerhof and Dittman-Kohli. It is especially useful to utilize a qualitative methodology, as Westerhof and Dittman-Kohli have, when examining the meanings of work for different individuals, in order to provide a rich description of the varied ways that people make sense of their employment status in relation to their personal identities (cf., Pernice, 1996).

Westerhof and Dittman-Kohli discuss their research in terms of personal meaning systems, which broaden the scope of self-concept from psychological aspects to include the ways in which a person relates to a broader environment. This environment includes the world of work and employment. Thus, the paper by Westerhof and Dittman-Kohli can be considered as an important bridge between social psychological identity research and research investigating aging and work.

In an area devoid of rich description, Westerhof and Dittman-Kohli make a valuable contribution to theory development. They concluded that there were clear differences in the centrality and the meaning of work-related selves according to age and work status. Work did not play a consistent role across the personal meaning systems of employees in various age groups. This supports one of the tenets of identity research: that the personal meaning we find in social groupings can change over time (Nkomo & Cox, 1996). Thus, not only should multiple aspects of identity be investigated, but identity should also be investigated over time. It would be fruitful to examine the relationships found by Westerhof and Dittman-Kohli in a longitudinal design, to reduce the potential contamination of results by cohort effects. Thus, a longitudinal design would be a valuable next step in this line of research.

In addition to considering identity changes over time, Frable (1997) suggests that a fruitful addition to current identification research would be to investigate multiple aspects of identity within the same study. Although we may talk about an individual's multiple identities as separate entities, they are undoubtedly interlocked into the same personal meaning system. Our identities are synergistic, not additive or independent, and thus we need to consider multiple identity measurement simultaneously (Nkomo & Cox, 1996). Westerhof and Dittman-Kohli do mention other meaning domains that they found through their qualitative methodology, including psychological and physical selves, activities, and material living conditions, but they present no specifics of these other identities. An interesting extension of the current Westerhof and Dittman-Kohli study would be an examination of what interactions occur among the various meaning domains, and how they interact in the formation of personal meaning systems, in order to provide a richer picture of the entire constellation of identification processes and structures.

THE ROLE OF CULTURE AND SOCIAL STRUCTURE

Culture can play a strong role in creating, maintaining, and revising our identities (Oyserman & Kemmelmeier, 1995). The way in which we answer the question, "Who am I?" is often curtailed by cultural traditions and social roles (Oyserman & Kemmelmeier, 1995). One of the most interesting characteristics of the sample population used in the Westerhof and Dittman-Kohli study was that it included individuals from both the former Federal Republic of Germany (FRG) and the German Democratic Republic (GDR), West and East Germany, respectively. There are two differences in social structure between the FRG and GDR that are highlighted by Westerhof and Dittman-Kohli: the difference in unemployment rates, and the difference in attitudes toward women as homemakers.

Prior to reunification, East Germany had been a communist country for over 40 years (all or nearly all of the likely working life of the members of Westerhof & Dittman-Kohli's sample). Thus, the government took responsibility for the totality of workers' lives, and the cultural mindset traditionally considered care of individuals "from cradle to grave" to be a government, and not an individual, responsibility. Most people who wanted to work had a job under the old Communist regime (Came, 1998). Yet now the unemployment rate in Germany overall is 10.6% of the workforce (4.1 million people), with areas of the former East Germany reaching up to 21% unemployment rates (Merseburg area; Came, 1998). Some of the negative sentiment expressed by the unemployed sample in the Westerhof and Dittman-Kohli study can likely be related to the changing culture of East Germany as people struggle to accept a more individualistic economy. Many former East Germans "seethe with a barely concealed outrage that the union of the two Germanys has produced neither the prosperity nor the 'flowering landscape' promised by Chancellor Helmut Kohl" (Came, 1998, p. 38). Some of the fears expressed by the unemployed individuals in the former East Germany may be explained by considering the discrepancy in skills and opportunities between the East and the West ends of Germany. Many individuals in the former East Germany report experiencing a "profound sense of inferiority" and "are feeling defeated, devalued, robbed of their self-esteem" (Came, 1998, p. 40). Perhaps the next generation of German employees will experience a different work identity than those included in Westerhof and Dittman-Kohli's study as adaptation to a reunified German social structure and economy occurs.

In addition to general differences between East and West German inhabitants, Westerhof and Dittman-Kohli report that there are differences in female attitudes toward unemployment in the former FRG and GDR. In the former FRG, women homemakers reinterpreted their situation ("unemployed") as homemakers. Thus, the Western homemakers in the study by Westerhof and Dittman-Kohli, unlike the other unemployed group, only sometimes had employment as a goal. In addition, as opposed to the unemployed, some of the homemakers defined what they were currently doing at home as "work." In the former GDR, however, state-run child care formerly permitted women to work, and staying at home was not common. These Eastern homemakers seem more like the unemployed groups than the Western homemakers do. Examining the effects that the social structure, such as availability of free child care, has had on the women homemakers highlights that not only is centrality of work status important in the Personal Meaning System of the homemakers, but there are differences in the very definition of "work."

A confound in Westerhof and Dittman-Kohli's research is that the homemakers were all female, which is reflective of the traditional social structure. Traditionally, women have been the individuals to stay at home and care for the children. More recently, dual-income households are becoming normative, as are one-parent families and even families where the father stays home to care for the children (Higgins, Duxbury, & Irving, 1992). Men who are homemakers may develop aspects of identity that are different from women who are homemakers because they act contrary to traditional social structure. An interesting extension of Westerhof and Dittman-Kohli's research would be to examine the role of work in the personal meaning systems of men who are homemakers.

The core of our personal identities is influenced by factors such as national culture and social structure. Although previous research investigates the role of culture in identity formation and comprehension (see, e.g., Oyserman & Kemmelmeier, 1995), the findings discussed above highlight the importance of social structure as an additional level or layer of the identity "onion" to consider.

RETIREMENT AND IDENTITY

The findings of Westerhof and Dittman-Kohli suggest that "persons in the second half of life clearly share the negative cultural construction of meaning of *un*-employment in social practices and political discourse." Thus, the idea that the institutionalization of the life course around work affects how people centralize work in their personal meaning systems appears to be supported. It is interesting to note, however, that Germany has a mandatory retirement age.

Thus, all individuals above a certain age are expected to be retired (and expect to be retired). The United States, on the other hand, illustrates a society in which there has been movement toward a general lack of mandatory retirement age.

The abolishment of mandatory retirement age for almost all occupations in the US has probably not been in effect for a sufficiently long period of time for this policy change to have had a strong and consistent impact on how US workers define the stages of typical employment, but it will be interesting to examine this effect in the coming years. Also, some researchers suggest that attractive early retirement incentive packages, while not acting as a legal enforcer of retirement, result in some employees feeling forced to retire at a certain age (Carter & Cook, 1995). Thus, although Westerhof and Dittman-Kohli did not find many negative responses from retirees, or wishes for reemployment, different results may be found in the United States.

In the United States, retirement may be experienced as positive or negative. It has been suggested that adaptation to retirement represents a period of strong adjustment and role redefinition (Carter & Cook, 1995). Westerhof and Dittman-Kohli's study helps to highlight some of the changes in identity and personal meaning systems that may occur as a result of retirement. Carter and Cook (1995) also suggest that self-efficacy and locus of control act as two psychological variables that may help to predict retirement adjustment. For example, individuals with a high internal locus of control may be more likely to engage in proactive planning to ready themselves for retirement and retirement activities, than are those with high external locuses of control (Carter & Cook, 1995). Additionally, people with high feelings of self-efficacy, or self-confidence in a particular realm, in this case, retirement, will be more likely to adjust well to retirement than those with low self-efficacy (Carter & Cook, 1995). Thus, examination of psychological factors may illuminate reasons for individual variation in adjustment to retirement.

It has been frequently suggested in the research literature that the factors which have influenced an individual's decision to retire play an important influence also on the individual's post-retirement adjustment (e.g., Feldman, 1994). Schultz, Morton, and Weckerle (1998) found that those retirees who believed that they had retired voluntarily had greater life satisfaction and rated themselves as healthier than those who believed that their retirement was involuntary. It seems a reasonable inference that the voluntary or involuntary nature of one's retirement might also affect both the centrality of work in retirees' personal meaning systems and the meaning contents of their work-related selves.

Westerhof and Dittman-Kohli discuss both negative and positive responses to their open-ended questions, which are indicative of both real and potential future selves. However, they fail to acknowledge whether these responses come from different individuals, or from the same individuals. Thus, it would be interesting to examine individual responses in more depth. Do the same people give both negative and positive responses? Or are some people more negative and some people more positive? In short, what are the potential individual-level mediators of positive and negative evaluations of self in the various work status conditions?

CENTRALITY AND WORK ADJUSTMENT

Nicholson (1984) proposed a two-factor theory of work-role transitions. An individual may adjust to transitions at work through role development, personal development, or some combination of the two. Role development refers to changes made in the work role itself, to better suit the individual. Personal development refers to change within the individual, due to alterations of values, beliefs, or identities. Four categories are thus created: replication (low on both role and personal development); absorption (low role development, high personal development); determination (high role development; low personal development); and exploration (high role and high personal development). One way to reconcile Nicholson's (1984) theory with the findings of Westerhof and Dittman-Kohli is to consider into which category of adjustment individuals best fit. For example, it appears that homemakers engage in determination by redefining the tasks they perform in their homes to be "work" in order to suit better their personal identities. They are, therefore, leaving a personal stamp of individuality on their work-role definition. The unemployed, however, seemed to be more concerned with finding a job (exploration). Westerhof and Dittman-Kohli, borrowing from Brandstädter and Greve (1994), used the terms "assimilation" for individuals who changed the situation to fit their own self-concept and "accommodation" for individuals who adjusted their self-concept to fit the situation. This terminology implies that only one type of adjustment is possible for a given individual. We suggest that an alternative vocabulary, based upon Nicholson's (1984) theory, may better highlight the theoretical connections between individual interpretation of, and reaction to, work events, including the possibility that both role and personal adjustments may be made by an individual. Thus, whether individuals chose strategies to adjust to work-role transitions that are high in role or personal development may affect the form and centrality of work in their personal meaning systems.

Role transitions or anticipated role transitions are also likely to be times when reflection, planning, prediction, and other forms of controlled cognitive processing are used by individuals in making decisions and anticipating outcomes of possible alternative decisions. This may account in part for the increase in the centrality of work in the older employed group (ages 55–69) in the Westerhof and Dittman-Kohli study. Work would be more salient to these individuals than those in the 40–54 age range who are much less likely on average to be thinking about retirement decisions and other employment-related transitions (e.g., to fewer working hours or to a part-time job).

RELATIONSHIP TO OUTCOMES

As industrial/organizational psychologists, we are concerned with the effects that work definition and personal meaning systems may have on organizational outcomes. For example, the relationship between age and performance is not clear. Older employees in maintenance or stable situations (e.g., jobs that do not require changes or transitions in job tasks, nor highly speeded performance) may not experience a decrement in job performance (Park, 1994). On the other hand, employees in jobs requiring high processing speeds may experience difficulties as they age, due to a decline in cognitive speed (Warr, 1994). Employee attitudes and withdrawal behaviors have also shown a relationship with age. Older employees are less likely to turn over, are generally higher in job satisfaction, exhibit less absenteeism, and are more committed to organizations than younger employees (Warr, 1994). One moderator of these relationships may be the centrality of work in an individual's personal meaning system. Presumably an individual who believes that work is central to his/her identity may, for example, exhibit lower absenteeism rates and be more satisfied and committed than an individual whose personal meaning system does not place work in as central a position.

Although the centrality of work in employees' personal meaning systems, as defined by Westerhof and Dittman-Kohli, has not been examined in the research in industrial/organizational psychology, two related variables, job involvement and work involvement, have been the subject of much research activity (cf., Brown, 1996; Kanungo, 1982). Job involvement is typically defined as one's psychological identification with one's current job and the degree to which the job situation is central to one's identity (Brown, 1996), while work involvement is focused on identification with work in general, especially influenced by past socialization about the centrality of work in one's life (Misra, Kanungo, von Rosenstiel, & Stuhler, 1985). Since most involvement research in organizational settings has been conducted with employed persons, it is not surprising that the bulk of the research studies have focused on job involvement. In a meta-analytic review of the research on job involvement, Brown (1996) found that the degree of job enrichment (the extent of challenge, autonomy, skill variety, and task significance in one's work activities) was significantly related to the level of job involvement. This suggests that those individuals who have more interesting and intrinsically motivating jobs also identify more with those jobs, or that the jobs are more central in their personal meaning systems (to use the terminology of Westerhof & Dittman-Kohli). What we do not know is how these job characteristics affect the meaning contents of work-related selves, although job involvement's usual significant correlation with job satisfaction (Brown, 1996) would lead us to predict that the content would be more positive for those with more enriched jobs than for those with less enriched ones.

An interesting extension of Westerhof and Dittman-Kohli's research would be to look for differences in meaning content for individuals employed in various kinds of jobs. Because organizational level and occupational status can be used as rough measures of job enrichment, it might be possible to categorize members of their research sample into job enrichment levels and see if differences in centrality and meaning exist. We would predict that work would be more central to personal identity and the meaning content more positive for those individuals in high-status occupations or high-level positions than for those in lower-status occupations or low-level positions. Examining age-related differences within each of these status and level groups might also reduce one potential confound that may affect the results presented by Westerhof and Dittman-Kohli. That is, since older workers typically have higher-level positions than younger workers, we cannot be sure how whether some of the apparent age-related differences noted by Westerhof and Dittman-Kohli are due to level or status differences, or to the associated differences in extent of job enrichment.

A final interesting extension of Westerhof and Dittman-Kohli's research that cannot be fully addressed for some time is to examine the impact of the changing nature of jobs, organizations, and employment relationships on the centrality and meaning of work. Certainly, many members of their sample from the former East Germany have experienced profound levels of change in their working conditions, as we have previously noted. However, observers of work organizations and the nature of work itself have commented on the substantial changes that all employed persons are facing today and will continue to face in the foreseeable future. Whereas many workers, especially those employed in large organizations, have traditionally anticipated a long career of upward progression with a single employer or at least within a single occupation or industry, an individual's work life in the 21st century will be characterized increasingly as one with numerous employers and several mini-careers (Howard, 1995, 1998). Individuals will also much more frequently be employed as temporary or contract workers, be assigned by their employer to work within a client organization, or be other kinds of "free agents" in the marketplace, selling their skills and needing to update and upgrade those skills to meet market demands. Such changes in the employing organization's commitment to workers are likely to be associated with parallel changes in employee commitment to those organizations and, perhaps, in their level of involvement in their work (see, e.g., Rousseau, 1995).

One recent organizational trend that is likely to be relevant for the role of work in individuals' personal meaning systems is the increasing responsibility that individual employees now have for their own careers and related skill updating. The individual for whom work is not central may not be strongly motivated to devote time and energy to career planning and work-related lifelong learning, and may have employment difficulties within those organizations that take little responsibility for developing their employees. We might expect that such employment difficulties will lead to additional negative meanings related to work and an even less central role for work within these employees' personal meaning systems. A likely result may be negative "spirals" (cf., Lindsley, Brass, & Thomas, 1995) in which the reduced importance of work and lowered motivation to spend personal time on skill improvement serve to create ever-increasing employment problems for the individual. At the same time, work may become even more central for those individuals who do proactively plan their careers and improve their work skills and then are rewarded for such behavior with employment success, leading to a positive spiral effect of increasing work-related efficacy and intrinsic motivation. Thus, we may see both positive and negative behavioral and attitudinal spirals regarding work and its place within individuals' lives. While we are speculating regarding such spirals with little or no empirical base, the possible implications of personal meaning systems regarding individual effectiveness at work are considerable.

CONCLUSIONS

The concept of a personal meaning system is a valuable addition to research and theory on the meaning of work and its relation to the self. As work organizations and the nature of work itself continue to evolve, increasing responsibility is being placed on individual employees at all organizational levels to manage their careers, to update and change their skill sets, and to contribute innovative ideas as an expected part of their job performance. As social, legal, and economic factors also create changes in the normative definitions of career and retirement, there is considerable need to understand better how work is integrated into the personal meaning systems of older individuals. The work of Westerhof and Dittman-Kohli is an important beginning to this understanding. As is expected with any important research, it does raise more questions than it answers. We look forward to reading the future work stimulated by this provocative paper.

REFERENCES

Brandstädter, J., & Greve, W. (1994). The aging self: Stabilizing and protective processes. *Developmental Review, 14*, 52–80.

Brown, S. P. (1996). A meta-analysis and review of organizational research on job involvement. *Psychological Bulletin, 120*, 235–255.

Came, B. (1998, September 28). Kohl's big test. *Maclean's, 111*(39), 38–40.

Carter, M. A. T., & Cook, K. (1995). Adaptation to retirement: Role changes and psychological resources. *The Career Development Quarterly, 44*, 67–82.

Feldman, D. C. (1994). The decision to retire early: A review and conceptualization. *Academy of Management Review, 19*, 285–311.

Frable, D. E. S. (1997). Gender, racial, ethnic, sexual, and class identities. *Annual Review of Psychology, 48*, 139–162.

Frone, M. R., Russell, M., & Cooper, M. L. (1995). Job stressors, job involvement and employee health: A test of identity theory. *Journal of Occupational and Organizational Psychology, 68*, 1–11.

Higgins, C. A., Duxbury, L. E., & Irving, R. H. (1992). Work-family conflict in the dual-career family. *Organizational Behavior and Human Decision Processes, 51*, 51–75.

Howard, A. (Ed.). (1995). *The changing nature of work.* San Francisco: Jossey-Bass.

Howard, A. (1998). Commentary: New careers and older workers. In K. W. Schaie & C. Schooler (Eds.), *Impact of work on older adults* (pp. 235–245). New York: Springer Publishing Company.

Kanungo, R. N. (1982). Measurement of job and work involvement. *Journal of Applied Psychology, 67*, 341–349.

Lindsley, D. H., Brass, D. J., & Thomas, J. B. (1995). Efficacy-performance spirals: A multilevel perspective. *Academy of Management Review, 20*, 645–678.

Misra, S., Kanungo, R. N., Von Rosenstiel, L., & Stuhler, E. A. (1985). The motivational formulation of job and work involvement: A cross-national study. *Human Relations, 38*, 501–518.

Nicholson, N. (1984). A theory of work role transitions. *Administrative Science Quarterly, 29*, 172–191.

Nkomo, S. M., & Cox, T., Jr. (1996). Diverse identities in organizations. In S. R. Clegg & C. Hardy (Eds.), *Handbook of organizational studies* (pp. 338–356). London, England: Sage Publications.

Oyserman, D., & Kemmelmeier, M. (1995, June). *Viewing oneself in light of others: Gendered impact of social comparisons in the achievement domain.* Paper presented at the 7th Annual Convention of the American Psychological Society, New York.

Park, D. C. (1994). Aging, cognition and work. *Human Performance, 7,* 181–205.

Pernice, R. (1996). Methodological issues in unemployment research: Quantitative and/or qualitative approaches? *Journal of Occupational and Organizational Psychology, 69,* 339–349.

Rousseau, D. M. (1995). *Psychological contracts in organizations.* Thousand Oaks, CA: Sage.

Schultz, K. S., Morton, K. R., & Weckerle, J. R. (1998). The influence of push and pull factors on voluntary and involuntary early retirees' retirement decision and adjustment. *Journal of Vocational Behavior, 53,* 45–57.

Warr, P. (1994). Age and employment. In H. C. Triandis, M. D. Dunnette, & L. M. Hough (Eds.), *Handbook of industrial and organizational psychology* (2nd ed., Vol. 4, pp. 485–549). Palo Alto, CA: Consulting Psychologists Press.

CHAPTER 4

Caution: Health Care Is Hazardous to the Aging Self

Robert L. Kane

INTRODUCTION

This chapter addresses a basic paradox. Seeking health care is one of the most egocentric acts in which most people engage. When we are ill, we are preoccupied with it; we tend to focus our attention on our bodies and the consequences of that illness. We want the undivided attention of those from whom we seek help. However, the health care system acts in almost the opposite way. For most people, most of the time, the cost of getting health care includes sacrificing one's sense of person. The process can become dehumanizing.

Medical care is designed to help people, but sometimes its consequences can be harmful as well. We refer to the risks of care as iatrogenic complications. Some of the risks are readily apparent, such as the side effects of medications. Others can be more insidious. The effects on an older person's sense of self are included among the latter. The cost of health care should not include the diminution of one's sense of self, but, too often, such is the case. Anyone who has been a patient in a hospital can quickly identify with the assaults on self, as one's identity is removed and one's dignity is stripped away. The medical care system does not especially target older person's for these insults; older people are simply more often exposed and vulnerable to them.

Americans are notoriously self-directed. The Declaration of Independence affirms "life, liberty, and the pursuit of happiness." Many Americans seem to be actively pursuing this goal. Some may question the potential for independence in an environment bombarded by behavior shaping advice (often in the form of advertising) and rules and regulations that seem to circumscribe behavioral choices, but many of the latter were introduced in response to excesses in self-fulfillment. Ours is a consumer society. We have high expectations of what society can do for us and tend to view most of this as close to a right, or at least an opportunity. Thus, Americans are self-centered. They place a high value on themselves (and consequently on human life). Given a choice, they will more likely than others seek the path that offers some hope, however feeble, of extending the life span, even for days.

WHAT DO PEOPLE WANT IN TREATING ILLNESS

The concept of self in the context of the health care system prompts Kafkaesque visions of patients struggling to find their way in a bureaucratic maze. The first question we need to address is whether this situation is particular to health care, or instead represents part of a larger shift to a more impersonal and complex society, where people no longer communicate, but engage in rituals. However, even if medical care is falling victim to larger societal forces, we may ask whether such behavior is acceptable for the caring setting.

It is no accident that health care traces its origins to priestly practices. Magical thinking still plays a strong role in healing and in allowing things to be done to our bodies. Medical care often entails an enormous invasion of privacy. Bestowing special status to medical practitioners is one means of easing the trauma of such intrusions. Medical care deals with scary things, like dreaded disease and death. In times of fear, we are all prone to resort to magical thinking, and welcome the opportunity to place our trust in some higher power. As medicine becomes more available to laypersons (e.g., through news releases and media stories), some of the magic is lost. One cost of the bright light and the even playing field is a loss of faith. As medicine becomes more of a commodity or another service to be supplied on demand, our expectations for service rise, but our satisfaction is bound to diminish.

Different generations will likely have different expectations of medical care. The current generation of older persons was raised to believe that doctors deserved respect by virtue of their position. It was far better to wait to see the doctor than to have him (for they were usually men) waste precious time waiting for a patient to arrive. Indeed, the longer the wait, the more prestige accrued to the doctor. Patients did not enjoy waiting, but they viewed the wait as inevitable.

Older patients may find it hard to play by modern rules that make the patient an equal partner in treatment decisions. Patient empowerment works only if the patient wants to be empowered. What does one do with the older patient who says that she is anxious because she has become aware of all the risks involved in treatment and balks at all the choices to be made? She turns to her doctor and asks him to make the decisions because she does not feel competent to decide and does not want the responsibility that comes with the decisions.

One mechanism for coping with serious disease is to place one's trust in those providing the care. The danger of this model comes when the providers begin to feel comfortable with this approach and view it as normal. This loss of insight can prove costly. It justifies establishing institutions that run to fit providers' needs rather than those of patients.

HISTORY OF THE PATIENT/SYSTEM RELATIONSHIP

The last several decades have seen a dramatic change in the relationship between patients and the health care system. The shift has been reflected in the jargon. We have moved from "patient" to "consumer" to "customer." These terms are heavy with significance.

The very word "patient" implies waiting. Until fairly recently, there was a large social distance between patients and physicians. Doctors were viewed as special people. Often, they represented the more educated members of society, and belonged to the near upper class. Patients were expected to pay deference to the doctor, whose time was seen as more valuable, and whose advice was to be followed as inspired revelation.

A number of things have changed over the last half century. Since the end of World War II, the population has become better educated. Whereas, years ago, most physicians practiced independently or in small partnerships, most physicians today practice as part of large groups or corporate enterprises. Hospitals have become palaces of technology, where the high daily costs of care produce strong pressures to discharge patients as quickly as possible.

The patient has become an impatient consumer. Daily lives are busier. More people (especially women) work. The pressures to fulfill multiple responsibilities place an ever-heavier burden on time. Even leisure has become task-oriented. As a result, medical encounters have become more businesslike. Time spent waiting is viewed as a cost. Many (but not all) older people have more free time. For them, a visit to the doctor's office may be a social occasion. The waiting room can be a place of interaction.

For an ego-centered society with an active agenda, visits to a physician present a paradox. On the one hand, no one wants to be kept waiting. We have an expectation of efficiency that implies prompt service production on a predetermined schedule. At the same time, no one wants to be treated as an anonymous being. Seeing a physician is still a very personal, individual experience. Given the narrowed social distance, if anything, today's patients expect their physicians to pay even closer attention to them. Once they are in treatment, they want full attention for as long as possible. The effect on the larger group of patients is ignored. No satisfactory answer to this conundrum has been found.

The response to this dilemma—of wanting maximum attention with minimum waiting—has been the marketing of medical care. As in other sectors, other personnel have been hired to act as intermediaries, to create a sense of attention and personal concern, and to follow through on the implementation of regimens. (Think of flight attendants on airlines, or greeters at Walmart.)

On the other hand, the change in terminology has moral implications. The physician's responsibility for a "patient" is likely to be much greater than that for a "customer." While this sense of beneficence can quickly evolve into paternalism, putting the patient in a dependent position, it offers a stronger sense of caring and a deeper commitment than would be found in a more commercial relationship. The role of customer implies a greater sense of individual responsibility. In the marketplace, buyers must beware.

The shift to a vocabulary that addresses consumers and customers implies more attention to the individual and a greater appreciation of the need to meet each person's expectations. This new emphasis is part of a larger transition towards a more businesslike approach to delivering medical care. The implications of the reconceptualization are profound. As patients became consumers, medical care came to be regarded as another service. As they become customers, their satisfaction takes on greater salience. However, quality in the business world is judged primarily by its effect on sales. High quality is that which is valued by the customer. Products and services are designed to be attractive and desirable. Quality in science is considered more of an inherent trait, reflecting professional beliefs about what is important. In the business paradigm, packaging is important, Attention to service access and personalized service may overwhelm the importance placed on doing the right things well. Satisfaction (and hence customer loyalty) may be better achieved by influencing how patients are handled than how well their medical conditions are managed.

THE CHANGING HEALTH CARE SYSTEM

America suffers from advanced technophilia. American physicians are driven by technology. Health care has become a much more complex undertaking. The old image of the family doctor working on his own to meet his patients' needs has given way to a much more sophisticated, if impersonal, model of care. Doctors need company. They need colleagues, usually specialists in specific areas of skill and knowledge. They need support staff. They need equipment. Numerous forces tend to press for more technology.

First, the very presence of a technology is an inducement to use it.

Second, payment systems have favored technology over time; doctors are paid more for technologically complex activities. Talking to patients and thinking are not well rewarded. (At least, they have not been under the fee-for-service payment scheme.) Moreover, in that fee-for-service world, technology generates income, and often costs the doctor nothing. Either the doctor orders the test to be done elsewhere (and may charge a fee for interpreting it), or he runs the test and bills separately for it. It is only when he is paid a single fee for all the components of an office visit that technology would be used only if it provided information that was worth the cost to the doctor. In the hospital the situation is different. The doctor assumes no responsibility for costs, but Medicare pays the hospital a single payment, regardless of how much technology is used. If the doctor owns the technology, the incentives to use it are even greater.

Third, professional standards of practice encourage the use of technology. Specialists owe their existence to technologies, and are continuously interested in maintaining their advanced position by keeping abreast of new developments. Malpractice concerns encourage physicians to get as much information as possible.

The hospital has emerged as a technology palace, one where the technology needed for sophisticated practice is provided to the practitioner at no cost. The increased technological sophistication of the hospital has had several consequences. Hospital care has become more expensive and hence the pressure to reduce lengths of stay has increased. This pressure to discharge quickly creates an atmosphere that does not encourage lengthy communications, and certainly does not encourage patients to become actively involved in decisions about their care. Many of these decisions are terribly complex. They require careful deliberate thought. Often, all parties are far from agreement. Such lengthy decision making threatens the efficient functioning of the technology enterprise. Making good decisions presupposes that one can get good information. Most experts involved in a technology are enthusiasts for that technology. Some may not even be aware of their predisposition, viewing it simply as informed opinion. In the best case, they are prone to bias in favor of the technology. In the worst case, they are unable to accept anyone who would challenge its role.

The pre-eminence of technology further serves to widen the gap between patients and care professionals. The hospital is seen as an institution for delivering technically sophisticated care. That care is expensive. The time of those involved in providing the care is at a premium. Hence, procedures should operate to maximize the efficiency of production. Patients' convenience and comfort come as secondary considerations. The situation deteriorated to such a point that books had to be written reminding nurses that patients are people (Brown, 1964).

Hospitals concerned about their image with the public began hiring ombudspersons. The major function of these personnel was to address patient complaints before they become litigations. In effect, they were a defense against malpractice suits (Mailick & Rehr, 1981).

Probably one of the worst areas in meeting patient needs, and, ironically, one of the most important, is discharge planning. Especially for older persons, discharge from a hospital may influence the care that person receives for the rest of her life. It may mark the beginning of a long-term care career. The decision about the location, type, and amount of post-hospital care to be provided should not be made lightly. Often, this decision requires careful consideration of options and the implications of each. Various family members have a stake in this decision, as potential care providers or simply as highly interested bystanders. The goals for such care address not merely the clinical trajectory of the older patient, but the physical and emotional health of the entire caregiving apparatus.

The circumstances for making such a crucial decision could hardly be worse. The pressures to shorten lengths of stay place great pressures on the discharge planners, whose effectiveness is measured in time, not results. Ideally, discharge decisions should follow a systematic process (Potthoff, Kane, & Franco, 1998). The first question is to assess the patient's status (or, more accurately her clinical trajectory, since few patients are any longer discharged in a stable condition) and to determine the benefits and risks associated with alternative types of post-hospital care. In order to decide among these alternatives, it is important that patients be clear about the outcomes they want to maximize. This type of decision making is not easy under the best circumstances. Few people can spontaneously identify their real priorities. Carefully structured assistance is needed from skilled professionals.

Another critical ingredient is time. It takes time to uncover what is most important to people. Most of us have never really stopped to clarify the complex value issues that are associated with the multiple possible outcomes from care. It takes even longer to resolve conflicts among family members who may have strong feelings (and invest-ments) in different outcomes. For example, some may be strongly concerned about issues of the patient's safety and willing to go to any lengths to avoid a catastrophe; others (including the patient) may be more anxious to maintain a greater level of autonomy.

The next step in discharge decision making is to select a vendor among those offering the service that best fits the patient's risk/benefit profile. The salient factors for choosing a vendor may be quite different from those involved in choosing a type of post-hospital service, which is often confounded with location (e.g., nursing home versus home care). Vendor issues may hinge on such things as ambi-ance, philosophy, location, and cost. When the decision involves making a major move, such as entering a nursing home, it would be better made after visiting several potential vendors to obtain firsthand knowledge about the environment. Such a step seems un-realistic in the context of contemporary hospital discharge planning. Too often, the most available place is the one chosen. Not only is self not the center of concern; it is virtually ignored.

The hospital with all its technological complexity has evolved into a larger structure, the medical center. This transition implies a network of services. One of the unexpected consequences of tech-nological development is the ability to deliver services once thought to be the exclusive purview of hospitals in a variety of settings. Such a shift should give the patient more options, but the decision about location of service is usually made by the payer, not the patient. Indeed, patient convenience is the often less well served. Patients may be asked to arrive at early hours for outpatient surgery, after fasting and doing their own bowel preparations, in order to avoid a night's hospitalization. They may be discharged soon after surgery to be cared for at home by family.

The medical network is seen by some hospitals as a universe in which the various components of care revolve around the hospital, but a new Copernican revolution may be occurring. The hospital's central position is being usurped. Hospitalization is being increas-ingly viewed as a treatment setting to be avoided.

The shift in locus of care has also been accompanied by a revision in thinking about health care costs. The rapidly rising costs of care prompted a major rethinking about how to organize the incentive system. Managed care emerged as the answer. Managed care is essentially hands-on health insurance. The health insurance company is no longer able to simply pass on the costs of care; they have an obligation to control these costs. There are basically only two ways to control costs: 1] pay providers less, or 2] provide less. Ideally, a third option would be to become more efficient by delivering care more efficiently or by preventing problems in the first place. Certainly neither of the first two options seems to benefit the consumer of care. Paying providers less encourages their spending even less time per encounter. Doing less is clearly antithetical to most health care users' goals.

The gap between the potential and the reality of managed care's effects on health care is especially important for the care of older persons. On the one hand, managed care could provide a vehicle for more effective care through improved coordination and better accountability. On the other hand, managed care could simply emphasize cost cutting and restricted access (Kane, 1998).

The shift to managed care is also a move toward a new locus of care. Health care has become less a professionally driven service and more a corporate enterprise. Those at the head are more inclined to measure success in terms of profitability than achieving some professional norms. Because profitability is likely to be affected by consumer loyalty, more attention is directed toward pleasing the customer. Ironically, the corporate model may be more attentive then to the customer's wishes (at least their superficial ones) than the solo-practitioner doctor model, in which the doctor prided himself on really knowing his patients.

ROLE OF LITIGATION

Fear of litigation has had a great influence on medical practice. Health professionals report practicing "defensive medicine," by which they mean ordering tests whenever there is a possibility of serious disease in order to avoid missing a treatable condition. Not only does this practice drive up costs, it is probably only modestly effective in reducing malpractice suits (Brennan, Sox, & Burstin, 1996). Ironically, the best defense against being sued is probably having a strong rapport with one's patients (Hickson et al., 1994). People who feel that their doctor cares about them are less likely to blame the doctor for poor results and more likely to react to poor care as part of the bargain. Nonetheless, the response to the fear of litigation has been more technological than personal.

PERFORMANCE OF OTHER PROFESSIONALS

While physicians are often characterized as spending too little time with patients and having inadequate interpersonal skills, other disciplines are supposed to be more adept at these. Nurses have long incorporated into their training a strong emphasis on patient-centeredness and the importance of communication. In truth, there is likely wide variation in the performance of nurses in these areas. At least part of the variation may be explained by setting. Nurses working in technologically intensive settings such as intensive care units may be little better than physicians in taking the time to communicate. Nurses or social workers placed in time-stressed roles such as discharge planning seem unable to achieve the needed levels of communication and attention to preferences that would be desired. Nurses in charge of hospital inpatient units seem to be too caught up in an endless stream of paperwork to develop rapport with patients in their charge. Ironically, one classic study found that the person hospital patients turned to for information on their condition was often the cleaning person (Duff & Hollingshead, 1968).

Nonetheless, nurses do appear to offer more personalized contact with patients than do physicians. Indeed, the rise of nurse practitioners as an alternative source of primary care seems to be based on nurses' interpersonal skills (Mundinger, 1994). Certainly, the basic trade-off is between someone presumed more clinically skilled and someone who will give more attention to the patient. Nurses are also more likely to emphasize preventive issues and take a more holistic view of health.

Dissatisfaction with traditional care has led to greater enthusiasm for alternative forms of care (Astin, 1998). Although the scientific value of chiropractic care is still not clear (Balon et al., 1998; Cherkin, Deyo, Battie, Street, & Barlow, 1998), interest in chiropractic care is growing, perhaps because chiropractors spend more time with their patients and legitimize their complaints, whereas physicians are more likely to dismiss functional complaints (Kane, Woolley, Leymaster, Olsen, & Fisher, 1974).

Social workers are expected to have strong patient skills. Much of their training is directed at listening to people and helping them to cope with their problems. As medical care has felt the pressure for efficiency, the role of social work has diminished. Social workers are most likely to be found in discharge planning units, where they face the same time pressures as their nursing colleagues, or functioning as mental health therapists, competing with physicians and psychologists. Few medical organizations continue to include within their purview an obligation to assist patients in coping with their diseases or their implications.

THE AGING SELF

As noted earlier, health care was not particularly designed to assault the aging self. Older people are simply at greater risk for several reasons:

1. They are more likely to get sick, especially with chronic conditions that may require extensive care. Hence, they are more likely to be more exposed.
2. Older persons are more likely to suffer from several simultaneous problems that affect different domains of life (e.g., physical, psychological, and social); each can exacerbate the deleterious effects of the other.
3. The health care system may have a different effect on people of different ages.

The mantra of gerontology includes recognizing the difference between age and cohort. In this context, at least some of the difference in how people relate to the health care system can be attributed to cohort effects. Older persons today have brought with them into old age a set of beliefs and expectations about how the health care system should operate. They seem to imbue it with a level of authority and pay deference in a way that may be incomprehensible to their children, and certainly to their grandchildren. Many are uncomfortable taking an active role in making decisions about their care; they prefer to leave such decisions in the hands of persons they believe to be much better informed. Many have only modest expectations from the medical care system, and appear grateful for the time spent by busy practitioners. Many who evince strong feelings in private seem to be transformed once in the doctor's presence into meek, compliant subjects, unable to express dissatisfaction or even to admit when they do not understand what is being said.

This pattern of ineffective communication can create further problems. Patients who fail to understand their regimens are unlikely to follow them. Hesitancy to ask questions can lead to delays in treatment and unnecessary complications. Acceptance of one's situation as inevitable can prevent early recognition of treatable problems.

At the same time, older persons do experience real change with frailty. They are less able to respond to the stresses of illness. The diminished response to stress can manifest as asymptomatic or dampened presentation of illness (Kane, Ouslander, & Abrass, 1994). Thus, those caring for older persons need special training to recognize that illnesses may not present in the same way they do with younger patients. Exacerbations of chronic conditions may be hard to detect amidst a pattern of generalized symptoms.

Frailty also diminishes an older person's ability to engage the system. They may lack the energy and resilience to pursue their cause, and end up passively accepting what is done to them.

LOSS OF SELF AS THE COST OF CARE

The way the current medical system is constructed, one expects to pay a price in terms of dignity and self when one enters a hospital. The unstated social contract runs something like this: You will forfeit your sense of self, your identity, and your dignity in exchange for the anticipated benefits of the care you are about to receive, although one could certainly challenge the premises of that contract by questioning whether such a sacrifice is necessary. The hospital (and the physician's office) is being operated to maximize the convenience and efficiency of the staff (although the staff would probably claim it was operated primarily for the physicians' convenience). Patients are moved around like game pieces.

While most younger patients can tolerate this type of treatment because it usually does not last long and because they are basically intact, such an approach may have terrible consequences for frail older patients. Hospitalized older people may become disoriented (i.e., delirious) and eventually may be labeled as demented. They can become incontinent because they are bedbound or placed in an unfamiliar setting. They may develop any of a number of complications associated with prolonged bed rest.

The basic social contract with the hospital promises a substantial potential for benefit in exchange for the risks entailed to one's self and one's person. As a general rule, one might argue that the value of this bargain to the older person diminishes as problems become more chronic and less amenable to promises of a cure. This contract is least useful in the context of the nursing home, where the potential benefits are much fewer. Unlike the hospital, nursing home care lasts a long time and is usually not expected to achieve any major improvement in one's condition. Indeed, the milieu of the nursing home constitutes much of the treatment. Unfortunately, too many nursing homes provide neither much nursing (most of the care is provided by nurses' aides) nor a homelike environment. The regimented, impersonal, routinized lifestyle is not conducive to individualization, and certainly does not respond to a sense of self. Ironically, most studies of satisfaction among nursing home residents have been unable to elicit high degrees of dissatisfaction, despite the deprivation noted. Part of the problem may be traced to fear of retribution, but another factor is accommodation. In essence, persons placed in deprived situations lower their expectations and hence are satisfied with much less. Circumstances that produce learned helplessness can lead to depression and withdrawal (Seligman, 1976).

The deprived level of existence can be appreciated in the responses demonstrated from extremely modest interventions, such as allowing nursing home residents to grow a plant or have a pet. (For a list of such studies, see Table 8.1 in Kane & Kane, 1987.) The fact that these simple acts have been shown in randomized studies to produce significant improvement in residents' quality of life points to just how close these nursing home residents must have been to their nadir.

The plight of nursing home patients, especially in light of their frailty, has spurred numerous efforts to regulate the nursing home industry. Most of the effort has been directed toward structural and process criteria, which suggest that a given level of staffing or approach to care will produce desired results. Little attention has been directed at directly examining the effects of care on the residents. Several years ago, federal law mandated the introduction of a systematic recording system to standardize the reporting of residents' status, the Minimum Data Set (MDS). However, this data is obtained exclusively by observing residents. No provisions are made to ask residents directly about how they feel. In effect, all residents are treated as though they were too cognitively impaired to be able to respond to specific questions (Kane, 1998). Such a process is a dramatic denial of the importance of self for these people. Data derived solely from observations is a very poor basis for addressing quality of life. Assuming the capability to infer another person's emotions or their sense of meaning, or even their satisfaction, simply from observations, is an act of hubris.

COMPLIANCE/ADHERENCE

Perhaps nothing illustrates the powerful relationship between doctor and patient as well as the terminology used to describe patient behavior under treatment. The common term is "compliance" (Roter et al., 1998). The very word conjures up an image of a passive object shaped by an active force. Efforts to find a more socially suitable word have not fared much better. The term currently in vogue is "adherence," but this term suggests some type of sticking to it, and is equally as passive. Indeed, the dominant model of care is one where the physician diagnoses and treats and the patient complies. The good patient will do as she is told. In some instances the treatment process may be some form of negotiation, whereby the doctor proposes a treatment and the patient indicates barriers to following through. Concessions may be made to address logistical problems, but once the bargain is struck, the patient is expected to comply.

The penalty for noncompliance varies. It may result in a mild rebuke, or it could be the basis for terminating the therapeutic relationship. Under this arrangement, the health professionals have an obligation to instruct and patients have a duty to learn. Studies of compliance indicate that it is influenced adversely by the complications of the treatment regimen (Haynes, Taylor, & Sackett, 1979). Simplification is one means to improve compliance. Skillful practitioners may seek ways to incorporate chronic regimens into patients' daily routines.

DECISION MAKING

One way to acknowledge the importance of the individual is to incorporate the patient as a key player in the decision-making process. Some allusion to decision making has already been made in the context of discharge planning, but clinical care requires decisions to be made at various stages. The key to decision making is who controls information. Inevitably, the health professional has a monopoly on clinical information. While some dedicated clinicians may attempt to provide patients and their families with a complete picture of the risks and benefits of alternative treatment approaches, most practitioners are biased in favor of one approach or another. However well intended, they are not the best sources of information.

Other approaches to facilitating decision making have attempted to slow down the process and make it more deliberate. These approaches offer unbiased information in fashions that make them accessible to the patient. One of the most ambitious approaches to this end was the Shared Decision-Making project, which used interactive video technology to provide information to patients that could be watched as often as necessary until the patient felt comfortable with the information. An impressive result of that experience was the number of patients who opted for watchful waiting in lieu of treatment (Barry, Mulley, Fowler, & Wennberg, 1988; Kasper, Mulley, & Wennberg, 1992).

Ironically, structuring better decision making through vehicles like Shared Decision-Making may provide a means to achieving the rationing that many factions seek. If, indeed, patients opt for less treatment after considering the consequences of the alternatives, it would be to everyone's advantage (except those providing the treatment) to encourage greater deliberation. One context where the treaters do hold such sway is managed care. In this setting, efficiency is defined as delivering the necessary service at the lowest possible price that does not compromise quality. One might expect that managed care operators would be more enthusiastic about improving decision making if it offers a means to reducing utilization of expensive services. Surprisingly, few managed care organizations have adopted such programs. Instead they seem to rely on external case managers who employ a variety of strategies to reduce utilization (Pacala et al., 1994).

Ironically, there seems to be more concern about how decisions will be made by people who can no longer express their will than for those who can. One area of decision making that has received a great deal of attention is advance directives. The dominant motivation for advance directives is to prevent what is viewed by many as the ineffective expenditure of large sums on fruitless care to prolong meaningless lives. In essence, the patient's self has been subordinated to the technology that permits life-sustaining treatment. A cynical perspective might suggest that the effort is really a modestly disguised effort at rationing care, beginning with those least able to protest.

While there is good reason to applaud efforts to prevent needless care, there is some cause for concern. Studies have shown that people's values and preferences can change rather dramatically with circumstances. Specifically, people's disutility (negative value) associated with avoiding a condition may be much greater than the utility held by those with the condition for getting rid of it (Sackett & Torrance, 1978; Torrance, 1987). In other words, fear of developing a condition may cause people to express an opinion about how they would like to be treated that may cause undertreatment should the case actually occur. One example of this phenomenon was the surprising finding that many older people with advanced disease were still anxious to cling to life and wanted active care (Tsevat et al., 1998).

HOSPICE CARE

One area where patients are likely to be treated as individuals and to have their selves recognized is hospice care. Such an observation reaffirms the idea that some sort of basic trade-off is involved. Health care's ability or enthusiasm to address the self seems to vary inversely with the perceived benefits of treatments. While hospice care is certainly an extreme case, many would argue that medical care should attend to the whole person. The increasing emphasis on quality of life as an outcome of care implies a redefinition of successful care. Especially in an era of chronic care, where cure is unlikely, care should include helping patients to deal with their problems and addressing the functional implications of illness and its treatment. Much of geriatric practice is designed to achieve just this end. Organized programs that systematically assess the whole older person have shown impressive benefits (Stuck, Siu, Wieland, Adams, & Rubenstein, 1993). The basis for the success of comprehensive geriatric assessment likely lies at least in part in its ability to broaden the definition of care to encompass the patient and her illness.

RECOMMENDATIONS FOR IMPROVING HOW THE HEALTH CARE SYSTEM TREATS THE SELF

The modern health care system has not been very successful at enhancing, or even addressing, the concept of self in older persons. It is too easy to suggest that loss of self is the price of technologically sophisticated care. Especially in an era of chronic disease, where the expectations of medical care must shift, the importance of acknowledging the effect of care on the individual takes on new salience.

There is some basis for optimism. At least the language of medicine is changing in a way that is more compatible with goals that encompass the whole person. More attention is being focused on quality-of-life issues, although much of that effort seems to be directed principally at finding a basis for rationing care.

Several steps can be taken now to improve the situation. In the context of long-term care, we need to acknowledge that the hospital-based model of the nursing home, which artificially combines the housing and service functions, is inappropriate. One way to remove the distinction between home and institutional care would be to separate programmatically the room and board and the service components of care (Kane & Kane, 1991). Such a division would leave institutional residents to be viewed primarily as tenants, to whom services could be brought more economically than if they were dispersed in the community. As tenants, they would control their environments and have much greater opportunities to exercise autonomy over everyday decisions. The services could be designed in more individualized ways to meet specific needs.

A second step would be to hold institutions accountable for the outcomes of the care they provide. While not all (perhaps even only a relatively small part) of the total variance in outcomes can be attributed to care, that portion should serve as the basis for accountability. If the outcomes are defined to include elements of both quality of care and quality of life, and if appropriate case-mix correction is applied, then the basis of regulation and reward can be shifted from an undue reliance on professional criteria to an emphasis on outcomes, leaving the providers more flexibility to create innovative approaches to care. Especially if satisfaction is included as a relevant outcome, such approaches may be more likely to address the psychosocial aspects of care than do the current systems.

The typical response to addressing a new area in the health care system is to create a new discipline to attend to it. If personalization is to become a more central feature of health care, it may prove necessary to create a new cadre (or to empower an extant group) of workers to attend to the problem. Paraprofessional workers could collect data on individual client preferences. This data could then be used by clinicians in framing recommendations, or even better, for structuring more thoughtful decision making. Several candidate groups to collect such data already exist. Case managers seem a likely choice, but they exist only sporadically, and at present seem more preoccupied with controlling utilization. We have already seen that discharge planners, who might be expected to play this role, are overwhelmed by the pressures placed on them to accomplish their primary task under conditions of hardship. Ombudsmen could also theoretically play this role, but they would have to become more proactive and be more universally available (Harris-Wehling, Feasley, & Estes, 1995). Different settings may find different ways to personalize care, but its accomplishment is the ultimate goal.

The penchant for using guidelines as a basis for care could extend to creating guidelines for decision making. The same structured approach to defining the elements for good care could be applied to outlining the steps involved in good decision making and used as criteria to judge the quality of that aspect of care.

A RESEARCH AGENDA

Many important questions remain to be answered about how the medical care system affects the aging self. At the simplest level are the "how" questions. How does one implement programs to make the medical system more attentive, more responsive? The next level are the "so whats." What difference would it make if the system did achieve these reforms? Would older persons be happier, better off? Would their clinical course reflect this alteration in style? Is such attention to the older self an added cost, or can it properly be viewed as a means toward a common end?

Some of these questions lead back to basic gerontological issues. Are older persons simply a more extreme case of patients in general, or do they respond differently to the stresses produced? In other words, is there an interaction of aging and susceptibility? Is the aging self at special risk simply because it resides in an older person, or can the different effects be traced to the attributes of the care provided and circumstances of its provision?

REFERENCES

Astin, J. A. (1998). Why patients use alternative medicine: Results of a national study. *Journal of the American Medical Association, 279,* 1548–1553.

Balon, J., Aker, P. D., Crowther, E. R., Danielson, C., Cox, P. G., O'Shaugnessy, D., Walker, C., Goldsmith, C. H., Duku, E., & Sears, M. R. (1998). A comparison of active and simulated chiropractic manipulation as adjunctive treatment for childhood asthma. *New England Journal of Medicine, 339,* 1013–1020.

Barry, M. J., Mulley, A. G. J., Fowler, F. J., & Wennberg, J. W. (1988). Watchful waiting vs. immediate transurethral resection for symptomatic prostatism: The importance of patients' preferences. *Journal of the American Medical Association, 259,* 3010–3017.

Brennan, T. A., Sox, C. M., & Burstin, H. R. (1996). Relation between negligent adverse events and the outcomes of medical-malpractice litigation. *New England Journal of Medicine, 335,* 1963–1967.

Brown, E. L. (1964). *Patients as people.* New York: Russell Sage Foundation.

Cherkin, D. C., Deyo, R. A., Battie, M., Street, J., & Barlow, W. (1998). A comparison of physical therapy, chiropractic manipulation, and provision of an educational booklet for the treatment of patients with low back pain. *New England Journal of Medicine, 339,* 1021–1029.

Duff, R. S., & Hollingshead, A. B. (1968). *Sickness and society.* New York: Harper & Row.

Harris-Wehling, J., Feasley, J. C., & Estes, C. L. (1995). *Real people, real problems: An evaluation of the long-term care ombudsman programs of the Older Americans Act.* Washington, DC: Institute of Medicine.

Haynes, R. B., Taylor, D. W., & Sackett, D. L. (Eds.). (1979). *Compliance in health care.* Baltimore: Johns Hopkins University Press.

Hickson, G. B., Clayton, E. W., Entman, S. S., Miller, C. S., Githens, P. B., Whetten-Goldstein, K., & Sloan, F. A. (1994). Obstetricians' prior malpractice experience and patients' satisfaction with care. *Journal of the American Medical Association, 272,* 1583–1587.

Kane, R. A., & Kane, R. L. (1987). *Long-term care: Principles, programs, and policies.* New York: Springer Publishing Company.

Kane, R. L. (1998). Assuring quality in nursing home care. *Journal of the American Geriatrics Society, 46,* 232–237.

Kane, R. L., & Kane, R. A. (1991). A nursing home in your future? *New England Journal of Medicine, 324*(9), 627–629.

Kane, R. L., Ouslander, J. C., & Abrass, I. B. (1994). *Essentials of clinical geriatrics* (3rd ed.). New York: McGraw-Hill.

Kane, R. L., Woolley, F. R., Leymaster, C., Olsen, D., & Fisher, F. D. (1974). Manipulating the patient: A comparison of the effectiveness of physician and chiropractic care. *Lancet, 1,* 1333–1336.

Kasper, J. F., Mulley, A. G., & Wennberg, J. E. (1992). Developing shared decision-making programs to improve the quality of health care. *Quality Review Bulletin, 18,* 183–190.

Mailick, M. D., & Rehr, H. (Eds.). (1981). *In the patient's interest: Access to hospital care.* New York: Prodist.

Mundinger, M. O. (1994). Advanced-practice nursing: Good medicine for physicians? *New England Journal of Medicine, 330,* 211–214.

Pacala, J. T., Boult, C., Hepburn, K., Kane, R. A., Kane, R. L., Malone, J., Morishita, L., & Reed, R. (1994). *Case management of older adults enrolled in health maintenance organizations. Final report of a study conducted under contract with the Robert Wood Johnson Foundation.* Minneapolis, MN: University of Minnesota.

Potthoff, S., Kane, R. L., & Franco, S. J. (1998). Improving hospital discharge planning for elderly patients. *Health Care Financing Review, 19*(2), 47–72.

Roter, D. L., Hall, J. A., Merisca, R., Nordstrom, B., Cretin, D., & Svarstad, B. (1998). Effectiveness of interventions to improve patient compliance: A meta-analysis. *Medical Care, 36,* 1138–1161.

Sackett, D. L., & Torrance, G. W. (1978). The utility of different health states as perceived by the general public. *Journal of Chronic Diseases, 31,* 697–704.

Seligman, M. E. P. (1976). *Learned helplessness and depression in animals and men.* Morristown, NJ: General Learning Press.

Stuck, A. E., Siu, A. L., Wieland, G. D., Adams, J., & Rubenstein, L. Z. (1993). Comprehensive geriatric assessment: A meta-analysis of controlled trials. *The Lancet, 342,* 1032–1036.

Torrance, G. W. (1987). Utility approach to measuring health-related quality of life. *Journal of Chronic Diseases, 40*(6), 593–600.

Tsevat, J., Dawson, N. V., Wu, A. W., Lynn, J., Soukup, J. R., Cook, E. F., Vidaillet, H., & Phillips, R. (1998). Health values of hospitalized patients 80 years or older: HELP Investigators. Hospitalized Elderly Longitudinal Project. *Journal of the American Medical Association, 279,* 371–375.

Commentary

Illness Narratives and the Aging Self

Dan G. Blazer

R obert Kane, in his chapter "Caution: Health Care Is Hazardous to the Aging Self" (this volume), has focused upon the loss of the aging self as it negotiates the evolving health care system in the United States. He specifically focuses upon loss of self during long-term care. Kane has investigated long-term care throughout his distinguished career. He suggests that, though persons might expect to forfeit their sense of self, identity, and dignity in exchange for the anticipated benefits of acute care, the same is not the case with long-term care. While the basic social contract with the hospital promises a substantial potential for benefits in exchange for the risks entailed to one's self, that same potential for benefits is far from being realized with long-term care in the nursing home. "The regimented, impersonal, routinized lifestyle is not conductive to individualization and certainly does not respond to the else of self" (Kane, p. 195, this volume).

I believe Kane is correct, that he has cut to the angst we experience as providers, investigators, and recipients of so-called long-term care in the United States. Yet this is an hypothesis. Dr. Kane does not provide guidance as to "Where do we go from here?" Few studies have addressed this hypothesis directly. We could benefit from studies which document and clarify the loss of self by older adults in long-term care settings. These studies should derive from a theoretical construct of the self. I will briefly provide one rather simple construct for such studies, recognizing that constructs of the self are manifold.

I bring to this volume the perhaps unique perspective of a practicing "social psychiatrist" whose focus is geriatric psychiatry. Geriatric psychiatry is a thriving subspecialty of psychiatry, yet social psychiatry is a largely forgotten discipline. Social psychiatry flourished during the 1960s (Kaplan, Wilson, & Leighton, 1976). The failure of the overly ambitious agenda of social psychiatry and the mental health center movement was due to the failure of social therapies to impact the mental health burden of the public; the perceived need to more closely associate psychiatry with mainstream medicine; and the explosion of the neurosciences coupled with new biological therapies. On balance, psychiatry has benefitted from its biological orientation; yet the social psychiatric perspective could be of great benefit to us today as an heuristic framework. Considering the suffering or fractured self (the ultimate focus of psychiatry) within the context of the social environment is essential if the ills of the health care system are to be understood, much less corrected.

The social environment at the turn of the century is not friendly to the sense of self. Self-concept requires a consistent and integrated view of who one is. Yet, persons today find themselves filling multiple and often competing roles simultaneously. For example, persons' elders may be both parent and child (and perhaps even grandparent and child). They may be professionals, such as professional educators, yet have lost virtually all contact with their profession. They may live in an affluent neighborhood, yet find themselves under financial pressure (are they rich or poor?). They may maintain a lifelong identity with a political party, yet find themselves at odds with the policy of that party. The fast-changing and often confusing social environment challenges the basics of self-concept, such as constant values, a permanent sense of identity, and the ability to project oneself into the future.

Self psychology has been of interest to psychiatrists and psychologists for most of this century and to philosophers since antiquity. During the 20th century, Heinz Kohut (1985) provided a correction to Freud's psychoanalytic theories via his emphasis upon the analysis

of the self. Carl Rogers (1961) implicitly elevated the self via his popular non-directed psychotherapy which utilizes paraphrase to encourage the self to emerge during the process of therapy. These therapeutic approaches, however, are not well suited to objective study. The work of Alexander Leighton (1959) on the other hand, does attempt to apply social theory to both psychiatric illness and therapy via epidemiological studies and therapeutic interventions via community mental health centers. His theory of social integration/ disintegration, however, failed in that it did not link the person and the environment. In other words, Leighton's theories and investigations were ecological. I suggest that narrative may be one link between self and the social environment, a concept not new to this group.

No single theoretical construct of self would be sufficient nor accepted by all or perhaps even most scientists interested in the study of self. Yet "self" is at the heart of our deliberations. Constructs of self are difficult, because they depend not only upon our theoretical orientation, but are at the very core of our personal self perceptions. Therefore I suggest a construct of self based on narrative. My assumption is that we can only recognize ourselves or other selves when we tell our stories or hear the stories of other persons. The self based in narrative is a core assumption of psychiatric/psychological assessments and therapies. I propose a series of parameters of the narrative self which might be used to examine the self in the context of long-term care. The parameters I identify may seem unusual, perhaps not objective at all, but I submit that these parameters are critical to recognizing, much less understanding, the aging self. My thesis is that, to the extent that narrative or story is lost, self is lost. If the older adult's narrative is recognized by the providers of long-term care, then the self can be preserved, even under the most difficult circumstances. In other words, narrative, to a large extent, contributes to the construction of the aging self, both from the perspective of the older adult and those with whom the older adult is in contact in the delivery of health care (Kleinman, 1988).

The idea of the self as narrative is not new to gerontologists. Butler (1963) noted that elderly patients may spend much time in their consultations with health care professionals, not to mention family and friends, discussing the many aspects of their lives, such as losses of friends and loved ones, past accomplishments, hobbies, and values prevalent in the past. This tendency to reminisce was central to Erikson's eighth stage of development, integration vs. despair. In other words, those who can tell their life stories effectively near the end of their lives have integrated their selves, whereas those who cannot despair of ever finding themselves (Erikson, Erikson, & Kivnick, 1987). Though very few persons actually script their lives to any real extent, that is, life is serendipitous, to maintain a sense of an integrated self it is important, when one looks back on one's life, to find a script. The story of one's life may evolve spontaneously, but it nevertheless should form a comprehensible whole.

I propose that four parameters of narrative are critical to the preservation of self in long-term care and that these parameters are subject to objective inquiry. The first is narrative of current personal concerns of the self in relation to his or her body (including the brain). This narrative has been reified in the medical history as the "chief complaint" (though frequently the current concerns of the older adult are not complaints as such in the long-term care setting). In other words, what is of chief concern to the older adult in long-term care? Even the elder with significant cognitive impairment voices current concerns, such as "I want out." Or "Hurts, that hurts." These brief comments say much more than is often appreciated. "I want out" is an expression of a desire for control. Loss of control, a feeling of being out of control coupled with a feeling of being controlled, is almost ubiquitous with the process of institutionalization, but it is a part of the narrative of each person who expresses a complaint. Likewise, the complaint of discomfort, perhaps the feeling of persistent discomfort, though it may be a major concern of the elder, may desensitize the caregiver in long-term care. Like the proverbial boy who cried "wolf" too often to be heard when he was attacked by a wolf, the elder who constantly complains of pain may not be heard when a new and important pain arises.

The second is narrative of the social network or the self in relation to others. This narrative has been reified, to some extent, in sociological and epidemiological research of "social support." Social support includes the actual network of persons who come in contact with the elder through various means (see below) but also the frequency of interaction and the quality of interaction. The elder's self is defined in large part by the elder's network. "I am a family man" may be evaluated in light of the observation of how often the elder speaks of family, of how often family visit or the concern and assistance provided by family. If the perception is discordant with the observation, then the self may be fragile.

The third is narrative through time. This narrative has been reified to a limited extent in the "past history" and "care plans" of medical management. Yet, narrative through time passes from the past through the present to the future. One of the most easily forgotten aspects of care in long-term care facilities is the future of the elder, however foreshortened. Tomorrow matters, just as yesterday and today matter. The provider of care of older persons in long-term care would do well to ask, "What are you going to do tomorrow?" or "What shall we do tomorrow if it is sunny?" This permits the elder to regain the sense of self as continuing intact into the future, essential for a concept of self.

The fourth is narrative of integration. This narrative has been reified at times in studies of spirituality and existential issues, though it has largely been neglected both in sociological/epidemiological research and in medical practice. As noted above, the work of Erik Erikson (Erikson et al., 1987) has grounded our understanding of the need for integration. Yet integration does not stop at the boundary of the person through time, but includes a history of family, race/ ethnicity and faith traditions. A statement such as "I am a Jew from Brooklyn" is pregnant with meaning, and should be remembered and pursued in the long-term care setting. The self is not only the physical person residing in a nursing home near University Park, Pennsylvania.

Narrative of current personal concerns would appear to be the most accessible of the four parameters in the long-term care setting. Yet this perception can be misleading. When the older adult visits a physician's office or is evaluated in an emergency room, the "reason" for the evaluation, the "chief complaint," is the focus of the initial dialogue between the elder and the caregiver. In long-term care, however, familiarity may breed neglect, if not contempt. A complaint of pain or hopelessness, witnessed over days, perhaps weeks, in a nursing home may be forgotten or repressed by the providers of care. Congruence of narrative between the older adult and caregivers potentially can be compared.

Narrative of social support can be investigated by recording the visits and phone calls of the older adult to determine the network and frequency of interaction as well as the type of social interaction engaged in by the older adult. In addition, the elder can be asked to describe her or his network through open-ended questions. The perceived as well as the observed network of the elder can be investigated. The perceived may be more important than the observed network. Regardless, the relationship between the observed and perceived networks is most important. Care providers should possess an understanding of the perceived and observed network. What is the congruence across the elder's perceived network, the observed evaluation of the network, and the care provider's perception of the network?

Narrative through time can be evaluated by emerging techniques which encourage the older adult to "tell her or his story." The story can then be compared with the "story" described by the nursing providers. The techniques for eliciting these "stories" are applicable to the care providers as well as the investigator. A care provider could spend 2 hours, perhaps divided into three or four interviews, during which time the explicit goal is to learn about the elder's life story (perhaps via interview with both the elder and a family member).

Narrative of integration can be determined by having the older adult, again through open-ended techniques, describe her or his faith tradition and what brings meaning into her or his life. This exploration has been described by both theologians and social scientists as fixing the individual story within a larger story, or fixing narrative within metanarrative. Recent studies suggest that such narrative explorations can provide most useful information. The taking of a "spiritual history" as part of the diagnostic work-up has become a recognized necessity in the delivery of health care. Even simple components of this narrative of integration, such as the faith tradition to which the older adult belongs or the older adult's particular views about the role of one's faith as it relates to one's health and well-being, could be most informative.

The methods for collecting the data to inform us regarding these four parameters of narrative are both available, and can easily enough be implemented in the study of older adults in long-term care. For example, biographical and life-history approaches to the life cycle have been explored by Bertaux (1981) and Kaufman (1986). Most of the authors who write of the methods reflect upon the tension between the macro- and micro-level approaches to personal narratives. Hughes (1971) referred to so-called objective and subjective careers, respectively. That is, as a community, we share ideas of what is expected from a normal life—the objective career—yet the subjective career may rebel or at least feel tension with the objective, such as the tension one feels when fit into the Procrustean bed of being a long-term care resident.

Of course, cognitive dysfunction, among other factors, will mitigate the use of these methods to some extent, and cognitive dysfunction is frequent in nursing homes. The challenge to investigators and clinicians alike is to synthesize these parameters. The very concept of self implies synthesis. Edmund Wilson (1998), in his recent book *Consilience,* has suggested that the greatest challenge to science is this synthetic task and that the social sciences, of all the sciences, struggle most with synthesis.

On a more positive note, synthesis proves not to be such a challenge to those of us who are care providers, for we intuit that which is difficult to systematically construct. We naturally take diverse bits of information and mold them into a perception of individual selves, ourselves and the selves of others. Perhaps what is most often missing in long-term care settings are the bits of information necessary to construct these selves. If we can find the time to hear the narratives, perhaps learn to retell the stories, of the persons for whom we provide care, then the selves of older adults, I believe, will emerge both for us and for the older adults.

REFERENCES

Bertaux, D. (Ed.) (1981). *Biography and society: The life history approach to the social sciences.* Beverly Hills, CA: Sage.

Butler, R. N. (1963). The life review: An interpretation of reminiscence in the aged. *Psychiatry, 26,* 65.

Erikson, E. H., Erikson, J. M., & Kivnick, H. Q. (1987). *Vital involvement in old age.* New York: W. W. Norton.

Hughes, E. C. (1971). *The sociological eye.* Chicago: Aldine-Atherton.

Kaplan, B., Wilson, R., & Leighton, A. (Eds.) (1976). *Further explorations in social psychiatry.* New York: Basic Books.

Kaufman, S. (1986). *The ageless self.* Madison, WI: University of Wisconsin Press.

Kleinman, A. (1988). *The illness narratives: Suffering, healing and the human condition.* New York: Basic Books.

Kohut, H. (1985). *Self psychology and the humanities: Reflections on a new psychoanalytic approach.* New York: Norton.

Leighton, A. (1959). *My name is Legion: Foundations for a theory of man in relation to culture.* New York: Basic Books.

Rogers, C. (1961). *On becoming a person.* New York: Houghton Mifflin.

Wilson, E. (1998). *Consilience: The unity of knowledge.* New York: Knopf.

Commentary

Preservation of Self Among Elders: Implications for Change in Health Care

Sarah Hall Gueldner

I found Kane's chapter (this volume) to be powerful and provocative, reflecting profound insight into what some would call the plight of aging within the social structures of today's world. His exposition profiles well the many ways that the present health care system unthinkingly compromises the self of older persons.

Most notably, encounters within the fast paced for-profit health care environment too often bypass the elder in the decision-making process, sending the subtle message either that they are incapable of making decisions, or that their input is not important. Under the pressure of cost-containment, the health care system is increasingly impersonal and inattentive to the personal identity of its clients. Services are provided at the convenience of the system, implying that the client's time is not valued. The system is complex and instruction is limited and hurried, creating the likelihood of confusion and mistakes. In these ways, the health care system tends to compromise the feelings of identity and mastery of virtually all of its clients. The threats to self inherent in this scenario may be exponentially compounded by declining function and limited resources among elders, placing them at greater risk than the general population for diminished self-esteem.

Kane's chapter has inspired me to reflect on correctable flaws within our social structure that can lessen the potential for harm to the self within our elders as they attempt to navigate the system of health care to obtain the services that they need. I will attempt to extend Kane's discourse in regard to four areas: 1) philosophical ambiguities that exist within the underlying premises of today's health care system, 2) attention to comprehensive elder-specific discharge planning, 3) the need for social policy that supports the system of informal caregivers, and 4) re-verification of right-to-die decisions.

Philosophical Ambiguities Within the Health Care System

I am struck by the outdated premise that continues to undergird our current health care system. It does not yet live up to its name, *health* system, but instead lingers conceptually beyond its time as an *illness* system, based on acute care aimed at curing disease, implying an unrealistic dichotomy between illness and wellness (Kane, 1999). But freedom from illness is becoming less of an option for contemporary society. Sophisticated pharmaceutical and other advanced therapies have curbed the threat of infections and many other life-threatening conditions, enabling more people to live longer. But as people live longer they develop chronic health problems. It is estimated that 80–95% of health expenditures today go to address chronic conditions (Hoffman, Rice, & Sung, 1996). Therefore, a more central health issue has become managing chronic illness, for which there usually is not a cure. As a society we are challenged to find ways to achieve a degree of health, even in the presence of serious and potentially disabling chronic illness.

Aggressive Elder-Specific Discharge Planning

I strongly agree with Kane's view that discharge planning is the weakest link in today's health care system. A large body of research confirms that many elders require care that is too complex for families to manage after discharge from the hospital, placing them at high risk for re-hospitalization (Naylor, 1986, 1990). In fact, the re-hospitalization of patients over 70 is estimated to be as high as 37% within the 6 weeks after discharge (Weinberger, Smith, Katz, & Moore, 1988), accounting for up to one-fourth of all admissions (Fethke, Smith, & Johnson, 1986) and incurring Medicare costs as high as $8 billion each year. It is important to note that re-hospitalization is particularly expensive, with costs ranging from 24% to 55% higher than the original hospitalization (Zook, Savickis, & Moore, 1980). Although hospitalized elderly have been found to need more assistance after discharge for a longer period of time than the general population, they are least likely to have the support they need at home. Yet research findings confirm that discharge planning is not considered a priority by most health professionals, and that it often suffers from delayed and inadequate assessment, poor documentation, and fragmented implementation (Department of Health and Human Services, 1987; Fink, Siu, Brook, Park, & Solomon, 1987; Johnson, 1989). A study by Johnson and Fethke (1985) revealed that only 20% of hospitalized elders received any discharge planning.

Over the past decade, increased attention has been given to the development and testing of comprehensive elder-specific discharge planning protocols designed to improve post-discharge outcomes. The more successful of these plans have included geriatric consultation and intensive post-discharge follow-up (Edelstein & Lang, 1991; Naylor, 1990; Naylor et al., 1994; Smith, Weinberger, Katz, & Moore, 1988). A research team headed by Naylor (1986, 1990; Naylor et al., 1994) demonstrated substantial post-discharge benefits using a discharge protocol developed specifically for the elderly and implemented by a gerontological nurse specialist (GNS).

A unique feature of the Naylor protocol is a thorough assessment of each patient by the GNS within 24 hours of admission, using the revised Enforced Social Dependency Scale (ESDS) (Moinpour, McCorkle, & Saunders, 1988) to measure functional status. Within this scale, enforced social dependency is defined as assistance from other people to perform activities or roles that under ordinary circumstances adults can do by themselves. The revised ESDS measures social as well as personal competence. Social competence is assessed around four categories judged central to performing as a normal adult, including activities in the home, work, recreational and social activities, and social competence. Personal competence includes six activities: eating, dressing, walking, traveling, bathing, and toileting. A high correlation has been established between the ESDS and the Sickness Impact Profile (Fink, 1985).

The GNS uses the data obtained during this early assessment to project the post-discharge needs of the elderly patient and his/her primary caregiver, and to develop a discharge plan. The discharge plan is immediately communicated to the patient's primary nurse, along with a list of specific teaching needs. Throughout the hospitalization, the GNS validates the understanding of the patient and their primary caregiver relative to the knowledge and skills that will be required after discharge. The discharge plan is re-evaluated and modified by the GNS within the 24 hours prior to discharge. The GSN is available by telephone throughout the hospitalization and after discharge, with a minimum of two telephone contacts with the patient within the first 2 weeks after discharge.

The findings from the work of Naylor and others have consistently confirmed the economical and personal benefits of elder-specific discharge planning and education, particularly in terms of the decrease in post discharge infections and incidents of re-hospitalization (Kennedy, Neidlinger, & Scroggins, 1987; Naylor, 1990; Naylor et al., 1994). Implementation of the discharge planning was not found to significantly increase the length of the primary hospitalization. These studies confirm the need to focus more attention on discharge planning, including educational programs for elders and their family members or friends who will care for them when they leave the hospital. It is imperative that a carefully developed discharge plan go home with each patient and their informal caregiver(s), replacing scattered instructions hastily disseminated as elders are being wheeled out to their car to leave.

Social Policy to Support the Informal Caregiver

A critically flawed entity within the social structure of our contemporary health care system, not addressed by Kane, is the lack of public policy supporting the role of informal caregivers, many of whom are frail elders themselves. The public cost of long-term care for elders is often lamented, but in truth most of the care of elders in our country is being provided in their homes by informal community caregivers—family and friends, most often women (National Alliance for Caregiving and American Association of Retired Persons, 1997). There is evidence that informal caregivers continue to provide a substantial part of their care, even when they are moved to the hospital or a long-term care facility (Kane, 1994).

Most elders prefer to be cared for at home by their family and friends, and most families and communities feel it is their responsibility to care for their elders. But the findings from more than 20 years of research on caregivers are alarming (Whitlatch, Zarit, Goodwin, & von Eye, 1995; Wright, Clipp, & George, 1993). Studies inform us that the life of many informal caregivers is incredibly difficult and stressful. We also know that they tend to neglect their own health care, and that they are twice as likely to die as their counterparts in the community who do not carry the heavy burden of caregiving (Wright et al., 1993).

Fortunately, research has also identified strategies that may help ease the caregiver's load. There is substantial evidence that adequate social support makes the load seem lighter, and that supplemental interventions, such as respite opportunities and psychoeducational programs, may help them to cope with the strain (Kane & Penrod, 1995; Whitlatch et al., 1995; Wright et al., 1993).

In spite of their tremendous contribution to society, informal caregivers seem to be taken for granted by most segments of society (Doty, 1995). For instance, even though we now have an adequate base of research findings to inform policy, the United States still lacks a coherent policy on family care for the elderly (Kane & Penrod, 1995).

I believe it is time to seriously revisit the present system of family caregiving. Care given by family is assumed to be more loving, attentive, and emotionally satisfying than care given by strangers (Kane & Penrod, 1995). While this is generally true, there are also instances of abusive care, perhaps due to unbearable stress. And the caregiver always experiences some loss—loss of free time, social contacts, or time with other members of the family. Some family caregivers even have to give up their work, or place their jobs in jeopardy because of absenteeism (Neal, Ingersoll-Dayton, & Starrels, 1997). For women, whose careers are already more fragile, this may feel like a terrible loss. For this reason, it is important that we be mindful of Neysmith's (1991) caution that models of societal caregiving should not continue to impose disproportionate costs on women.

I believe that we must consider ways to provide the societal support necessary to sustain our informal caregivers. It has been suggested that public funds be designated to purchase supplemental services that would lighten their load. Given that informal caregivers save society a great deal of money, it seems reasonable that a system of payment be devised that would enable informal caregivers to purchase the help they need in order to avoid becoming sick themselves. We must continue to test supportive interventions, and perhaps above all, we must be sure that neither the caregiver or their care recipient slips from the mainstream of society. That is too great a price for them, and for society, to pay.

It is important that we consider innovative community-based models, such as those being implemented in the United Kingdom and Canada, and recently in the United States (Arno, Levine, & Memmott, 1999; Kane & Penrod, 1995), that are based on public payment for some aspects of care previously provided without charge by family caregivers. Some argue that paying informal caregivers "puts a price tag on filial duty" and undermines the family's role (Kane & Penrod, 1995, p. 162). However, there is considerable evidence that families will remain involved with their older relatives, even when the public pays for some services that the families now provide (Kane & Penrod, 1995). Data from these programs show that community care for the elderly remains the overwhelming preference of older people and family caregivers alike. It should be emphasized that all such programs are designed to augment, not replace, the care that families give.

Linsk, Keigher, Simon-Russinowitz, and England (1992) take a positive view of such a payment system for family caregivers, and describe it within an income redistribution policy. As Kane and Penrod (1995) observed, it seems "absurd to pay someone to care for a stranger and pay someone else to care for his or her own mother" (p. 163). Paying family caregivers would provide additional income to low-income families, who are the most affected by the devastating effects of family caregiving, and vulnerable older people with disabilities would theoretically enjoy a stronger power base from the income.

But such a major social reform will take time, and some relief must be found for informal caregivers in the meantime. A less daunting modification in the social structure that bears consideration as both an interim and long-term partial solution is the expansion of the concept of flexible hours and/or caregiver leave at the workplace. Some work organizations have become more sensitive to caregivers, and have developed policies that provide flexibility in the scheduling of work hours (Neal et al., 1997). Other work organizations offer formal services to help their employees find and manage satisfactory care arrangements for their family members who need assistance.

It is also time that we, as a society, begin to change our misconception that women are at home each day, and that caregiving is a female role. Statistics inform us that 58% of all American women 16 years of age and older are in the labor force, and that percentage is estimated to grow to 63% by the year 2005 (Doty, 1998). Given this trend, it seems certain that men will increasingly have to assume or participate in the role of informal care (Harris, 1998). Toward that end, it is important that boys and girls alike be socialized as children to nurture and care for others (Neal et al., 1997).

Kane and Wilson (1993) encourage us to "move toward a hopeful new paradigm" as we search for "efficient and humane care of people with disabilities in living settings that they recognize as normal" (p. 167). These authors further advocate that older people who have disabilities that affect their ability to care for themselves and function in their homes and communities are entitled to long-term benefits for assistance with these functional needs. They also argue that such benefits should be considered separately from any health benefits.

Re-verification of Right to Die Decisions

Finally, I am haunted by Kane's assertion that, in contrast with our generation's seeming obsession with living wills, number of days alive do matter a great deal to some elders who are facing death. I think this possibility requires that we revisit our zealous Right to Die/Living Will movement, to be sure it accurately reflects the views of those nearing the potential implementation of such a document.

It seems possible that we may view that choice a bit more cavalierly in our younger years than in our later years, as the option becomes more vivid. It seems some may have agreed to conditions that they might later wish to change, if given the opportunity. We must be sure that they have that opportunity.

A growing body of research indicates that while some individuals may come to welcome end of life, at least some others value life intensely, and cling to it as long as possible, even in the face of severe health problems (Lawton et al., 1999; Tsevat et al., 1998). Lawton and colleagues (1999) demonstrated a complex relationship between value of life (VOL) and years of desired life (YDL). The findings of this study in a sample ($n = 600$) of individuals 70 years of age or older revealed that African American subjects, those naming more family members, and those at the younger end of the age spectrum were more likely to desire to live "as long as possible." It was important to note that African American subjects, who comprised one half of the large sample, wished to live significantly longer under all ten of the conditions measured, no matter how devastating the circumstances. Even the hypothetically posed condition of severe pain reduced the wish to live by only a very small amount. Likewise, age was not always found to be a significant variable. In general, men wished for a longer life than women. It is important to note that the Quality of Life (QOL) indicators used in most previous studies as a correlate of desire to live rarely correlated to Years of Desired Life in this study.

These findings raise questions about the growing assumption that persons faced with diminished health related quality of life wish to live for a shorter amount of time. The work of Lawton and his colleagues clearly documents that there is more to the wish to live than health alone, and gives evidence that one's health status may in fact represent the least potent influence on one's wish to live.

CONCLUSIONS

As a society, we must restructure the health care delivery system so that it embraces the self of elders and their informal caregivers, rather than needlessly desecrating their identity and undermining their confidence. Specifically, we must delete those characteristics of the system that compromise self-worth, overcome the tension between cost and convenience, and arrive at a better balance between high-tech and high-touch. We must embrace new interdisciplinary models of health care that operate at the convenience of all clients—but especially at the convenience of our elders, who are less mobile and have fewer options than the population in general. The system must foster healing relationships built through rapport that takes time to establish.

But changing the health care system to better meet the needs of our elders will require a wide-scale shift in our present view of both aging and health, moving our emphasis from *illness* and *disability* to *health* and *ability*, even in the face of serious, perhaps incurable illness. Society must also change its expectation of the health care system from cure of disease to the management of chronic conditions. And we must come to see that one doesn't earn or not earn health care, at any age. Likewise, we must continue to develop comprehensive elder-specific discharge plans and social policy that supports the forgotten group of informal caregivers, who provide most of the care for elders. Finally, we must not presume to know when another wishes to die, regardless of age or health status.

REFERENCES

Arno, P. S., Levine, C. & Memmott, M. M. (1999). The economic value of informal caregiving. *Health Affairs, 18,* 182–188.

Department of Health and Human Services. (1987). *Posthospital care: Discharge planners report increasing difficulty in planning medicare patients.* (GAO/PMED-87-5BR). Washington, DC: U.S. Government Printing Office.

Doty, P. (1995). Family caregiving and access to publicly funded home care. In R. A. Kane & J. D. Penrod (Eds.), *Family caregiving in an aging society: Policy perspectives* (pp. 92–122). Thousand Oaks, CA: Sage.

Doty, P. (1998). The impact of female caregivers' employment status on patterns of formal and informal eldercare. *Gerontologist, 38,* 331–341.

Edelstein, H., & Lang, A. (1991). Post-hospital care for older people: A collaborative solution. *The Gerontologist, 31,* 267–270.

Fethke, C. C., Smith, I. M., & Johnson, N. (1986). Risk factors affecting readmission of the elderly into the health care system. *Medical Care, 24,* 429.

Fink, A. (1985). *Social dependency and self care agency: A descriptive correlation study of ALS patients.* Unpublished master's thesis, University of Washington, Seattle, WA.

Fink, A., Siu, A., Brook, R., Park, R., & Solomon, D. (1987). Assuring the quality of health care for older persons. *Journal of the American Medical Association, 258,* 1905–1908.

Harris, P. B. (1998). Listening to caregiving sons: Misunderstood realities. *The Gerontologist, 38,* 342–352.

Hoffman, C., Rice, D., & Sung, H. Y. (1996). Persons with chronic conditions: Their prevalence and costs. *Journal of the American Medical Association, 276,* 1973–79.

Johnson, J. (1989). Where's discharge planning on your list? *Geriatric Nursing, 10,* 148–149.

Johnson, N., & Fethke, C. (1985). Post-discharge outcomes and care planning for the hospitalized elderly. In E. McClelland, K. Kelly, & K. Buckwater (Eds.), *Continuity of care: Advancing the concept of discharge planning* (pp. 229–240). New York: Grune and Stratton.

Kane, R. A., & Penrod, J. D. (1995). Toward a caregiving policy for the aging family. In R. A. Kane & J. D. Penrod (Eds.), *Family caregiving in an aging society: Policy perspectives* (pp. 145–153). Thousand Oaks, CA: Sage.

Kane, R. A., & Wilson, K. B. (1993). *Assisted living in the United States: A new paradigm for residential care for older persons?* Washington, DC: American Association of Retired Persons.

Kane, R. L. (1994). *A study of post-acute care* (Final report, Health Care Financing Administration, Grant No. 17-C98891). Minneapolis: University of Minnesota Institute for Health Services Research.

Kane, R. L. (1999). A new model of chronic care. *Generations: The Journal of the American Society on Aging, 23,* 35–37.

Kennedy, L., Neidlinger, S., & Scroggins, K. (1987). Effective comprehensive discharge planning for hospitalized elderly. *The Gerontologist, 27,* 577–580.

Lawton, M. P., Moss, M., Hoffman, C., Grant, R., Ten Have, T., & Kleban, M. H. (1999). Health, valuation of life, and the wish to live. *The Gerontologist, 39,* 406–416.

Linsk, N. L., Keigher, S. M., Simon-Russinowitz, L., & England, S. E. (1992). *Wages for caring: Compensating family care of the elderly.* New York: Praeger.

Moinpour, C., McCorkle, R., & Saunders, J. (1988). The measurement of functional status in illness. In M. Strombord (Ed.), *Instruments for clinical nursing research* (pp. 23–45). East Norwalk, CT: Appleton-Century-Crofts.

National Alliance for Caregiving and American Association of Retired Persons. (1997). *Family caregiving in the U.S.* Bethesda, MD and Washington, DC. Website: http://www.caregiving.org/content/reports/finalreport.pdf

Naylor, M. (1986). *The health status and health care needs of older Americans.* (U.S. Senate Special Committee on Aging, Serial No. 99-L). Washington, DC: U.S. Government Printing Office.

Naylor, M., Brooten, D., Jones, R., Lavizzo-Mourey, R., Mezey, M., & Pauly, M. (1994). Comprehensive discharge planning for the hospitalized elderly: A randomized clinical trial. *Annals of Internal Medicine, 120,* 999–1006.

Naylor, M. D. (1990). Comprehensive discharge planning for hospitalized elderly: A pilot study. *Nursing Research, 39,* 156–161.

Neal, M. B., Ingersoll-Dayton, B., & Starrels, M. E. (1997). Gender and relationship differences in caregiving patterns and consequences among employed caregivers. *The Gerontologist, 37,* 804–816.

Neysmith, S. M. (1991). From community care to social model of care. In C. T. Baines, P. M. Evans, & S. M. Neysmith (Eds.), *Women's caring: Feminist perspectives on social welfare* (pp. 272–299). Toronto: McClelland & Stewart.

Smith, D., Weinberger, M., Katz, B., & Moore, P. (1988). Postdischarge care and readmissions. *Medical Care, 26,* 699–708.

Tsevat, J., Dawson, N. V., Wu, A. W., Lynn, J., Soukup, J. R., Cook, E. F., Vidaillet, H., & Phillips, R. S. (1998). Health values of hospitalized patients 80 years or older: HELP Investigators. Hospitalized Elderly Longitudinal Project. *JAMA, 279,* 371–375.

Whitlatch, C. J., Zarit, S. H., Goodwin, P. E., & von Eye, A. (1995). Influence of the success of psychoeducational interventions on the course of family care. *Clinical Gerontologist, 16,* 17–30.

Wright, L. K., Clipp, E. C., & George, L. K. (1993). Health consequences of caregiver stress. *Medicine, Exercise, Nutrition & Health, 2,* 181–195.

Weinberger, M., Smith, D. M., Katz, B. P., & Moore, T. S. (1988). The cost effectiveness of an intensive postdischarge care. *Medical Care, 26,* 1092–1101.

Zook, J., Savickis, S. F., & Moore, F. D. (1980). Repeated hospitalization for the same disease: A multiplier of national health costs. *Millbank Memorial Fund Quarterly: Health and Society, 58,* 454–471.

CHAPTER 5

Risk, Rationality, and Modernity: Social Policy and the Aging Self

Angela M. O'Rand

INTRODUCTION: DEFINING TERMS

The modern self is the subject of new sociological interest at the turn of the century, among both mainstream social theorists (Castells, 1996; Giddens, 1991) and popular commentators (Beck, 1992). At the core of conceptions of the modern self are the ideas of individualization and risk as the central existential conditions of aging and the life course process. Modernity is a "risk culture" (Giddens, 1991)—rife with greater knowledge constrained by uncertainty, multiple choices with changing probabilistic outcomes, and individual vulnerability to distant (usually unrecognized and very likely uncontrollable) happenings as well as to proximate contexts. The ascendance of individualized risk as the principal factor in aging is the paradoxical result of the convergence of demographic and structural trends that define the modern age: these include longer (active) life expectancy, informational technology, globalization, and privatization. All these trends affect social policy and the aging self.

In the following essay, I will explore the aging self in the context of modern social policy. Social policies bear upon the organization of the life course. They influence the order, tempo, and steady or unsteady progression of social roles and transitions in the aging process. Market- and state-based policies affecting the aging self vary across societies, but the mutual contingency of these policies in a rapidly globalizing private capital economy is reconfiguring the private-public mix of policies across societies. This general process of policy reorganization is in the direction of privatization—i.e., towards greater individual responsibility and the market-centered, as opposed to state-centered, provision for normal life transitions and for more randomly encountered life-course risks. The privatization of social policy is requiring the individual to assume new risk-taking roles and responsibilities in matters of wealth and health.

I define "social policy" as the interdependent system of market practices and state or government statutes and administrative provisions that organizes and regulates the content and conduct of economic and civic life of individuals. The private-public systems of social policy across nations pursue jointly considered—though differentially valued—goals that include economic productivity/growth, social integration, general welfare or well-being, and equity. The extent to which these systems are more market-based (or residual) versus more state-based has had considerable impact on the forms and the inclusiveness of social policies protecting individuals against life-course threats or risks such as poverty, unemployment, or illness (see Leisering & Walker, 1998; O'Rand & Henretta, 1999; Pampel, 1998).

I define the aging self with the assistance of Giddens' recent reflections on the trajectory of self-identity (1991). The self is a reflexive project (an identity) that continuously links the known past (biography) with the less knowable future (anticipated life-span) in response to options confronted in the present. Reflexivity is directed towards balancing two processes: the constant revision of knowledge and practice to facilitate the control of time (work time, family time, leisure time) and the body (physical age, reproduction, illness, and health maintenance) in the present; and the preservation of a coherent self across successive contexts. The second process is further described by Giddens as a narrative of the self that preserves continuity while undergoing constant revision—and one that is continuously shaped and reshaped through social interaction and identity re-formation.

The life course is a series of passages or major transitions that presents the self with both institutionalized and personalized options, which are best defined as socially constrained opportunities and risks. As such, the life course is shaped by social forces that differentiate life experiences and outcomes (Dannefer & Uhlenberg, 1999). In the U.S. and other industrialized societies, the "normal life course"—i.e., the general lifetime sequence of social roles characteristic of the population as a whole—is demarcated as a tripartite order that (1) begins with childhood dependency and preparation for participation in the economy as a worker and in the state as a citizen; (2) is centrally defined by the trajectory of economic and family roles of adulthood; and (3) ends with a post-employment and post-child-rearing phase.

Across industrialized societies, the relative predominance of state or public supports for roles across these phases serves to standardize them and their temporal organization, while the relative predomi-nance of market institutions leads to less standardization and tempo-ral homogeneity and greater heterogeneity and inequality (Leisering & Walker, 1998). In addition, more marketized societies with weaker welfare state structures provide fewer public protections against life-course risks, leading to even more heterogeneity and inequality across the life-span (O'Rand & Henretta, 1999).

Some life-course passages are more 'fateful' (Giddens, 1991) or consequential than others over the long run. Among the latter are what sociologists have called the transition to adulthood, which is comprised of a bundle of transitions variously ordered and timed across young lives that anchors diverse life trajectories that follow. The bundle of transitions usually comprises a diverse set of statuses and a variable schedule of status changes in education, marriage, parenthood, and employment, with consequences extending to late life. For example, the longer duration of education has prolonged and robust positive effects on later wealth and health (Mirowsky & Ross, 1998). Premarital parenthood, on the other hand, has more depressing average effects on later wealth and health (Furstenberg, Brooks-Gunn, & Morgan, 1987).

Other consequential passages may relate to lifestyle changes oc-curring later and more randomly over the life course within cohorts, including the adoption of selected health behaviors (smoking, jogging) or voluntary changes in work environments or family roles. Still other fateful passages may relate more to life chances than to lifestyles. Unexpected or accidental events (such as job loss, divorce, physical injury, or disability) and highly constrained opportunity structures (such as the limited availability of life-course protections in health, disability, and pension insurance) can preclude the successful negotiation of crises and the coherent preservation of the self.

I define "risk" as the probability or relative uncertainty of an anticipated opportunity or outcome. As such, risk denotes a likelihood function based on limited information. The irony of risk in modern society is twofold. First, many old risks to the life course have largely disappeared. Old risks were based on an absence of information. The uninformed or unprotected exposure to life-threatening diseases, such as polio, or to life-threatening lifestyles, like smoking, has been significantly reduced. The unplanned for or involuntary transition from work to retirement has declined over the long stretch of the 20th century, albeit with interruptions in this trend resulting from cyclical disruptions and, more recently, from economic restructuring and labor force downsizing. Similarly, the risk for extreme poverty in old age has been reduced through social policies (e.g., Medicaid, Supplemental Security Income) developed over the 1960s and 1970s that recognized the inevitable vulnerability of segments of the aging population to poverty that had been previously underestimated and misunderstood. Meanwhile, new risks involve access to relatively more information, but information usually available in the form of probabilities or likelihoods, rather than certainties. Accordingly, the life expectancy of the oldest, frail population presents individuals and policymakers with probabilistic alternatives related to morbidity, mortality, and formal versus informal care options and their costs.

Second, in the presence of relative ignorance, old risks were considered from a societal perspective to be exogenous factors, i.e., as external shocks to which individuals within the collective were randomly and, therefore, equally vulnerable. This conception of risk facilitated collective (public) policies and solutions. In the presence of greater information, new risks are considered to be more endogenous. Accordingly, individuals' relative access to and understanding and use of information regarding, say, health risks or retirement savings strategies bear directly on their own outcomes. This conception of risk encourages more individualized (private) policies and solutions. It also challenges individuals' perceptions of personal efficacy and their sense of common fate.

Indeed, in spite of increased average life expectancy, assurances of the population's general better health, and improved material well-being reflected in employment rates and consumer behavior, Americans believe that life is getting riskier. The overwhelming majority (over four-fifths) of Americans polled over the past decade believe they are subject to more risks today than 20 years ago (Covello & Johnson, 1987). Philosophical, economic, sociological, and anthropological interpretations of this apparent paradox range between reductionist theories of rational choice and relativist theories of cultural determinism (Douglas & Wildavsky, 1982; Kelsey & Quiggin, 1989; Shrader-Frechette, 1991). All theories are converging on the idea that risk is not an "objective reality," but an informational process subject to temporal and social factors. We will return to these theoretical concerns later in this essay. For the time being, Herbert A. Simon's (1969) reflections on human behavior provide the frame for what follows: the complexity of human behavior largely reflects the complexity of the environment.

RISK ACROSS THE LENGTHENING LIFE COURSE

Increased life expectancy—also referred to as the "compression of mortality" (i.e., the increased survival and concentration of deaths around the mean age of death)—results from the success of the directed actions of institutions and individuals in overcoming traditional threats of earlier death (including infectious diseases, some chronic diseases, and selected environmental life threats) (Wilmoth, 1998). The most recent Social Security Administration projections of the life expectancy of the baby boom cohort in the U.S. at age 65 for men range between 12.9 and 13.1 years (depending on birth in 1946 or in 1959—the beginning and the end of the baby boom period) and, respectively, for women between 14.6 and 15.9 years. These projections produce expected mean ages at death that range between 78 and 81 for men and women—projections that some demographers consider conservative, given the dramatic recent declines in mortality at older ages (Manton & Stallard, 1996).

The age distribution of a population has implications for the economy and for existing pay-as-you-go welfare redistribution policies predicated on a different population age structure. The most recent Report of the Social Security Trustees (Social Security and Medicare Boards of Trustees, 1996) projects that the old age security and disability trust fund will remain in close actuarial balance for only 35 years (until 2030). The Medicare system presents more immediate concerns regarding solvency. Accordingly, policy analysts are considering alternative scenarios for economic and welfare policies that will achieve balance in the longer run.

Uhlenberg (1992) identifies three general social policy alternatives in the face of an aging population. The first is to intervene in the demographic process. Pro-natalism, high and selective immigration of the young, and the age-specific rationing of health care are options for changing the age structure itself. The second is to increase the productivity—or alternatively to decrease the dependence—of the older population. This implies the social reconstruction of the life course by resetting the boundaries of the work life, specifically extending the institutionalized threshold to retirement to later ages or by redefining the meaning of productivity. The third is to shift the locus of responsibility for maintenance of the life course away from the public and more towards the individual.

Numerous specific policy proposals that have been advanced have been less general, and have focused on incremental changes, such as cutting benefits and raising payroll taxes (Gramlich, 1997). Proposals for cutting benefits include (a) raising the retirement age, (b) deleting or suspending cost indexing, (c) reducing benefits for high-income retirees, (d) changing the benefit formula over time to reduce the replacement rates of higher-income groups, and (e) making benefits fully taxable within the income tax code. Proposals for increasing payroll taxes include removing the wage/salary ceiling and raising the tax rate. The most recent variants of these approaches are to raise payroll taxes immediately and invest these revenues in government bonds following current policy (Aaron, Bosworth, & Burtless, 1989) and/or in private equities with putatively higher returns than bonds (Bosworth, 1996). In spite of the relative unpopularity of most of these proposals across subgroups of the population—

and excluding the proposal to invest tax revenues in the equity market—they do not depart radically from the redistributive principles of the current system. And, even the proposal to invest in equities preserves a collective approach to income maintenance in old age.

Proposals for more fundamental change to the public Social Security system, on the other hand, call for higher levels of mandatory saving by individuals for retirement and/or health emergencies or long-term care and greater involvement in market-based as opposed to state-based approaches. The models for privatization are already in place in the U.S. occupational welfare system—which has drifted steadily for decades towards more highly individualized income and health protection mechanisms. More recently, the U.S. system has accelerated in this direction, fueled by the decline of collectively based models in the market (specifically labor or professional union plans) and the retreat by employers from long-term benefit coverage (Farkas & O'Rand, 1998). Privatized models are also being advocated on a worldwide basis as the social welfare states of Europe are faced with fiscal crises and the newly developing countries elsewhere are perhaps best characterized as weak states drifting in a hegemonic global economy dominated by multinational corporations (Castells, 1996).

The extension of these models to the public sector in the U.S. involves mandated savings in pension and/or selected health accounts (such as proposals for long-term care insurance) that are defined by constrained choices among vendors and across types and levels of insurance. The Federal Thrift Plan (FTP) of pension saving for federal employees is the exemplar in this area (the FTP program will be discussed in more detail later in this essay). The multiplex health insurance system under the rubric of "managed care" is already a privatized, individualized system of cost-graded alternatives.

In effect, the aging of the population is provoking numerous policy proposals that fall largely within two of Uhlenberg's categories (1992): the reconstruction of the life course through the decreased dependence of aging populations on public systems, and the relocation of more and more responsibility to the individual as saver and risk-taker. Uhlenberg's "demographic fix" is less directly evident, although the extent to which immigration policies are tied to labor policies (and therefore to welfare policies) and the extent to which health rationing ascends to a central position in national health insurance debates could move social policy more strongly in these directions.

MODERNITY, SOCIAL POLICY AND RISK-TAKING

Nowhere is the shift towards privatization and individualization in the U.S. more evident than in its pension and health policies. The welfare regime of the U.S. approximates the liberal model identified by Esping-Anderson (1990); this model provides minimal public insurance against life-course risks to income maintenance and health. Instead, the employment system is the primary source of direct or indirect access to protective benefits. The Social Security (including Disability) and Medicare systems provide only safety-net support structures for workers and their dependents and beneficiaries. Private pensions and health insurance are tied even more tightly to employment, since they are available unevenly across industrial and occupational sectors. Health insurance is becoming more and more rationalized (rule-bound) and constrains the choices of individuals and health professionals to option sets that defy easy decision making and at times obstruct or delay diagnosis and treatment. Unemployment insurance is regulated by a highly decentralized system with rigid minimum earnings requirements and the provision that only (legally defined) "involuntary" separations from jobs qualify for support. All of these characteristics of the U.S. occupational welfare system permit higher levels of inequality across age groups and among the aged than found among nearly all other advanced countries (Smeeding, 1997).

It might be useful at this point to provide the rationale for why inequality measured in the aggregate (e.g., as Gini or Theil indices, coefficients of variation, or other distributional measures) has implications for the self and issues of identity. Economic or social inequality reflects degrees of dispersion within and across subpopulations of hierarchically arrayed or valued attributes (e.g., health, prestige, power, wealth). Dispersion also implies social distance and variability in life experiences and outcomes. Lower dispersion (lower variability, greater equality) thus is positively associated with common experience and perceptions of shared identity, while higher dispersion (higher variability, greater inequality) is positively associated with more individualized life experiences and perceptions of *un*shared identities. Comparisons of populations across countries with different welfare state structures provide evidence for this rationale. In strong welfare states where economic and social equality are higher, ideologies of solidarity and citizenship are predominant; in weak welfare states where economic and social *in*equality are higher, ideologies of individualism are predominant (Leisering & Walker, 1998).

Important for our discussion is the growing individualization of private pension and health insurance in the U.S. with new consequences for the aging self. Since the early 1970s, several structural and compositional trends accompanied by business cycles in the workplace have developed that place more and more responsibility on individual workers to provide for the protection of their incomes and their health. First, growing global competition in major U.S. manufacturing industries has led to massive restructuring, which has included downsizing, plant closing, and the contracting of cheaper labor pools in other countries. Second, the decline of the manufacturing sector in the U.S. has been accompanied by the expansion of the service industries and occupations. These sectors have several distinctive characteristics:

(1) they are bifurcated by a majority of low-skilled jobs held by minority and marginal labor forces, on the one hand, and smaller but growing sectors of highly skilled jobs in high-end services such as health, communications, and finance, on the other;

(2) part-time and contingent work are highly prevalent;

(3) women are relatively highly concentrated in jobs distributed across these sectors;

(4) smaller firms are more prevalent; and

(5) average wages and benefits are among the lowest in these sectors.

The general outcome of these structural arrangements is increased heterogeneity and inequality in the provision of income and health protections (O'Rand & Henretta, 1999).

The third trend—emanating from the previous two—is away from the so-called long-term employment contract. Employers in large and small enterprises alike are retreating from long-term contracts through the use of several practices, including among them: (1) the trimming of internalized labor pools and expansion of contingent labor pools, and (2) the replacement of long-term employee benefits requiring extended employer promises with shorter-term employment benefits or benefits requiring greater worker volition and contribution. Exemplary of these practices is the shift towards the provision of new pension plans—termed defined contribution plans—which do not obligate the employer with the "promise" of a fixed lifetime annuity upon retirement. Rather, these new pensions are savings or investment accounts of the worker with tax shelter, loan, and portability features that impose limited employer obligations, including the likelihood in some plans of no employer contribution, and require worker discretion and risk-taking. Health insurance plans also present workers with individualized option sets, rule-structures, and obligations.

Defined contribution plans account for six out of every seven pension plans in the U.S. and cover about half of all workers with pensions. One-fifth of workers are saving exclusively in these plans. The projection is that over the next 30 years the significant majority of covered workers will have access only to defined contribution (DC) plans (Gordon, Mitchell, & Twinney, 1997; U.S. Department of Labor, 1995).

PENSION RISK AND ACCOUNT MANAGEMENT

From the perspective of risk, the difference between Social Security and defined benefit pension plans, on the one hand, and defined contributions plans (like 401ks), on the other, is the simple difference between an insured, specific monthly annuity in the future and an account balance that the worker must build, respectively. Defined contribution plan participants are confronted with uncertainty regarding their expected level of benefits and with increased investment risk in the years immediately preceding retirement. The social-psychological implications of this on a cognitive level have probably not been addressed in the literature. But several studies of risk-taking and risk aversion in DC plans are instructive.

The Employee Benefit Research Institute (1993) reports that over two-thirds of American workers prefer low-risk, low-return investments. Other surveys also corroborate this finding: Hewitt Associates (1993) reported that low-risk investments like fixed-income accounts are favored by nearly half of participants. The sources of heterogeneity in this pattern appear to be associated with gender, age, education, earnings levels, and job tenure. Studies using the Survey of Consumer Finances (for the years 1983 and 1989) find that women are less willing to take financial risks than men, even after controlling for income (cited in Hinz, McCarthy, & Turner, 1997).

A recently published study of 20,000 managerial workers in a large national firm investigated the patterns by which workers allocate assets in DC/401k plans (Bajtelsmit & Van Derhei, 1997). Investment choices fall into three major categories: employer stock ownership plans (ESOPs), diversified equity portfolios, and fixed income accounts (complements of government bonds and guaranteed investment contracts—GICs). Overall, workers prefer employer stock (42% of men; 44% of women) and fixed income accounts (39% of men and 40% of women) relative to equity assets (19% of men, 17% of women).

Multivariate likelihood (tobit) estimates of allocations across these three accounts reveal several patterns—which generally point to risk-aversion. First, controlling for age (and age^2), tenure (and tenure^2), salary, race, and level of DC wealth, women are more likely to invest in fixed income accounts than men, and less likely to invest in employer stock. No gender effects are detected in equity investment. Second, age has a significant average negative effect on fixed income allocation, but at higher ages, individuals increase their fixed income investment. The reverse pattern is observed for employer stock options. Third, tenure has a significant average positive effect on fixed income allocation, but at longer tenures, individuals begin decreasing fixed income allocations. The tenure effect on equity allocations is also nonlinear: allocations decrease with tenure, after which they increase. Finally, earnings and wealth effects further document risk aversion. Salary is positively associated with allocations to equity and fixed income accounts, and negatively associated with investment in employer stock. Allocations to equities increase with level of pension wealth, but at a decreasing rate.

A study of 36,000 participants in 24 nationwide defined contribution plans covering a cross-section of employers-employees reveals similar patterns (Goodfellow & Schieber, 1997). Over one-half

(58.1%) of total assets were allocated to fixed-income funds with the average asset balance in these accounts ($32,204) more than twice the amount of any other account type (e.g., balanced funds, company stock, domestic equities, and international equities). They report strong age, earnings, and wealth relationships that are consistent with those reported in the previous study.

Finally, a study of the federal government's Thrift Savings Plan (TSP) for federal employees in 1990 provides further evidence of patterns of risk aversion (Hinz et al., 1997). The federal government contributes 1% of all federal workers' salaries in the TSP and also matches up to 5% of pre-tax contributions made by workers. The TSP has three plans among which workers choose to participate: the G, F, and C funds. The G fund consists of short-term non-marketable U.S. Treasury securities. The F fund is a fixed-income index fund of government and corporate bonds. The C fund is a Standard & Poor's 500 index common stock fund. The riskiness of these funds increases across plans, making the common stock C fund the most speculative of the three. Higher earners are more likely to invest in common stock. Women are less likely than men to choose the higher risk plans. Only 28% of women, compared to 45% of men participate in the common stock fund. Also, although married men and unmarried women take similar investment risks, married women are the most conservative, while unmarried men are the least conservative. Gender differences in plan choice persist after controlling for other factors including age, marital status, earnings, and other economic characteristic, and result in widely varying portfolio sizes.

What are the implications of risk-averse or risk-taking behaviors in a volatile financial market? Economic simulations of the outcomes of different defined contribution plan investment scenarios support the rationality of risk-averse behaviors among pre-retirement workers whose tolerance of fluctuations are less. But among younger midlife workers, the selection among alternative plans produces wide variations (inequalities) in prospective retirement account balances. Rappaport, Young, Levell, and Blalock (1997) report a simulation comparing four investment scenarios among DC plans: a diversified portfolio; a GIC or fixed income investment; a bad-luck scenario based on poor choices and wrong timing in switches between assets; and (proposed) a "cash balance" alternative that combines investment maximizing elements of DB and DC plans. After 10 years, their simulation shows that the three luckier scenarios produce nearly equivalent account balances, with the fixed income investment the lowest of the three (diversified portfolio $37,300; GIC $33,800; cash balance $35,500). The unlucky scenario yields $22,400. At age 65 their simulation yields the following outcomes for the three luckier scenarios: $610,600, $424,000, and $506,900 respectively for the diversified portfolio, GIC, and cash balance account. The bad luck scenario results in $122,800—a four- to five-fold lower balance when compared to the other scenarios.

HEALTH RISK, HEALTH EQUITY, AND HEALTH RATIONING

Approximately three-fourths of the U.S. population under age 65 and age 65 and over are covered by private health insurance in any given year (U.S. Bureau of the Census, 1995). Those outside the private system include approximately 16% not covered by any insurance under the age of 65, with the remainder covered by Medicare and/or Medicaid. Among those without any health care coverage are disproportionate shares of African-Americans (22%), those in poverty (36%), the unemployed (39%), workers in firms with fewer than 25 employees (71%), the foreign-born (33%), and the least educated (those without high school diplomas, 30%).

Yet, given the essentially voluntary character and the high cost of private health coverage, the rate of private health insurance coverage is a remarkable figure. It suggests that health risks are salient to individuals in the maintenance of their lives and those of their families. These risks are also more immediate, prevalent, and unpredictable over the life course, unlike the risk for poverty in old age posing a threat sometime in the longer-term future. Health risks are immanent, have fateful consequences, and can derail the "normal life course" (O'Rand & Henretta, 1999).

Alternatively, the widespread coverage by health insurance can obscure the heterogeneity of options available by cost grade. Several types of managed care have emerged over the past 15 years: Health Maintenance Organizations (HMOs), Preferred Provider Organizations (PPOs), Point of Service Plans (POSs), Individual Practice

Associations (IPAs), Physician Hospital Organizations (PHOs), and Management Service Organizations (MSOs). These options can be arrayed in ascending order according to cost and relative freedom of choice with respect to specialized or intensive levels of health services. The HMO, which in most respects includes the most restricted plans, is a highly specified, prepaid system of care that generally requires patients to use only the health care providers (physicians and hospitals) under the HMO contract. The PPO is not prepaid or fixed and is less narrowly specific in the range of illnesses or conditions normally covered by the system. Patients are permitted to obtain services outside the system, but normal costs are higher and higher fees are levied on patients going outside of the system. The POSs, like the PPOs, come closer to the traditional fee-for-service system that predated managed care, permit going outside the system, and cost even more.

The array of alternative systems is wide, and the devil is in the details of each plan. Workers do not usually have choices across all types of plans, but do confront choices and restraints within them. Once participating in some of these plans, especially HMOs, choices disappear and new risks emerge. For example, whether a specific condition is covered (such as a pre-existing condition) under the plan is problematic. Whether the same physician will be treating the same condition is not certain. Whether a so-called "physician extender" (nurse practitioner, physicians assistant) provides treatment, instead of a physician, is uncertain. Whether the time period of coverage of selected conditions (especially chronic conditions) runs out is a risk. And whether emergencies are covered either inside or outside the system is often problematic.

This system represents an unambiguous and, perhaps inevitable, rationalization and commodification of health care within a market characterized by exploding costs. Individual risks are embedded in a complex mix of choice and non-choice. And the transparent pursuit of managed costs over equitably delivered health care speaks for itself. But even this brief overview of health insurance cannot be concluded without some reference to the idea of health rationing—as a cost-cutting and population control mechanism (Uhlenberg, 1992). New medical technology and the reduced mortality among the elderly are major sources of health care expenditures in modern societies. Indeed, the Clinton Administration's Health Care Task Force's Ethics Working group argued in 1993 that technological developments were the major driving force behind rising medical costs throughout the world, forcing even the most universalistic national health insurance systems to ration beneficial services, often below U.S. levels (Daniels, 1998).

A specific form of health rationing has been proposed to alleviate this cost problem. Callahan (1987) proposes the rationing of government-financed health care at about age 80 and beyond (i.e., at an age close to the putative life-span). The logic of this approach is both redistributive and bluntly rational. The ethical implications reside in the domain of values. At this time in the debate over health rationing, social (humanistic) values probably supersede specific proposals based on algorithms akin to equations estimating income distributions as the sums of individual utilities (Diamond, 1998). Individual utilities can be defined as individuals' subjective determinations of the market value (also referred to as "welfare") of alternative outcomes. Neoclassical economic theories advocate that individuals behave in ways that maximize their utilities.

And it is with the issue of values that I am closing this section and introducing the next. Sociological considerations of the tension between human values and market rationality extend at least as far back as Simmel's observations on money and social life (1978). Historical episodes of the tension between values and market rationality—ranging from the resistance to life insurance in the 19th century (Zelizer, 1978) to the social relations underlying blood donation in the 20th century (Titmuss, 1971)—all suggest that the ascendance of values over markets is most likely to occur under what are defined as life-and-death conditions. In the face of tragic or cruel choices, as between the young and the old, value preferences within situations are likely to prevail. And, even within rationalized systems, situated value preferences will probably operate. A significant body of social psychological research distinguishes between "outcome" and "process" justice and how these two value sets vary in their salience across selected problem-solving tasks (see Cook & Hegtvedt, 1983, for a review). The case of health rationing provides a strategic context for the study of distributive justice (Daniels, 1998).

THE SOCIOLOGY OF RISK: PERSPECTIVE AND ANALYTICAL RATIONALITY

Gordon C. Winston (1988) draws the distinction between analytical and perspective time in micro-economic theory and their respective assumptions regarding rationality in human behavior. Analytical time is time taken from the vantage point of the researcher and is predicated on a general model of causal associations among attributes of actors. In life-cycle economic models, causal associations are driven by assumptions regarding how actors orient their current behavior in light of expected (probable) future outcomes. And though unmeasured heterogeneity and uncertainty have come to be more acknowledged in the application of these models, explanation follows from how researchers value outcomes on behalf of actors.

In perspective time, following Winston's definition (1988), actors perceive and act primarily in terms of the present. The future is not knowable under even the most liberal assumptions of relative certainty. He argues that all the actors have to make decisions with relative knowledge of their proximate environments in temporal and spatial terms. The future is thus better conceived as uncertain, and better conceptualized in terms of risk.

But is this enough? Winston omits any reference to the self, defined earlier in this essay as a biographically anchored but ongoing reflexive project (an identity) embedded in social relations. Knowledge and practice are revised and directed in response to present conditions, and in light of past experiences. Actions in the present involve identities responding to present contexts. The manner and degree to which identities project themselves into the future may influence responses to the present, but neither future orientation nor present-centeredness is the singular or the inevitable rationale for these responses. Biographically shaped identities respond to life conditions and carry the past into the present and into future orientations.

The perspective rationality of the aging self in modern society consists of value-constrained decision making in the face of information whose meaning and value are defined by a biographically shaped identity. Information is partial in an objective sense. In a subjective sense, information is also relative, that is it is meaningful only as it is relevant to the experience of the self. Thus, participants in defined contribution pension plans like those described earlier (e.g., The

Federal Thrift Plan) vary widely in their risk-taking propensities for equity funds because of their social-biographical experiences, not because of their universal access to partial information.

Modern theories of risk-seeking/taking converge on the assumption that all risks are perceived (although not wholly relative) (Shrader-Frechette, 1991). There is also general agreement that long-term risk-taking is probably not based on rational optimization of utilities, but on a set of "conventional" expectations which do not necessarily change as new facts present themselves (Kelsey & Quiggin, 1989). Conventional expectations are derived of personal experience and social comparison and are reminiscent of the rigidity of scientific paradigms—that is, they are prone to resist change. Moreover, conventional expectations in risky situations concentrate on extreme outcomes. They rely on the maximum (best-case) and the minimum (worst-case) outcomes of a situation, not on some rational-analytical average likelihood. In other words, individuals' worst fears or highest hopes are weighed in assessments of risk. The worst possible consequences are avoided and may weigh more heavily.

Research on the relationship between risk-seeking and the marginal utility of wealth suggests further that social factors influence the weight of fears relative to hopes. Studies of this relationship actually find curvilinear utility functions: the utility function is concave for low income levels and convex for high income levels (Kelsey & Quiggin, 1989). Lower risk-seeking occurs among less advantaged groups and higher risk-seeking among more advantaged groups. Perspective rationality is shaped by biography and conventional expectations.

ECONOMISTS' POLICY PREFERENCES: A SELF-EXEMPLIFYING CASE OF THE TENSION BETWEEN ANALYTICAL AND PERSPECTIVE RATIONALITY

The problem of risk and the aging self provides a strategic opportunity to explore two kinds of rationality. First is the generic case above of the aging self working in a value-constrained decision-making process. Risk-taking over the life course is founded on cumulative experience, biographically shaped perceptions, and social comparison with others presumed to have similar life chances. This represents perspective rationality. An equally interesting exploration is provided fortuitously in the more specific case of some aging experts, who often must adjudicate between their scientific knowledge—or analytic rationality—and their value preferences (their perspective rationality). This second case is briefly discussed here.

Information defines risk in modern societies. More information is available, but it usually comes in the form of probabilistic alternatives provided by intermediate authorities (or experts) (Giddens, 1991). Few social scientists come as close to influencing social policy (including aging and welfare policies) in the U.S. as elsewhere as economists. Their influence stems from relatively robust models of individual behavior that shape market practices and state policies. As such, economists provide a strategic case for the observation of analytical rationality. However, they also provide a convenient self-study in perspective and analytical rationalities. Several recent efforts in what might be called "professional self reflexivity" by economists give us some more insight into perspective rationality as it pertains to all of us. Such efforts are rare in the sciences and to be admired when they are undertaken.

At least three recent surveys of economists provide a revealing picture of what economists think they know about individual risk-taking behavior and whether their knowledge translates into their own policy preferences (Alston, Kearl, & Vaughan, 1992; Fuchs, 1996; Fuchs, Krueger, & Poterba, 1997). Some of the motives for these self-studies came from the policy debates on national health planning in the early 1990s, which revealed divisions among economists participating in the research and policymaking in this area. In general, these studies find a relatively high degree of consensus on positive economics among selected groups of economics specialists and far less consensus on economic policy. In other words, economists agree on what the determinants of economic behavior are but they disagree on what to do about economically related problems— even given what they think they know about individual behavior. Their agreement on positive economics is explained by analytical rationality. Their disagreement on social policy is probably better explained by perspective rationality.

The most recent survey by Fuchs et al. (1997) is particularly instructive for our interests in aging and social policy. They surveyed specialists in labor and public economics at 40 leading research universities from departments of economics and from programs and schools in business and public policy. The purpose of the survey was to determine the relative importance of agreed-upon economic parameters, values, and political party on policy preferences. Their survey instrument included items that estimated economic parameters (some within 95% confidence intervals) within their fields, items that proposed policies, items that measured personal values, and a measure of political party identification. (The response rates were 39% from labor economists and 66% from public economists.)

The policy items included proposals to: increase AFDC benefits, eliminate the OASI cap, eliminate affirmative action, increase the minimum wage, eliminate job training, increase unionization, adopt a value added tax, expand IRAs, increase state financing of education, increase mandatory savings accounts, and increase the gasoline tax by 25 cents per gallon. The personal values items, intended to reflect fiscal liberalism-conservatism, were measured on continuous scales and included questions on preferences for (1) greater or lesser government involvement in income distribution; (2) the use of transfers to accomplish redistribution; (3) more or less emphasis on equity relative to efficiency; and (4) more or less weight placed on individual responsibility relative to social responsibility (Fuchs et al., 1997, pp. 45, 49).

Their general findings included the following: (1) Only one of 13 policy proposals—a 25 cent per gallon increase in the gasoline tax—elicited a 75% consensus within each group of economists [labor economists opposed, public economists in favor]; (2) Policy positions were better predicted by differences in value preferences than by differences in estimates of economic parameters; (3) Average best estimates of economic parameters agreed well with the extant literature though dispersion around the mean was considerable; and (4) Confidence intervals tended to be too narrow—suggesting some over-confidence.

The observed agreement on selected economic parameters is relevant to analytical rationality. For example, one question in the Public Economist survey (Q14) asked about the price of individual annuity contracts available in the private market relative to their actuarially fair value. Their responses conformed closely with documented estimates in Friedman and Warshawsky (1990). These estimates suggest strongly that individuals with this information would prefer Social Security as it is presently constituted over private annuity accounts, since the former provides them with greater certainty in receiving future benefits.

A second question in this survey (Q19) comparing the administrative costs of a mandatory privatized annuity versus Social Security provides similar evidence. The median estimate was a cost ratio of 1.5 to 1, suggesting that individuals with this information would be inclined (though perhaps also ambivalent) to change to the new system. But consensus on this question was weaker: the 25th percentile estimate was 1 to 1, and the 75th percentile estimate was 3 to 1. The wide dispersion of responses is evident (also reflected in the mean response of 2.6 when compared to the median).

The model predicting opinions about moving towards a mandatory savings account reveals that neither of these economic parameters (Q14, Q19) significantly predicted this policy preference. Indeed, none of the predictors (parameter estimates, values, party affiliation) of this policy preference was significant. Also, labor and public economists were asked their preferences with regard to eliminating the OASI cap in the payroll tax. In both models, economic parameter variables and party affiliation were not significant but values were. Respondents with more liberal ("left") values were likely to support the elimination of the OASDI cap.

What does this say about rationality and risk? Scientific consensus is affirmed by the survey. But the application of scientific information to the determination of policy preference—a choice analogous to those made on a day-to-day basis by ordinary people with limited information on pension and health insurance—is shaky at best. Value preferences prevail. And where do preferences come from? This question falls outside the boundaries of economics, but does preoccupy many of us in aging research.

CONCLUSION: RISK, RATIONALITY AND SOCIAL POLICY

Twenty or more years of the study of modern welfare systems and their respective social policies has documented that these social forms are historically contingent (Achenbaum, 1986; Esping-Anderson, 1990; Pampel, 1998). While they are the products of the direct actions of institutions and individuals applying systems of rationality to the solution of societal problems, they emerge piecemeal in reaction to new problems and become patchworks of targeted, categorical policies. Only in the last decade have more global forces emerged to influence social policy formation and to make it less nation-bound or culturally specific. Population aging and market globalization have converged (along with a few other forces related to technological change) to present new problems and new solutions. Public welfare structures are all but failing to efficiently manage the costs of population aging. Global markets are offering private and individualized solutions: private pensions and private health insurance.

The ascendance of market solutions in the U.S. context is not very surprising, given the history of our welfare ideology and system. But if a qualitative shift cannot be documented, a quantitative change is clear. The rapid spread of private individualized pensions and a graded mix of private health maintenance alternatives are pushing individuals to become more self-reflexive and calculating in the planning and control of their lives. Yet, the unequal distributions of information, resources, and power do not translate into greater freedom for individuals. Rather, individuals respond to newer choices based on their diverse social locations, past experiences, limited vantage points, and value preferences. The future is more uncertain in many respects and elicits a general response of risk-aversion and a retreat in many ways to the more familiar.

Individuals are faced with choices today regarding the insurance for risk classifications to which they will be assigned tomorrow (Diamond, 1998). Rational formulations of economic theory notwithstanding, we have little evidence that the future is very clear to anyone. In addition, we have some evidence that even with more access to information about the future, individuals fall back upon values more rapidly than on rationality. Finally, if most research documents an average tendency towards risk aversion, then how much of an increase in social and psychological stress can we expect in the future?

The apparent trade-off is between individual responsibility and societal protection. Yet, is it a necessary trade-off? Widespread trends in voluntary early retirement across welfare regimes suggest that the onset of retirement resides more at the individual level in a market-dominated environment. But should dependency be assigned to the same jurisdiction? The social model of insurance appears better suited—in terms of efficiency and equity—to the case of dependency.

Finally, the generic case of the aging self requires more attention from social science. The risk process is another mechanism that drives the life course, but we have hardly begun to understand it. Aging selves are continuously confronted with choices between what they expect to gain and what they expect to lose. Unlike gamblers, who have been distinguished by the greater value they place on what they expect to win than on what they have already lost (Wagenaar, 1988), aging selves place greater value on what they expect to lose, than on what they have already gained.

REFERENCES

Aaron, H., Bosworth, B., & Burtless, G. (1989). *Can America afford to grow old? Paying for Social Security.* Washington, DC: Brookings.

Achenbaum, W. A. (1986). *Social security: Visions and revisions.* Cambridge, England: Cambridge University Press.

Alston, R. M., Kearl, J. R., & Vaughan, M. B. (1992). Is there a consensus among economists in the 1990s? *American Economic Review, 82,* 203–209.

Bajtelsmit, V. L., & VanDerhei, J. L. (1997). Risk aversion and pension investment choices. In M. S. Gordon, O. S. Mitchell, & M. M. Twinney (Eds.), *Positioning pensions for the twenty-first century* (pp. 45–66). Philadelphia, PA: University of Pennsylvania Pension Research Council.

Beck, U. (1992). *Risk society: Towards a new modernity.* (Translated by Mark Ritter). London, England: Sage.

Bosworth, B. P. (1996). Fund accumulation: How much? How managed? In P. C. Diamond, D. C. Lindeman, & H. Young (Eds.), *Social security: What role for the future?* (pp. 89–115). Washington, DC: National Academy of Social Insurance.

Callahan, D. (1987). *Setting limits: Medical goals in an aging society.* New York: Simon and Schuster.

Castells, M. (1996). *The rise of the network society.* New York: Blackwell.

Cook, K. S., & Hegtvedt, K. A. (1983). Distributive justice, equity and equality. *Annual Review of Sociology, 9,* 217–241.

Covello, V. T., & Johnson, B. B. (1987). The social and cultural construction of risk: Issues, methods, and case studies. In B. B. Johnson & V. T. Covello (Eds.), *The social and cultural construction of risk* (pp. vii–xiii). Dordrecht, The Netherlands: D. Reidel.

Daniels, N. (1998). Symposium on the rationing of health care: 2. Rationing medical care: A philosopher's perspective on outcomes and process. *Economics and Philosophy, 14,* 27–52.

Dannefer, D., & Uhlenberg, P. (1999). Paths of the life course: A typology. In V. L. Bengtson & K. W. Schaie (Eds.), *Handbook of theories of aging* (pp. 306–326). New York: Springer.

Diamond, P. (1998). Symposium on the rationing of health care: 1. Rationing medical care: An economist's perspective. *Economics and Philosophy, 14,* 1–26.

Douglas, M., & Wildavsky, A. (1982). *Risk and culture.* Berkeley, CA: University of California Press.

Employee Benefits Research Institute. (1993). *Public attitudes on investment preferences.* Washington, DC: EBRI.

Esping-Anderson, G. (1990). *The three worlds of welfare capitalism.* Princeton, NJ: Princeton University Press.

Farkas, J. I., & O'Rand, A. M. (1998). The pension mix for women in middle and late life: The changing employment relationship. *Social Forces, 76,* 1007–1032.

Friedman, B., & Warshawsky, M. (1990). The cost of annuities: Implications for saving behavior and bequests. *Quarterly Journal of Economics, 105,* 135–154.

Fuchs, V. R. (1996). Economics, values, and health care reform. *American Economic Review, 86,* 1–24.

Fuchs, V. R., Krueger, A. B., & Poterba, J. M. (1997). Why do economists disagree about policy? The roles of beliefs about parameters and values (NBER Working Paper 6151). Cambridge, MA: National Bureau of Economic Research.

Furstenberg, F. F., Jr., Brooks-Gunn, J., & Morgan, S. P. (1987). *Adolescent mothers in later life.* New York: Cambridge University Press.

Giddens, A. (1991). *Modernity and self-identity: Self and society in the late modern age.* Palo Alto, CA: Stanford University Press.

Goodfellow, G. P., & Schieber, S. L. (1997). Investment of assets in self-directed retirement plans. In M. S. Gordon, O. S. Mitchell, & M. M. Twinney (Eds.), *Positioning pensions for the twenty-first century* (pp. 67–90). Philadelphia, PA: University of Pennsylvania Pension Research Council.

Gordon, M. S., Mitchell, O. S., & Twinney, M. M. (Eds.) (1997). *Positioning pensions for the twenty-first century.* Philadelphia, PA: University of Pennsylvania Pension Research Council.

Gramlich, E. M. (1997). Reforming social security. In M. S. Gordon, O. S. Mitchell, & M. M. Twinney (Eds.), *Positioning pensions for the twenty-first century* (pp. 220–229). Philadelphia, PA: University of Pennsylvania Pension Research Council.

Hewitt Associates. (1993). *401k hot plan topics.* Lincolnshire, IL: Hewitt Associates.

Hinz, R. P., McCarthy, D. D., & Turner, J. A. (1997). Are women conservative investors? Gender differences in participant-directed pension investments. In M. S. Gordon, O. S. Mitchell, & M. M. Twinney (Eds.), *Positioning pensions for the twenty-first century* (pp. 91–106). Philadelphia, PA: University of Pennsylvania Pension Research Council.

Kelsey, D., & Quiggin, J. (1989). Behind the veil: A survey of theories of choice under ignorance and uncertainty. *Working Papers in Economics and Econometrics,* 183. Canberra, Australia: The Australian National University.

Leisering, L., & Walker, R. (1998). *The dynamics of modern society: Poverty, policy and welfare.* Bristol, UK: The Policy Press.

Manton, K. G., & Stallard, E. (1996). Longevity in the United States: Age and sex-specific evidence on life span limits from mortality patterns 1960–1990. *Journal of Gerontology: Biological Sciences, 51A,* B362–B375.

Mirowsky, J., & Ross, C. E. (1998). Education, personal control, lifestyle and health: A human capital hypothesis. *Research on Aging, 21,* 415–449.

O'Rand, A. M., & Henretta, J. C. (1999). *Aging and inequality: Diverse pathways through later life.* Boulder, CO: Westview Press.

Pampel, F. C. (1998). *Aging, social inequality and public policy.* Thousand Oaks, CA: Pine Forge Press.

Rappaport, A. M., Young, M. L., Levell, C. A., & Blalock, B. A. (1997). Cash balance pension plans. In M. S. Gordon, O. S. Mitchell, & M. M. Twinney (Eds.), *Positioning pensions for the twenty-first century* (pp. 29–44). Philadelphia, PA: University of Pennsylvania Pension Research Council.

Shrader-Frechette, K. S. (1991). *Risk and rationality: Philosophical foundations for populist reforms.* Berkeley, CA: University of California Press.

Simmel, G. (1978). *The philosophy of money.* London, UK: Routledge.

Simon, H. A. (1969). *The sciences of the artificial.* Cambridge, MA: MIT Press.

Smeeding, T. M. (1997). Financial poverty in developed countries: The evidence from LIS. (Working Paper 155, Luxembourg Income Study). Syracuse, NY: Syracuse University.

Social Security and Medicare Boards of Trustees. (1996). *Status of the Social Security and Medicare programs.* Washington, DC: U.S. Government Printing Office.

Titmuss, R. M. (1971). *The gift relationship.* New York: Vintage.

Uhlenberg, P. (1992). Population aging and social policy. *Annual Review of Sociology, 18,* 449–474.

U.S. Bureau of the Census. (1995). Health insurance coverage, 1995. *Health insurance coverage status of all persons by selected characteristics.* Website: http://www.census.gov/hhes/hlthins/cover95/c95tabb.html.

U.S. Department of Labor. (1995). *Private pension plan bulletin: Abstract of 1993 form 5500 annual reports, table F-5.* Washington, DC: U.S. Government Printing Office.

Wagenaar, W. A. (1988). *Paradoxes of gambling behavior.* Hillsdale, NJ: Erlbaum.

Wilmoth, J. R. (1998). The future of human longevity: A demographer's perspective. *Science, 280,* 395–397.

Winston, G. C. (1988). Three problems with the treatment of time in economics: Perspectives, repetitiveness and time units. In G. C. Winston & R. F. Teichgraeber III (Eds.), *The boundaries of economics* (pp. 30–52). New York: Cambridge University Press.

Zelizer, V. A. (1978). Human values and the market: The case of life insurance and death in 19th-century America. *American Journal of Sociology, 84,* 591–610.

Commentary

Control, Choice, and Collective Concerns: Challenges of Individualized Social Policy

Melissa A. Hardy

N otions of the self and the boundaries of individuation are cultural products, historically contingent, and necessarily embedded in, many aspects of social life (Hazelrigg, 2000). U.S. culture has historically valued self-reliance and the assignment of both praise and blame to individuals. Perhaps this bias toward individualization is one reason why the discipline of sociology in the U.S. looks rather different from its European counterparts. The American mantra of the value of individual achievement has also muted the more European tendency to search for collective solutions to social problems. In her chapter, O'Rand argues that this emphasis on individualization and more particularly, individualized risk, is a principal factor in aging and in the redefinition of the aging self (O'Rand, this volume). Although the current trend toward the individualization of social policy and the privatization of what have been government-run programs is frequently viewed as an unfortunate turn away from New Deal approaches to policy, this contemporary emphasis may be a return to a previously charted course.

One of the central issues behind the shift in social welfare policy is that of subsidization. The growing popularity of policies that are oriented toward changing the behavior of individuals by constructing regimes of reward and punishment pleases some, but alarms others. Nevertheless, proponents of increasing or even maintaining the utilization of collectivized solutions to social problems appear to be swimming against the tide (Hardy & Shuey, 1998). The value of collectivized approaches, they argue, lies in the pooling of risk: the larger the pool, the lower the costs to any particular individual for "insurance" that can provide a hedge against the cost of negative events. The growth in the insurance industry is evidence of the popularity of this idea. But the insurance industry also sorts people into risk pools, charging higher premiums to those who share characteristics with groups considered at higher risk, refusing to accept those at highest risk, and canceling the policies of those whose claims make them undesirable. Even so, people in low-risk groups regularly pay their premiums to help pay the claims filed disproportionately often by those in higher-risk groups. And they wonder whether they would do better to save the money they send to the insurance company and place it in a special account for their own use, should the negative outcome occur. This approach seems reasonable, allowing them to control the funds themselves. But what if the event they fear occurs sooner rather than later? Then, having paid the premiums for that relatively short time period would allow them to claim reimbursement for their losses. Without the insurance, they must borrow the money and spend years paying off the debt. Here lies the dilemma of those thinking about buying insurance: how likely is the negative outcome, and what are the likely costs if it does occur? The answer to the second question and the subsequent sense of panic it creates can lead people to think carefully about the likelihood of certain—or should we say uncertain—events.

Among the issues that must be addressed as we consider restructuring social policies are the likely outcome distributions—the relative frequencies of success versus failure. How do we reconcile the actual versus perceived distributions of risk and reward? How do we assess the actual versus perceived ability of individuals to exercise sufficient human agency to eliminate, or at least drastically reduce, the risk of negative outcomes and maximize to near-certainty the likelihood of the desired outcome? Nowhere are these issues cast in sharper contrast than in the realm of pensions—the combination of government-financed, employer-financed, and individually financed plans to secure sufficient income for retirement. The fact that people must plan for sufficient income implies a relatively long-term view that allows a series of good choices made under conditions of uncertainty, or pure luck.

This categorization of pension financing is, to some degree, artificial. Governments finance through the collection of individual taxes and business taxes (which are passed on to consumers) and employers finance through a combination of tax breaks (which must be made up by other forms of taxes) and reduced labor costs (which generally translate into lower levels of compensation for workers). In other words, there is considerable merit to the argument that all financing schemes ultimately are based on the collection of individual or household resources. An important difference lies in the agency of collection. Governments set tax rates, and employers negotiate rates of compensation; therefore, the argument must be made less on the issue of "whose money is it," and more on the issue of the agency whose control of the funds generates the least concern. Historically, allowing organizations such as the federal government or firms (under federal regulation and oversight) to manage the funds was appealing, because it required these organizations to protect against losses. Governments and medium-to-large firms are in a better position to manage these funds for large numbers of people, again pooling the risk of individual investments and allowing diversification to allow growth without excessive risk. Of course, workers lose control of their individual contributions. Nevertheless, pooling the funds from many workers was exchanged for a promise to pay monthly benefits to those who survive to collect it (or to the dependents of those who did not). This approach was a straightforward way to deal with the sufficiency concern (assuming a reasonable benefit structure) since the time frame for payments is open-ended.

O'Rand argues that "old risks" were considered exogenous, whereas "new risks" are coupled with new information structures that recommend avenues of control. The pooling of risk makes the most sense when threats are exogenous, i.e., when injuries appear random, or when the threat (with resultant injury) is so widespread that any given individual appears powerless to influence the outcome. The Great Depression created such a sense of powerlessness and, in the wake of that perceived powerlessness, generated cultural conditions conducive to collectivized solutions. In contrast, to the extent that the available information suggests cause-and-effect connections between individual behaviors and undesirable outcomes, the actual incidence of these outcomes becomes predictable in a probabilistic sense, though not determinant in any individual case. However, the meaning of that difference can be lost. The mantra of post-World War II America has been anything but a message of powerlessness. The steady economic growth, coupled with the rise of the U.S. to a position of political and military preeminence, has reinvigorated our underlying belief in our ability to produce our own futures and create our own security. Whether our confidence is well-founded is a question to be answered in the future, but an important difference between those who promote collectivist solutions over individualized responses lies in the optimism (or pessimism) of these projections.

Which returns us to the issue of subsidization. When threats are considered exogenous, the probability distribution appears uniform and the incidence seems random; therefore, the lucky subsidize the unlucky. However, when risks are assumed to be endogenous, sets of probabilities are organized by strata, or by strata-defining characteristics. Depending on a person's background, or behavior, or genes, that person is linked to particular conditional probability distributions. Within each stratum of risk, the distribution may be random, but the average risk is variable by stratum. Variation in the incidence of illness may be linked to genetics; variation in the risk of addictions may be linked to predispositions; and variation in the risk of injury or loss may be linked to precaution. Nonuniformity in the probability of risk may correlate with individual actions that either increase or decrease the risk. This perceived predictability of outcome changes the structure of subsidy: the careful subsidize the careless; the cautious subsidize the incautious; responsible people subsidize irresponsible people.

But how does this apply to pensions? Whether discussing Social Security or defined benefit pension plans, all those who contribute beyond some floor or meet some minimum standard (generally measured by time) ultimately gain when they collect benefits. But is it the incidence of benefit receipt that is at issue, or the distribution of benefit amounts? Collective schemes tend to reduce variability in outcome. They reduce inequalities. If the benefit amount is based on earnings history, then those with a common earnings history collect the same monthly benefits. Those with different earnings histories collect somewhat different benefits. However, those with significantly different earnings histories may collect only somewhat different benefits, as in the case of Social Security, where the benefit formula is progressive with respect to benefit ratios: those with lower earnings receive a proportionately larger return on their contributions.

The case of defined benefit pension plans is similar to that of Social Security. Contributions (and coverage) occur automatically, rather than as a result of workers' decisions to participate. In neither case does the worker have the option of recapturing even a portion of these contributions for alternative investments. The benefits paid out at retirement are determined by a formula that takes into account continuity in employment and wage rate; those with continuous employment histories receive benefits that are, to some extent, linked to their wage rates, with higher wage workers earning somewhat higher benefits. But here, as in Social Security, the dispersion of benefits is somewhat collapsed relative to the dispersion of annual earnings. When risk of loss, insecurity, and unpredictability are dominant, collective solutions—and their relative uniformity of outcomes—can create a sense of stability and security. However, when we perceive an opportunity for gain and feel confident in our ability to manifest that gain, uniformity of outcome appears unnecessarily restrictive. Whether we need always choose one or the other is an important question for policymakers. In this essay, we will explore the issue of individual decision making. Are we skilled at making choices? How susceptible are we to misinformation or faulty logic? And even when the decision-making process is sound, what are the boundaries of human agency in domains governed by a complex network of interrelated actors with very different scales of operation? The methodology used in quantitative research provides us with some benchmarks to use in assessing various aspects of individual decision making. It is to a review of the formal versus everyday methods of individual decision-makers that we now turn.

ISSUES OF INDIVIDUAL CONTROL

Many of the proposals for reshaping pension opportunities include increased provisions for individual workers to exercise more control over their own contributions and contributions that are made on their behalf. This issue of control is currently focused most directly on Social Security. Defined benefit pension plans do not place pension funds under workers' control. However, many companies with defined benefit pension plans are adding supplemental defined contribution plans to the menu and providing workers who leave the company prior to retirement age the option of a lump sum payment of accumulated pension assets (Olsen & Van Derhei, 1997). In addition, the original Employee Retirement Income Security Act of 1974 (ERISA) and subsequent ERISA legislation have increasingly regulated defined benefit pension plans in an effort to increase the likelihood that workers will collect benefits equivalent to their expectations upon their retirement. Although workers themselves generally do not make investment decisions, plan managers are constrained by federal regulation to meet certain standards of funding, diversification, and risk in their investment decisions.

The dispersion of defined contribution plans coupled with talk of privatizing (or partially privatizing) Social Security places control of retirement investment funds in the hands of individuals and households. O'Rand's chapter recalls the well-documented trends in private pensions and health insurance in the U.S. These trends reflect the shift away from collective and towards individual responsibility and place the assessment of risk and the distribution of risk aversion relative to risk tolerance at center stage. When actors make decisions, at issue is what information or knowledge they have, how they weigh the different pieces of information, and how frequently and easily they add new information and reevaluate their decisions. Also of concern is the complexity of decision making that individuals are capable of managing. Here we deal with issues of human agency, the ability of individuals to overcome limited initial endowments, the general ability of people to shape their own destinies (Eells, 1982; Harsanyi, 1976). The presumption behind this increasingly confident move toward privatization is that actors can make good decisions under conditions of risk and uncertainty, relative to variable time frames, while monitoring the influence of "new" information in assessing both risk and the match between choices currently in play and desired goals. These requirements sound quite similar to those of producing sound research, both as an explanatory and as a predictive tool.

WHY STUDY INDIVIDUAL DECISION MAKING?

People make decisions everyday about things both important and mundane. Their decisions are limited by institutional constraints—the options from which to choose, the speed with which a choice becomes irrevocable, the costs associated with different types of exchanges—or facilitated by institutional actors who choose on their behalf. Institutional networks can camouflage choices by creating distance between the actor and the outcome. For example, some workers accumulate pension assets through employer-sponsored defined benefit accounts. When they retire, they will be paid benefits through the earnings of the firm's pension fund. Although these earnings derive from fund investments, the exact investments are generally unknown to the workers; nor are they subject to worker approval. However, the thickness of the institutional veil between the individual and the investment may be important to the investment outcome, since many experts believe that institutional forces correct the errors of individual decision-makers (Camerer, 1995). Studying individual decision making is an attempt to determine how people choose when the institutional veil is thin and thereby reveal the types of systematic errors made by individuals.

Much of what we know about individual decision-making derives from experimental studies in psychology and, more recently, economics (see for example Camerer, 1995; Chernoff & Moses, 1959; Jeffrey, 1965; Raiffa, 1970; Yates, 1990). These studies are designed to test the decision-making abilities of experimental subjects under a variety of circumstances. The more popular theories developed to explain errors in choices assume a limited ability on the part of the individual agent to perform the needed calculations to make the "best" choice. Experimental studies are limited by the artificiality of context; one cannot put subjects in a situation with "real" costs, since human subjects concerns require that no subject be harmed because of their participation in the research. Even so, these experimental studies provide useful information about the way individuals solve problems. Ultimately, the question of decision making is one of information and analytic ability—whether an individual can bring to bear the necessary information, analyze it in an appropriate way, and reach a proper solution (Kyburg, 1983).

MAKING DECISIONS UNDER CONDITIONS OF UNCERTAINTY

When, as in school exams or tests of other sorts, a "correct" answer can be determined, the problem-solving exercise has a definite outcome. However, many real decision-making situations require us to make choices under conditions of uncertainty. We confront a set of options with some amount of information about the relative frequency of alternative outcomes. The ranking of decisions from best to worst must be made relative to the outcome that occurs after the choice is made versus the counterfactual alternatives. Therefore, evaluations are always post-hoc. Given the outcome at time t+1, we decide what the best decision at time t would appear to have been. Even then, we can only speculate about alternative pathways, recognizing that a different choice would have been linked to a different distribution of outcomes, but a similarly uncertain future. When outcomes are linked to probability distributions, the outcome information is often framed as an aggregate rate. But the probabilistic nature of the problem implies that the correct decision will lead to an undesirable outcome some percentage of the time. Herein lies the element of risk. The notion of aggregation provides some comfort if the probability of success is high; however, individual decision-makers are concerned with their individual lives. To know that a medical procedure has a high success rate is of little comfort if you are one of the cases in which the procedure proves ineffective.

Making decisions under conditions of uncertainty is an accepted part of research methodology. Testing hypotheses is an exercise in managing error: accepting that a certain percentage of the time, the correct procedures will lead to errors; setting the error rates for your own study as low as possible; and then moving ahead with the hope that your study (based on a particular sample of observations) is not one of the few in which all the correct procedures for decision making nevertheless lead you to a false conclusion. The irony is that this reality is a commonly cited "limitation" of quantitative research, the implication being that actors engaged in other categories of endeavor suffer no such "limitations" of uncertainty. That many people believe that probability judgments characterize science but are not relevant to decisions of everyday life is both a puzzle and a concern to those who try to evaluate the capabilities of individual decision-makers.

PREDICTION, CONFIDENCE, AND RESOLUTION

One reason researchers employ quantitative models is to be able to predict future outcomes. For this prediction function to hold, one must assume that the process generating the outcome is in equilibrium, which is really just another way of saying the process has settled and can be reliably described. When a process is in equilibrium, a model that explains how an observed outcome is linked to characteristics or other features involved in the underlying process can also be used to predict likely outcomes for actors with the same characteristics operating in an environment with the same features. We must, then, assume stability and often infer causality from the correlative evidence—points to which we will return. Of course, the fact that we predict "likely" outcomes suggests that our predictions are themselves linked to probability distributions. Therefore, predictions are coupled with a level of confidence. Rather than predict specific outcomes, researchers often prefer to cite sets of outcomes, i.e., to use interval rather than point estimates. The wider the interval we cite (or the larger the set of values), the greater our confidence; the narrower the interval, the lower our confidence. We explain to our students the intuitive sense of this relationship: wider intervals provide more options that may be correct; narrow intervals provide limited options. On the other hand, very wide intervals are next to useless. To say, for example, that increasing one's skill may be linked to higher compensation, to lower compensation, or may have nothing to do with compensation is a response set that is unlikely to be judged incorrect; it also provide us with no leverage for deciding how to proceed. So in research, we balance confidence with precision:

confidence is not helpful if the prediction is not sufficiently precise to inform our actions.

Unfortunately, this reasoning does not necessarily coincide with everyday notions of precision and confidence. People tend to relate confidence to precision in the opposite way. So, for example, if we ask two individuals to predict the first playing card to be dealt from a standard deck, Individual A may say "the jack of diamonds"; Individual B may say "a jack." Individual A has limited herself to one chance in 52 of being correct, whereas Individual B has one chance in 13 of being correct—because individual B was less precise. But because individual B was less precise, a casual observer may determine that Individual A is more confident than Individual B; failure to state a specific outcome can be viewed as indecisiveness or evasion. In this framework, confidence seems to refer to individuals' belief in their own ability to make correct predictions. In quantitative modeling, confidence refers to the likelihood that the prediction is correct over the long run. It may seem a subtle difference, especially since in both cases, predictions are evaluated relative to their accuracy. If, in fact, the first card dealt is a jack, Individual B is correct; but if the card is the jack of spades, Individual A is not. Even so, a common reaction may be to regard Individual A as more decisive, since A was "as correct" as B, and bold enough to be more precise. But if this game had been linked to a wager of $100, with Individual A betting $100 on the jack of diamonds, and Individual B betting $25 on each of the four jacks, Individual B walks away with winnings, Individual A with nothing. Confidence in a decision and self-confidence are not the same thing.

Experimental studies report that subjects are overconfident in their predictions, i.e. that their confidence exceeds their accuracy (Keren, 1991; McClelland & Bolger, 1994). Evidence based on a series of calibration studies indicates that overconfidence is common, and it is related to the specificity and difficulty of the question (Kahnman, Slovic, & Tversky, 1982; Liberman & Tversky, 1993). First, rather than think in terms of interval estimates, subjects tend to focus on a point estimate. When asked to expand the point estimate to an interval, they build too narrow a range (Alpert & Raiffa, 1982). *Even after subjects undergo training specific to the issue,* they continue to build intervals that are too narrow. The training produces some improvement in degree, but the underlying tendency towards overconfidence continues to dominate. When asked to address *generic* outcomes rather than *specific* outcomes, overconfidence diminishes. Overconfidence is also lower when people are asked to answer easy questions than when they are asked to answer difficult questions: they are overconfident in their responses to the hard questions and underconfident in their responses to the easy questions (Lichtenstein & Fischhoff, 1977). Finally, people can be confident in making judgments, even when they are aware that specific knowledge clearly relevant to the question is unknown by them (Brenner, Koehler, Liberman, & Tversky, 1996).

COLLECTING AND ANALYZING INFORMATION

How do people absorb information, and how do they weigh information at hand to reach a decision? From the standpoint of quantitative modeling, we must address these issues through sampling and through the estimation of coefficient magnitude. In decision-making, the situation is directly analogous. It seems reasonable to assume that people collect information before they make a decision. From choosing a restaurant for an evening meal or a movie for weekend entertainment, to deciding what home to buy or which health insurance plan to purchase, most people make some effort to collect "data." They may note the opinions of friends who've dined at particular places, and allow their decision to be influenced by these recommendations; they may read a food critic's review; they may go by the restaurant and look over the menu. From the standpoint of sampling theory, the utility of the data depends on the number of observations and how those observations were chosen. Observations can be generated by different rules of probability; however, the information being supplied must be adjusted for the probability of selection. Observations generated without reference to a particular population and/or without known rules of selection are of little use in making probability judgments. Using information to guide decisions requires people to assess the strength of new information relative to whatever baseline data are available.

Using an example from quantitative modeling, if one determines that variable X is a strong predictor of variable Y, but the number of observations on which this determination is based is small and

gathered in a haphazard way, other researchers will be unconvinced
by the findings. However, if a strong effect is estimated in a large
sample systematically selected, the evidence is much more convinc-
ing. Exactly what that effect means may be disputed, but not the
fact that the association is "real." How does this relate to individual
decisions? People often collect their information in a manner less
systematic than scientists for several reasons. First, systematic sampling can be difficult to accomplish. A typical worker cannot acquire
the patient lists of the various health organizations and randomly
choose people to question about their experiences securing care.
But even when people think in terms of a "random" mix of view-
points, they are not very good at choosing randomly. In most cases,
the series of selections people view as random are actually negatively
correlated (Camerer, 1995). One might ask, for example, for a random series of six coin tosses and be given the following: heads, tails,
heads, tails, heads, tails. Hardly a random series, this result requires
alternating outcomes.

Perhaps a better example lies in how people choose lottery numbers. Asked to pick six numbers between 1 and 45, people frequently
scatter their choices across the full range, believing that choosing
1, 2, 3, 4, 5, 6 is a far less probable outcome than 4, 12, 20, 32, 38,
44. The likelihood of the first series winning is exactly the same as
the second, but to many people it does not appear that way because
they view the first series as a sequence. Actually, both series are "in
sequence;" however, the rules of sequencing for the two series are
different. The rule for the first is obvious; the rule for the second,
less obvious. The point is that, given that each pick is independent,
sequencing is irrelevant.

When the desired outcome requires a long-term planning horizon,
confidence in the aggregation of many individual decision-makers
implies that people can absorb new information and adjust their
thinking to shifts in the process that may occur over time. So long
as people are making decisions in areas where they have some expertise, the length of time is less important. However, when people
are making decisions in areas that are unfamiliar to them, they
experience errors in absorbing new information. Absorption errors
are correlated with how unusual the information is to the actor—one
reason why eyewitness testimony can be so unreliable. People tend
to misperceive surprising events. People are also sensitive to how

information is presented or framed; they rely too much on memory; and they often ignore baseline or prior information that should clearly be taken into account in making their decisions. This last point is often addressed as the issue of representation.

For example, suppose you were a member of an informal investment group. You are trying to decide which type of mutual fund to purchase. For the sake of simplicity, assume you have narrowed the choice to two types of funds. The prior information that is available is the past performance of the types of funds you are considering: one group has outperformed the market 7 out of the last 10 years; the second group outperformed the market 3 out of the last 10 years. A member of your group reports that his colleague recommends buying the second group. When asked for the past performance of the colleague, the member reports that the colleague has been correct making similar types of picks 8 out of the last 10 tries. Under these circumstances, the tendency is to ignore the prior information and place the probability at .8 that by buying the second group, you will have made the correct choice. The actual probability is much lower than that, if one assumes that the past performance of the funds as well as the past performance of the colleague need to be taken into account.

The error in judgment occurs because people tend to focus on the wrong conditional probability. Again, the tendency is to restate the problem as determining the probability that, given that the colleague chose the second group, what is the probability that the second group will pay off? Here, that probability is .8, the performance record of the colleague. However, the members of this group should actually be asking a different question: What is the probability that the second group will pay off, given that someone who is correct 80% of the time has chosen it? This calculation requires that we use Bayes' Theorem (see, e.g., Resnik, 1987, 53).

THE ILLUSION OF CONTROL

That people often behave as though they can influence purely random events comes as no surprise. What some people view as superstition, others regard as their personal "systems" for ensuring success (Hazelrigg, 1991). Within both sociology and psychology, researchers have employed scales that measure locus of control. Subjects are asked to respond to a series of statements that place them somewhere on a continuum of perceived control. The extremes of the scale range from the belief that "we determine our own destiny" to the belief that we are merely pawns in a world over which we have little or no influence. Needless to say, the former view is regarded as the "healthier," the latter view as either jaded or symptomatic of depression.

We might expect that, under external conditions that make success very difficult, the former view would become unhealthy; need and hardship are not necessarily the fault of the actor. But when times are good, it is easier to slip into the mindset that success is a function of individual behaviors and abilities, rather than an indiscriminate blessing. Such may be our current situation. It is difficult to find losers in the stock market over the last decade. Clearly some are bigger winners than others, but the idea that one simply puts money in the stock market and watches while it grows has been legitimized by the recent experiences of millions of Americans. It has not always been so, but that knowledge is lived knowledge for a smaller and smaller portion of the population. That people overestimate the influence of personal control may reflect a peculiarly American attitude toward success and failure.

CONCLUSIONS

Although O'Rand is not surprised by the ascendance of market solutions in the U.S. context, she cautions that distributional inequalities preclude translating a greater reliance on markets into greater individual freedom. While markets promise more efficiency, one unintended consequence of market solutions coupled with widespread risk aversion may simply be greater social and psychological stress coupled with lower levels of retirement savings.

Almost a half-century ago, Milton Friedman (1953) noted that market-level predictions may be approximately right, even if the model of individual behavior from which the predictions are derived is incorrect. In recent decades, researchers have attempted to understand how individuals make decisions, to identify the rationalities and the irrationalities of the decision-making process. An understanding of this process is not easily obtained, since we frequently judge people by their behaviors, assuming that "choice" and "preference" are the same thing; they are not (Sen, 1970). People's choices often reflect errors—errors in judgment, errors in calculation, errors of understanding. A substantial amount of coursework and training are required to produce researchers skilled in quantitative methodology. Consider the typical high school graduate, or the typical college graduate. How well prepared are they for these challenges?

And it has also become clear that moving from a consideration of individual gains and losses to societal gain or loss is not a simple function of aggregation (Hazelrigg, 1991; Sen, 1970). It is not sufficient to sum individual outcomes as a measure of social welfare; nor is it a straightforward process of disaggregation to move from descriptions of societal behavior or cumulative resources to the everyday behaviors and living standards of ordinary people.

To perceive an underlying rationality at the macro level, a correlation of outcomes or rates or accounts does not require that the same type or level of rationality occurs around the kitchen-tabled board rooms of American households. The sociological dilemma has always been to try to understand how we analytically disentangle the collective inputs and outputs into individual contributions and costs without distorting or corrupting the underlying dynamic that makes the collective work.

It is true that recent cohorts of retirees enjoy a higher average standard of living than that of previous retirees, but the average standard of living has been increasing for all Americans. And averages never tell the whole story. The distribution is what tells the tale, and the distribution of financial resources among those 65 and older not only reproduces the inequalities that characterized these households at younger ages; the inequality is expanded (Pampel & Hardy, 1994). As members of the baby boom generation move into retirement, inequality will increase even more (Hardy & Shuey, 1998). As we move toward an increasingly individualized social policy, people will have more options to consider and more choices to make. They will make mistakes. How will we apportion the costs of those miscalculations? How will we evaluate the success of the new approach?

The answers to those questions depends on how we move back and forth from the micro-level of individual households and individual lives to the macro-level of societal accounts. Recall that the push toward privatization coincided with the decline in savings rates that occurred in the 1980s, and that the economy requires these savings in order to sustain current rates of growth. If the goal of privatization is to increase rates of savings by providing the incentive of personal control, the evidence remains mixed (Engen, Gale, & Scholz, 1996; Poterba, Venti, & Wise, 1996). Whereas some researchers believe that the tax and control incentives have increased savings, others argue that households have simply redistributed what was already being saved. But an important part of the problem is that we know very little about how and why individual households save as they do. We know that current households enter retirement with very little in personal financial assets. We also know that there is considerable heterogeneity in savings behavior, both between and within groups. Many households increase their savings as they near retirement age, but some households do not save. Without understanding what explains these differences, how can we develop incentives to promote more savings? And if we do encourage some households to save more while creating opportunities for other households to spend more, have we succeeded? If our proof lies in the financial security of future cohorts entering retirement, we will have to wait to learn the answer. And what a price to pay if we discover that overconfidence, an illusion of control, a misinterpretation of correlation as causation, inadequate information, and a misuse of prior information led us to the wrong choice.

REFERENCES

Alpert, M., & Raiffa, H. (1982). A progress report on the training of probability assessors. In D. Kahneman, P. Slovic, & A. Tversky (Eds.), *Judgment under uncertainty: Heuristics and biases* (pp. 294–305). New York: Cambridge University Press.

Brenner, L. A., Koehler, D. J., Liberman, V., & Tversky, A. (1996). Overconfidence in probability and frequency judgments: A critical examination. *Organizational Behavior and Human Decision Processes, 65*(3), 212–219.

Camerer, C. (1995). Individual decision making. In J. Kagel & A. Roth (Eds.), *Handbook of experimental economics* (pp. 587–686). Princeton, NJ: Princeton University Press.

Chernoff, H., & Moses, L. (1959). *Elementary decision theory.* New York: Wiley.

Eells, E. (1982). *Rational decision and causality.* Cambridge: Cambridge University Press.

Engen, E. M., Gale, W. G., & Scholz, J. K. (1996). The illusory effects of saving incentives on saving. *Journal of Economic Perspective, 76,* 113–138.

Friedman, M. (1953). *Essays in positive economics.* Chicago: University of Chicago Press.

Harsanyi, J. (1976). *Essays on ethics, social behavior, and scientific explanation.* Dordrecht: Reidel.

Hardy, M. A., & Shuey, K. (1998). Realigning retirement income: The politics of growth. *Generations, 22,* 22–28.

Hazelrigg, L. E. (2000). Individualism. In E. Borgatta & R. Montgomery (Eds.), *Encyclopedia of sociology* (pp. 901–907). New York: Macmillan.

Hazelrigg, L. E. (1991). The problem of micro-macro linkages: Rethinking questions of the individual, social structure, and autonomy of action. *Current Perspectives in Social Research, 11,* 229–254.

Jeffrey, R. (1965). *The logic of decision.* New York: McGraw-Hill.

Kahneman, D., Slovic, P., & Tversky, A. (1982). *Judgment under uncertainty: Heuristics and biases.* Cambridge, UK: Cambridge University Press.

Keren, G. (1991). Calibration and probability judgments: Conceptual and methodological issues. *Acta Psychologica, 77,* 217–273.

Kyburg, H. (1983). *Epistemology and inference.* Minneapolis: University of Minnesota Press.

Liberman, V., & Tversky, A. (1993). On the evaluation of probability judgments: Calibration, resolution, and monotonicity. *Psychological Bulletin, 114,* 162–173.

Lichtenstein, S., & Fischhoff, B. (1977). Do those who know more also know more about how much they know? *Organizational Behavior and Human Performance, 20,* 159–183.

McClelland, A. G. R., & Bolger, F. (1994). The calibration of subjective probabilities: Theories and models 1980–1993. In G. Wright & P. Ayton (Eds.), *Subjective probability* (pp. 453–482). Chichester, England: Wiley.

Olsen, K., & Van Derhei, J. (1997). *Defined contribution plan dominance grows across sectors and employer sizes, while mega defined benefit plans remain strong: Where we are and where we are going.* EBRI Issue Brief No. 190. Washington, DC: Employee Benefit Research Institute.

Pampel, F. C., & Hardy, M. A. (1994). Status maintenance and change during old age. *Social Forces, 73,* 289–314.

Poterba, J. M., Venti, S. F., & Wise, D. A. (1996). *Do retirement saving programs increase saving: Reconciling the evidence.* (National Bureau of Economic Research: Working Paper, No. 5599). Cambridge, MA: National Bureau of Economic Research.

Raiffa, H. (1970). *Decision analysis.* Reading, MA: Adison-Wesley.

Resnik, M. D. (1987). *Choice: An introduction to decision theory.* Minneapolis, MN: University of Minnesota Press.

Sen, A. (1970). *Collective choice and social welfare.* San Francisco, CA: Holden-Day.

Yates, J. F. (1990). *Judgment and decision making.* Englewood Cliffs, NJ: Prentice-Hall.

Commentary

Bringing Risk Back In: The Regulation of the Self in the Postmodern State

Dale Dannefer

RISK AND ITS UNILATERAL PRIVATIZATION

The proposition that modernity is a "risk culture" seems, at first, paradoxical. Technology, science, and bureaucracy—three hallmark forces of modernity—all share the goal of increasing control over nature and events, and hence of reducing uncertainty and risk. The organizing force of these enterprises has in the twentieth century expanded across the developed Western societies to define the paradigmatic logics of modern states. Indeed, the word "statistics" owes its origin to the emergence of the modern state; its initial meaning was "matters pertaining to the state" (Hacking, 1990).

These tendencies toward greater order and predictability in society have extended to the standardization of biographies, of institutionalization of the life course itself (Kohli & Meyer, 1986). This standardization has involved not only the emergence of the "three boxes of life," but also the fairly steady 20th-century trend toward a progressively greater uniformity in the timing of each cohort's movement through the transitions of leaving school, entering the work force, getting married, and retiring (e.g., Hogan, 1981; Riley, 1978). In many respects, these changes have meant a reduction in disorder or unpredictability and hence—for better or worse—a reduction in risk. In an epoch of risk reduction in virtually every aspect of social and personal life, the idea of "risk"—even when specified as endogenous risk—appears more than a little incongruous.

Ironically, a key force behind the privatization of economic risk has been precisely the reduction of risks in other spheres. Employers, health-care insurers and providers and government have all sought to limit the increasing financial exposure created by the ability to survive acute illnesses, and by increasing longevity itself. The exogenous risks of natural processes are replaced by the endogenous risks of institutional liability and potential insolvency. These new risks are displaced downward to the individual citizen, as O'Rand shows: defined contributions replace defined benefits; managed care replaces what was widely assumed to be accessible and effective health care. In short, corporate and state uncertainties are transferred to citizens—protecting large institutions while exposing individuals to possible catastrophe in the domains of health care and personal finances, justified to the public by the claim that the pensioner can do better on his or her own, and that Social Security can do better diversified into equity markets.

Understandably, these changes are framed for the public mainly in terms of choice, autonomy, and opportunity, rather than risk. Although it takes distinctive forms for different ages, "opportunity" now permeates the U.S. life course, and self-reliance has been identified by leading business trend watchers as "the first building block for the New Millenium" in an "America that has turned itself around . . . and is now rebuilding itself on a new foundation" of entrepreneurship and individualism (Keller, 1998). Through the 1990s, "choice" has become an increasingly prominent buzzword in discussions of K-12 schooling issues, and the business press celebrated a dramatic growth of interest in entrepreneurship among Generation Xers (e.g., Lane, 1995). Recently, more than half of survey respondents aged 18 to 24 reported interest in being self-employed (Opinion Research Corp., 1995). And of course, those whose enterprises do not work out can join others taking the "opportunity" to play state-controlled lotteries. Through them, legalized gambling has expanded enormously, and their aggressive hawking has become a staple of media advertising (e.g., O'Brien, 1998). All such "opportunities" entail substantial risks.

Infusing retirement with risk is especially significant in view of the modernist view of later life as a biographical time of relative freedom from risk, when a threshold of security could be counted on, earned by decades of work and taxpaying. But through the same ideological reframing that celebrates risk as opportunity, the collective pension base is redefined as an entitlement and then declared to be in a crisis (Quadagno, 1996). In a carefully documented argument, Ekerdt (1998) has recently shown that the public definition of these issues by media can be carefully regulated to produce a systematic reframing that displaces the normative and moral sense of responsibility, as well as financial liability, to the individual level. This displacement will likely have implications for one's sense of self, as she confronts uncertainly a new set of issues that bear directly upon her future life chances.

RISK AND THE AGING SELF

Paradoxical and troubling as are the historic shifts surrounding the privatization of risk, it is likely that their effects upon the self will be consequential. O'Rand offers some intriguing speculations about how the "biographically anchored project of self" may react to these shifts, in ways that range from restructuring investments to staying in the work force longer than planned, to moving to Reno. The impact upon the self of these shifts is, however, unlikely to be only behavioral in nature.

In this section, I attempt to extend O'Rand's provocative macro-analysis by combining it with a microsociological perspective on the self. I believe this extension brings into view some additional implications for the self of the social imposition of new risks upon aging individuals.

The social-constitutive approach to self articulated by Giddens and adopted by O'Rand is well suited to an analysis that combines macro- and micro-approaches. A fully social-constitutive approach to self recognizes that the reflexivity of the self necessarily extends to the very nature of the self. That is, the self is not a fixed entity that operates reflexively on its environment, but is initially created and continuously sustained and reconstituted in the experience and interaction of everyday life in historically specific ways (Castells, 1997; Giddens, 1991). I will develop the implications of the interactive and reconstitutive nature of the self in the context of discussing three aspects of the self likely to be affected by the collective transformation of risk that O'Rand analyzed: Self-concept, roles, and values.

Self-Concept

In contemplating what the new experience of risk may imply for the self, a first task requires making explicit the point just emphasized: That the "biographically anchored and reflexive project" of self is always, and irreducibly, an interactively reflexive project that is realized in conversation with others and with oneself (e.g., Berger & Luckmann, 1967; Giddens, 1991, 1994; Mead, 1934) and that is constituted and reconstituted in the flow of that conversation. The extent of stability or change in the self depends heavily on the character of that conversation. As interactionists understand, this principle can readily explain phenomena that generate angst in those self theorists still perplexed by the logical and empirical contradictions posed by the old stability-change debate (for related discussions, see George and Whitbourne's chapter, this volume).

In being reflexive, a large part of what the actor responds to is her own perception of how others are defining her. She adjusts her own lines of action and her own self-definition in response to those perceptions, along with other exigencies (Berger & Luckmann, 1967; Mead, 1934; Stokes & Hewitt, 1976). The articulation of preferences for investment strategies is a moment of externalization and expression of the self, to be sure. But the self is not only observed in the act of expressing its preferences; it is also reconstituted, through action and interaction with others.

Consider how an individual reacts when a new set of social rules (of which one may learn, for example, by way of a letter from one's health care provider or employer) unexpectedly dictates that she must adopt a new level of responsibility for her investment strategy, for checking out what a doctor tells her, or figuring out how to pay for a medical visit. Such a rule change has implications for how the actor will spend time and energy, what she will read, whom she will talk to, what kinds of conversations she will have, and what kinds of knowledge will convey status in those conversations. It also defines a new sphere in which she needs to act competently. Her actions will not only affect her health and prosperity; it will also affect how she, and perhaps others close to her, appraise her competence in managing her limited resources. For many aging citizens, privatization of risks means that performance in new and unfamiliar domains of decision making cannot be altogether avoided.

These experiences of self-appraisal, internalization of the perceived appraisals of others, and the resultant possible modification of one's own self-concept, are all part of the reflexivity of the self (cf. Rosenberg, 1979). Analyzing it requires understanding how the particular configuration of social rules, imposed choices and risks can affect who I feel that I am. This is a direct effect, in the sense that it derives from the immediacy of interaction and activity, but there are also indirect effects upon the self of equal importance for the self, also for social well-being.

For example, it is now well understood that psychological stress affects physical health. There are many dimensions to this dynamic. For example, mood has a very clear effect upon the functioning of the immune system (Ader, Cohen, & Felten, 1995.) Is having to take a new level of responsibility for allocating my portfolio—and make decisions which I am ill-equipped to make in terms of information and knowledge—likely to be a source of negative stress (e.g., Aldwin, 1994) If so, and if such stress has physical consequences which lead me to decide I am sick or getting old or am no longer able to cope, that is an also an effect upon the self. It will likely mean that I come to see myself as a somewhat different person, perhaps as someone for whom life is becoming too much, or who envisages a newly delimited life space and temporal horizon.

The implications of these dynamics for both theory and policy become considerably sharpened when viewed in the context of Professor O'Rand's related point, that access to information is a key factor in defining risk. This connection deserves to be developed further than the space allocated to her chapter permitted. Since risk is neither evenly nor randomly distributed throughout the population, a stratification of information, of access to information and, ultimately, of self-concepts, will likely follow the increasingly bifurcated lines of occupational stratification traced in O'Rand's discussion and, increasingly, overtly exploited by marketing analysts (Keller, 1998). Such an effect is precisely the opposite of the likely psychosocial effects of Social Security and of defined contribution plans, which leave the aged relatively freer from some of these sources of invidiousness and anxiety, and which provide a measure of uniform security that reduces rather than accentuates economic differences. In selfhood as in economics, then, the tendencies toward cumulation of advantage and disadvantage (Dannefer, 1987; O'Rand, 1996) appear robust and enduring.

Roles

The privatization of decision making about matters such as retirement financing and health care may imply more general changes in the shape of retirement roles. Analytically, such changes may provide an opportunity to specify empirically some mechanisms of cohort norm formation (Riley, 1978; cf. Riley, Kahn, & Foner, 1994). For example, will individuals in general, and those nearing retirement in particular, strive to develop, en masse, new roles (and new identities) as master portfolio managers? Even the casual observer can pick up signs that argue in favor of such a hypothesis: the proliferation of neighborhood investment clubs, of print media and talk radio devoted to personal finances and investing, of software packages and websites promising investment expertise, of anecdotal reports of the popularity of investing as a topic to pass the time among retirees. *Wall Street Week*, one of the longest-running shows on U.S. public television continues to expand its popularity, and the record run-up in stock prices in the 1990s was, in part, a result of increasing numbers of small investors pouring money into equities (either directly or through mutual funds).

Second, will people evaluate themselves and calibrate their own self-esteem based on their role performance, on their adroitness as investors? Will health either improve or suffer in response to mood swings or changing self-appraisals tied to one's shrewdness as a health care consumer or market savvy?

In sum, the privatization of risks may invade the self and identity with a new set of tasks, a new set of topics, a new set of personal and social agendas, new domains of role captivity (Pearlin, 1975). No one could oppose being vigilant and knowledgeable about either one's personal finances or health care options. And even though it is a fearful prospect for many, for others it may be an unexpected source of fun and positive energizing (especially when the market is up)—as good a hedge against disengagement as it is against deflation. However, if procuring knowledge in these areas is not a matter of choice, but is imposed as a necessary preoccupation of responsible citizens, some basic policy questions must be confronted—questions that counterpose public interest to portfolio value.

Values

In the current situation in the U.S., retirement and pension policies generally encourage individual citizens to spend an increasing amount of time and energy, both pre- and post-retirement, preoccupied with enhancing private net worth.

Without question, it is important for people to save and to be fiscally prudent. Conserving and marshalling one's resources skillfully is important in every domain of activity—diet, exercise, and social and intellectual nourishment, no less than personal finances. In the area of personal finances, however, a policy that requires a preoccupation with solvency cannot avoid encouraging a preoccupation with acquiring wealth. As noted earlier, the infrastructure supporting and celebrating "opportunity" throughout the life course has been nurtured and expanded by corporate, media, policy, and educational institutions, but the salience to the aged is especially acute because their earning power is often curtailed.

It is worth pondering the general social and cultural implications of policies that encourage and compel individuals to focus on the accumulation of personal capital. Will such a private preoccupation reduce the energy that individuals can or will give to civic concerns? Will it erode further the collective awareness on matters of important public debate, and the democratic ideal of an informed citizenry?

SELF-INTEREST, PUBLIC INTEREST AND POLICY

The intellectual, social, and civic talents of the retired population will continue to grow dramatically into the 21st century, as they have through the 20th. Given the potential value of those talents, this foundational principle is proposed for policymakers: Policies that promote individual self-interest should be implemented only to the extent that they do not undermine or compete with public interest.

Under the present system, that competition is very real. For how many capable retirees will the pressure to become savvy as an investor squelch a willingness to engage in activities that are genuinely socially productive, as well as psychically rewarding? Having the right portfolio allocation creates value for no one but the investor and his or her heirs. Tutoring or befriending a needy child, visiting homebound elders, or becoming informed in the public debate over complex problems (e.g., using one's accumulated experience and expertise to advise how to deal with child labor or environmental problems, whether local or international in scope)—how much energy will be drained against such pursuits by a war of all portfolios against all that ensures nothing so much as inflated equity prices and the attendant eroded returns?

In short, Uhlenberg's (1992) second option of enhancing the productivity of the aged may be as important for what it implies about the potentials of retirees for constructive social participation as it is in the narrower sense of the individual self-sufficiency that results from earned income. Policy can be used as a tool to encourage continued productivity that offers substantial public value, value that can in many cases translate into an enhancement of the value of a tax base.

What are the broader consequences of a societal change which leads people to spend a sizeable and increasing amount of free time, and perhaps retirement time, preoccupied with enhancing personal value? In which people are assumed (and largely erroneously) to be personally responsible for the outcomes of their decisions, blaming themselves if they are disappointed, and perhaps assuming an unrealistic and inflated sense of competence if they are pleased?

For some people, this may understandably be fun, energizing, exhilarating—as good a hedge against disengagement as it is against inflation (or deflation). But for others, possibly very many others, it will be exactly the opposite. But even for the former, it is well to consider the consequences of creating "isolated, lonely, striving" selves (Wexler, 1996; cf. Habermas, 1987). One may well ask, would the general interest not be better served by policies that encourage elders to see the neglect of children or the destruction of the environment as the moral equivalent of war, and to engage these issues as central preoccupations of their consciousness and conversation, energy and expertise?

RESEARCH IMPLICATIONS

These questions, which follow from the problems that O'Rand poses, suggest a number of lines of possible research to link the external contingencies with which institutional change confronts the self, with the self's own internal dynamics. Thus, these are questions with the potential for contributing to basic theoretical understanding as well as to illuminating the discussion of policy issues. Carefully designed studies to address both the cognitive and behavioral dimensions of how people interpret and respond to the new survivalist challenges in middle and later adulthood provide an opportunity to examine the degree to which basic values and aspects of personality remain stable under conditions of change and uncertainty. Ideally, such analyses would require individual-level data to link resource and pension information to individual expectations and behavior. Such analyses could potentially illuminate the impact of risk on the three domains of self-concept, roles, and values. With regard to policy, these issues have significant implications for productivity, especially the social productivity of older people, and for quality of life at the societal level, implications that may ultimately be linked to issues as diverse as physical and mental health and civic participation. Addressing such questions requires 1) detailed study of actual options available to individuals for retirement planning, pensions, options, and how these may have changed; 2) linking such options, and especially changes in them, with the individual's cognitive appraisal of her situation, with her strategies for responding to the alternatives available to her; and 3) examining how the responses impact the lifestyles and activity routines of retired citizens.

CONCLUSION

In the context of a century of increasing retirement benefits as the secure biographical anchor following decades of hard work, the risk society confronts the aging self with a reversal of fortune. The transfer of health care and pension risks to individuals imposes upon retirees and those looking toward retirement the same preoccupation with self-reliance, with the continued need for vigilance and, possibly productivity, that is heralded as a general cultural triumph by the business press and pollsters. In the case of public funds and pension-related policies, it entails the use—mostly the unwitting use—of policy as a tool to reorient the preoccupations of everyday life, ensuring their privatization and monetarization. These consequences for the consciousness and patterns of activity and relationship of the entire society have probably not been clearly anticipated, but they comport well with capitalist ideology. The prospect of such consequences raises questions of how policy might, however, be used as a tool for the publicly constructive shaping of consciousness—by rewarding participation in matters of general concern to the public interest, whether in the form of nurturing neglected children—or elders—or in the form of working to reduce the environmental damage of post-industrial pollution. It is suggested that rewarding such publicly useful engagement, rather than a preoccupation with stock market dynamics, is a way to reengage the productive potentials of the aging self for the benefit of the entire collectivity.

ACKNOWLEDGMENTS

The author wishes to thank Elaine F. Dannefer, Ivor Goodson, Joe Hendricks, K. Warner Schaie, and the panelists and audience participants in the Penn State Conference on Social Structure and the Aging Self for comments and constructive criticisms on earlier versions of the paper.

REFERENCES

Ader, R., Cohen, N., & Felten, D. (1995). Psychoneuroimmunology: Interactions between the nervous system and the immune system. *Lancet, 345*, 99–103.

Aldwin, C. (1994). *Stress, coping and development: An integrative perspective.* New York: Guilford.

Berger, P. L., & Luckmann, T. (1967). *The social construction of reality: A treatise in the sociology of knowledge.* New York: Anchor.

Castells, M. (1997). *The information age: Economy, society and culture, Vol. II: The Power of identity.* Oxford, UK: Blackwell.

Dannefer, D. (1987). Accentuation, the Matthew effect, and the life course: Aging as intracohort differentiation. *Sociological Forum, 2,* 11–30.

Ekerdt, D. J. (1998). Entitlements, generational equity and public-opinion manipulation in Kansas City. *Gerontologist, 38,* 525–536.

Giddens, A. (1991). *Modernity and self-identity: Self and identity in the late modern age.* Palo Alto, CA: Stanford University Press.

Giddens, A. (1994.) *The transformation of intimacy.* Palo Alto, CA: Stanford University Press.

Habermas, J. (1987). *The theory of communicative action.* Boston: Beacon.

Hacking, I. (1990). *The taming of chance.* New York: Cambridge University Press.

Hogan, D. (1981). *Transitions and social change: The early lives of American men.* New York: Academic.

Keller, E. (1998, September). Report on Roper's Managing and Mastering Change Conference. *Public Pulse,* p. 2.

Kohli, M., & Meyer, J. W. (1986). Social structure and the construction of life stages. *Human Development, 29,* 145–180.

Lane, R. (1995, May). Computers are our friends. *Forbes, 155,* 102–108.

Mead, G. H. (1934). *Mind, self and society.* Chicago: University of Chicago Press.

O'Brien, T. L. (1998). *Bad bet: The inside story of the glamour, glitz and danger of America's gambling industry.* New York: Times Books.

O'Rand, A. (1996). The precious and the precocious: Understanding cumulative disadvantage and cumulative advantage over the life course. *Gerontologist, 36,* 230–239.

O'Rand, A. (1998, August). *Labor markets, pension mix and job mobility among two cohorts of women workers.* Paper presented at the Special Session on Pensions, Labor Markets, and Choice. Annual Meeting of the American Sociological Association, San Francisco.

Opinion Research Corp. (1995). *Caravan research: Project summary.* Princeton, NJ: Author.

Pearlin, L. (1975). Sex roles and depression. In N. Datan & L. Ginsberg (Eds.), *Life span developmental psychology: Normative life crises* (pp. 191–207). New York: Academic.

Quadagno, J. (1996). Social security and the myth of the entitlement "crisis." *Gerontologist, 36,* 391–399.

Riley, M. W. (1978). Social change and the power of ideas. *Daedaelus, 107,* 39–52.

Riley, M. W., Kahn, R. L., & Foner, A. (1994). Introduction: The mismatch between people and structures. In M. W. Riley, R. K. Kahn, & A. Foner (Eds.), *Age and structural lag: Society's failure to provide meaningful opportunities in work, family and leisure* (pp. 1–36). New York: Wiley.

Rosenberg, M. (1979). *Conceiving the self.* New York: Basic.

Stokes, R., & Hewitt, J. P. (1976). Aligning actions. *American Sociological Review, 41,* 838–849.

Uhlenberg, P. (1992). Population aging and social policy. *Annual Review of Sociology, 18,* 449–474.

Wexler, P. (1996, July). *Reselfing after postmodern culture: Sacred social psychology.* Paper presented at Crossroads in Cultural Studies Conference, Tampere, Finland.

CHAPTER 6

The New Aging: Self Construction and Social Values

Kenneth J. Gergen and Mary M. Gergen

> To look at people over 65 in terms of work, health, and productivity would be to treat them like full people again, not just objects of compassionate or contemptuous care.
>
> —Betty Friedan, *The Fountain of Age*

> Old age is best understood as a form of post-modern existence in which the mobilization of meaning is fluid and constant and confrontation with the self is continuous.
>
> —Haim Hazan, *Old Age, Constructions and Deconstructions*

Historically speaking, the aged in the United States have largely suffered through what may be characterized as a Dark Age. As Michael Harrington characterized it in 1969, "America tends to make its people miserable when they become old. [They are] plagued by ill health; they do not have enough money; they are socially isolated" (p. 32). Richard Margolis (1990) suggests that we have given "in to a heavy fatalism that recalls Seneca's dismissal of old age as 'an incurable disease.' We see feebleness, helplessness, mindlessness. The evidence . . . is all around us" (p. 112). There is a habit of seeing a population of "frail elders, locked within their homes, as rather passive and as prisoners of their illnesses" (Rubinstein, Kilbride, & Nagy, 1992, *x*). As Margaret Gullette (1997), proposes, our history is such that we treat longevity as "solely a disaster. (Perhaps men should congratulate themselves on dying younger!)" (p. 186). And as the Gray Panthers' television monitoring task force concluded in the late 1970s, older people were typically depicted as "ugly, toothless, sexless, incontinent, senile, confused and helpless . . . " (see http://www.progway.org/BGP.html).

This Dark Age condition has been intensified by certain dominant values in American culture. Two of these bear special attention. First the individualist tradition—holding each person to be a free agent, capable of making his/her own decisions, choosing his/her own way of life—has long been a cultural mainstay of American life (Rubinstein et al., 1992). While broadly celebrated, the value placed on the self-determining agent is also deeply problematic (cf. Lasch, 1979; Sampson, 1988). It invites attention to one's self—"my development, aspirations, emotions, needs" and the like. Other persons are thereby relegated to a secondary status. As Bellah, Madsen, Sullivan, Swindler, and Tipton (1985) propose, such a value threatens close ties of intimacy—both in the family and community.

Individualist values serve as a double-edged sword to the elderly. Through various exigencies, maintaining one's own individual status as an independent person may be threatened. Becoming vulnerable to illnesses and disabilities and/or losing economic self-sufficiency, the elderly have often reduced the freedom of those on whom they rely. When self-agency is primary, the aging dependent is an imposition on others. At the same time the aged person becomes dependent, he/she may suffer from the sense of diminished agency: "I am no longer capable of free action or expression; I am a dead weight." On the other hand, those who remain healthy and economically self-sufficient chose to remain alone, often separated geographically from family. Not being a burden means preserving one's individuality, and this entails not asking for greater connection to family members.

Also contributing to the Dark Ages of aging has been the traditional value of productivity. With deep roots in Protestant ethics and the spirit of pragmatism, there is a strong tendency to equate personal worth with productive achievement (Hochschild, 1989). Within the capitalist economy, productive achievement is typically associated with the earning of wages. Thus as one retires from the workplace, one's personal worth becomes questionable. This occurs despite the possibility that other measures of productivity could be made. One is "sidelined," "put out to pasture," or becomes a "has been." This displacement is especially important to men, for whom one's career success is directly entwined with one's sense of identity (M. Gergen, 1992). As feminist critics point out, being productive also affects the valuation of the maturing woman (Martin, 1997). Because women's "production" is so frequently allied with their capacity to bear children, they are doubly vulnerable to being found wanting. The onset of menopause signals for them a loss of worth. Women thus suffer from the sense of being "barren," "empty," or "without a nest." Within this context of values, women face the specter of being "finished at forty" when their biological productivity begins to cease (M. Gergen, 1990).

Yet, in our view, history is not destiny, and we now stand on the threshold of an entirely new range of conceptions and practices. As we shall hope to demonstrate, the Dark Ages of aging are giving way to a New Aging. To appreciate this movement and its potentials, we shall set the stage by briefly laying out the social constructionist perspective from which we approach the issues. Then we shall consider the changing conditions of aging, with special attention to demographic and economic factors. This will enable us to appreciate what we feel is a substantial and pervasive movement toward the reconstruction of aging in contemporary society. In particular, movements toward the erasure of age, re-empowerment, and sybaritic lifestyles will occupy our attention. Finally we shall propose that these altered images and practices are now transforming the matrix of values and practices within the culture more generally. The aged are ceasing to be the byproducts of a cultural mainstream, but are instead altering the very character of mainstream society.

THE SOCIAL CONSTRUCTION OF VALUE AND THE AGING SELF

We approach the issues of cultural values and the aging self from the standpoint of social constructionism (K. Gergen, 1994, 1999;

M. Gergen, 2000; Gergen & Davis, 1997). Social constructionism in social science was born within dialogues spanning a variety of disciplines—including science and technology studies, the history of science, cultural anthropology, literary theory, women's studies, and cultural studies among them. Of focal importance in social constructionist writings are the social processes giving rise to our common understandings of the world—what we take to be the real and the good. For the constructionist, all that has meaning in our lives—that which we take to be knowledge, reason, and right—has its origins within the matrix of relationships in which we are engaged. This is not the place for a full treatment of the constructionist standpoint. However, it is important to understand key implications for the present undertaking. Let us briefly consider the pivotal concepts of value and the aging self.

Regarding cultural values, social constructionism is scarcely controversial. We commonly hold that values vary greatly across cultures and across history. We are not by nature of our genes required to place a strong value on money, conquering space, or having a slim figure. Some may bridle when it comes to issues of universal value—perhaps there are, or at least should be, universal goods (e.g., freedom from oppression). And there may be economists and sociobiologists who will plump for the intrinsic desire for self gain or selfishness. However, from our standpoint, we are inclined to see all value as having its genesis in human relationship—including the value placed on human life, longevity, and health. In terms of the aging process in society, we are thus inclined to emphasize malleability. The cultural values that inform our conceptions of aging, along with the value we derive (or fail to derive) from aging itself, are thus subject to fluctuation and transformation (cf. Hashimoto, 1996; Shwezder, 1998). Further, and most essential for the present thesis, the aging population may serve as a source for creating its own values. Rather than being merely the recipients of description, older voices are adding and altering the ways in which important social values are being made. They are speaking to and for themselves with the broader society.

With regard to the concept of the aging self, constructionist theses are particularly catalytic. There is a widespread tendency within the social and biological sciences to search for the naturalized life course, that is, to chart the innate development and decline of human capacities, tendencies, proclivities and so on over the lifespan (Gubrium, Holstein, & Buckholdt, 1994; Turnbull, 1984). This tendency is strongest in the sciences of child development and aging, with the first largely devoted to setting standards for normal growth and the latter for decline (cf. Cunningham & Brookbank, 1988; Erikson, 1963; Kagan, 1984; Levinson, 1978; Santrock, 1992). In particular, studies of separate age cohorts suggest that many possible life trajectories are possible, and that what is fixed about human change may be small (Helson, Mitchell, & Moane, 1984; Neugarten, 1969, 1979; Stewart & Ostgrove, 1998). With its strong emphasis on culturally and historically situated knowledge, social constructionism serves as a challenge to these efforts. In this respect, much lifespan developmental literature is helpful (Bengtson, Schaie, & Burton, 1995). As lifespan doyen Bernice Neugarten (1980), proposed almost 20 years ago, we are slowly becoming an age-irrelevant society, in the sense that we are "becoming accustomed to the 28-year-old mayor . . . the 50-year old-retiree, the 65-year-old father of a preschooler and the 70-year-old student."

Social constructionist dialogues add important dimension to this possibility. For the constructionist, whatever we may observe about human action over time places no necessary demands on our interpretations. In this sense, there is nothing about changes in the human body that require a concept of age, of development, or decline. There is no process of aging *in itself*; the discourse of aging is born of relations within a given culture at a given time (Hazan, 1994). In other cultural conditions, alternative interpretations are invited. For example, as Richard Shweder (1998) observes, for the Gusii people of West Kenya, "decline and obsolescence are not the meanings associated with the increased sense of 'seniority' that a Gusii man or woman develops over time. Seniority is associated instead with respect, obedience, prestige, and social esteem" (p. *xv*). More dramatically, there is nothing about the conditions of what we call the "human body" that demands such terms as "disease" and "incapacity." Not only is what we call "the body" subject to widely differing conceptions (Young, 1997), but the suffering associated with a "disease" may depend strongly on the interpretive stance one takes toward it. For example, as Frank (1995) proposes, viewing oneself as "a victim" of disease, as opposed to "a moral witness," has powerful implications for one's sense of well-being.

Of special relevance to the present offering, we must also view the scientific literature of late-life decline as culturally constructed. That is, the extensive research demonstrating deterioration of physical and psychological functioning during the latter span of life is not a simple reflection of what is there. Rather, that a given configuration constitutes "decline"—or indeed, is worth mentioning at all—derives from a particular domain of values (such as productivity and individualism), sets of assumptions, ways of talking and measuring, and so on. In effect, to find someone biologically or cognitively impaired constitutes what Gubrium et al. (1994) call a "collaborative accomplishment". It is an accomplishment of a particular professional group, working with particular assumptions and values, within a supportive culture. And so it is that we must continuously reflect on the way in which the sciences construct the life-course, and most particularly accounts that treat decline as a natural fact of growing older. As Dannefer (1988) puts the case, "Naturalization is a highly effective mechanism of social legitimation because it is difficult to oppose that which is seen as natural. When (the rhetoric of naturalization) remains unacknowledged in scientific discourse, science is itself engaged in the legitimation of prevailing social arrangements" (p. 17). (Also see Tiefer, 1997, for a discussion of the ways in which natural is used as a term of social control.)

It is also when we avoid tendencies toward naturalization, when we become conscious of contingency, that we begin to appreciate possibilities of cultural transformation. When the taken-for-granted becomes "one supposition among many," we are alerted to the potentials of reconstructing the course of aging in more positive ways (Hazan, 1994). The American construction of aging has yielded enormous suffering, and it could be otherwise (cf. Campioni, 1997; K. Gergen, 1996; Kaplan, 1997). We shall return to this challenge shortly.

It should be noted, however, that constructionism cautions us to be aware, as well, of the constructed character of the present contribution. Our remarks should not be taken, then, as accurate and objective reports on what is the case, but as a way of understanding our world. Our primary hope is that this particular form of understanding will harbor promising potentials for our collective future.

CONTEMPORARY CONDITIONS OF AGING

As suggested earlier, our central argument is that major transformations in the construction of aging are currently taking place in the United States. In our view, the origin of these transformations may be traced to emerging conditions of society. In effect, the Dark Ages of aging were tied closely to a particular configuration of social and economic conditions. As these conditions disappear into the maw of history, the way is opened for transformations in construction. Before exploring the specific forms of transformation, it is thus essential to glimpse some central changes in societal conditions. Pivotally important are changes in demographics, economics, and technology.

Population: The Elder Explosion

Of chief significance to our thesis are demographic changes in the population, and particularly the growth in the population over 60 years of age. With steady increases in health and longevity along with simultaneous decrements in the birthrate, the proportion of the population over 60 has been steadily increasing. By the year 2030, one in five Americans will be 65 or older, the majority of which will be women (Hagestad, 1991; Peterson & Somit, 1994). This demographic pattern also means that the potential political power of the aging population is also steadily increasing. By the 21st century, a full 25% of the voters in American elections will be over 65. Political power may be even greater than the numbers indicate because older voters are increasingly more likely to cast a ballot. In the 1988 U.S. presidential election, for example, 66% of those eligible to vote did so; among those 60–79, 80% voted! (Peterson & Somit, 1994). This imbalance favoring the participation of older voters over young ones has continued unabated. According to the U.S. Bureau of the Census Current Population Reports, nearly 70% of Americans 65 and older voted in the 1996 national elections, compared with 33% of those 18–24 (Dychtwald, 1999).

The old are not only becoming more numerous and active politically, but they are also becoming better organized. For example, the American Association of Retired Persons (AARP)—which began as a small marketing venture for insurance products—has now become one of the strongest lobbying voices in political life. Its membership now exceeds 32 million. With lobbying organizations such as this, political wisdom has been shaped to the extent that certain entitlements for the older population have become unassailable. As Tip O'Neill, then Senior Congressman from Massachusetts, described it, programs for older people, such as Social Security and Medicare, are the "third rail of American politics. 'Touch it and you die' " (Morris, 1996, p. *xi*).

Finally, with respect to the construction of meaning, the aging have more peers with whom to interact than ever before, and with increasing alacrity are seeking them out. In earlier times, the aging were scattered minority members in most communities, often sequestered in homes with younger relatives (Rose & Peterson, 1965); now in some areas of the country (e.g., in Florida, Arizona, and Southern California) they are in the majority. With increasing numbers have come forms of self-organized segregation. Communities have been established exclusively for people over a certain age; young adults and children are prohibited as permanent residents. Limits are even set on how long younger people may visit. Essentially this means that in negotiating issues of value, self, and aging, the aging may rely on others like themselves, as opposed to a younger population for whom aging is an alien and often threatening stage of life.

Economics: Elder Power

A second cultural shift accentuates the effects of the first. Not only are the aging becoming proportionally more numerous, but they are also becoming increasingly powerful economically. As Charles Morris comments:

> One of the great embarrassments of American's 1960's War on Poverty was the discovery that the largest number of poor Americans were not Appalachian cabin dwellers or minorities in urban slums but old people living on Social Security. Payroll taxes had been kept low over the years . . . until Richard Nixon and a Democratic Congress massively liberalized the system in 1973 and 1974. Over the two years benefit levels were raised by about 35 percent and they were indexed for inflation. From that point on benefits were automatically increased each year to keep pace with the Consumer Price Index. . . . The bene-

fit increases . . . were enormously successful in lifting the nation's old
people out of poverty. (Morris, 1996, pp. 77–78)

Between 1966 and 1974, the poverty rate among the elderly was cut
in half; today, American's elderly are less likely than nonelderly to
be poor. From 1995 onward, the poverty rate of the those over 65
has hovered around 10%, according to the U.S. Census Bureau's
Current Population Survey. Between 1988 and 1991, senior wealth
grew by 20%, while median wealth for the country as a whole grew
by about 2%. In 1986, the average 70-year-old had 71% of the buying
power of a 30-year-old. Just 10 years later, in 1996, the 70-year-old
has acquired 18% more to spend than the 30-year-old (Morris, 1996).
Today, those over 65 control 70% of the total wealth and 77% of
all financial assets; are 66% of the stockholders; and are more likely
to own their own homes outright than any other group (80% have
paid off their mortgages) (Dychtwald, 1999, p. 20). While it is still
true that pockets of deep poverty characterize certain groups of the
elderly, especially African American women, the general economic
gains are immense.

Technology: Generational Arrival

A third shift in cultural conditions also demands brief attention—
perhaps more as a precis of the future than a posit of the present.
One of the most profound transformations of the present century
has been the insinuation of communication technologies into everyday life. From the early development of the telephone, telegraph
and radio to the more recent mushrooming of television, mobile
phones, and the computer, American society has been moving into
a condition of intense sociation (see K. Gergen, 2000). The availability of others—whether face-to-face, or mediated electronically—
steadily increases. Multitudes await the mere flicking of a television
or computer switch. Perhaps the most dramatic transformation lies
within the domain of computer technology, where—through the
Internet and World Wide Web—two-way communication is facilitated on a global scale. With these technologies not only are relations
easily generated and sustained, but like-minded persons can rapidly
organize around a given issue and make their cause known to
thousands.

While the majority of the elderly population still tends toward technophobia, a cohort of technologically sophisticated individuals are now entering retirement. Increasingly, the aging population is becoming "wired." Numerous bulletin boards, self-help groups, and chat lines devoted to issues of aging are beginning to emerge. Many individuals are available for dialogue any hour of the day or night. Further, because age markers can be removed, an elderly person can enter into discussions on virtually any topic with people from around the country—or the world—without encountering the prejudices otherwise often confronted in face-to-face interactions. Equally important, these technologies now facilitate an increasing degree of organization among the elderly. Opinions can be shared, agendas put forward, funds generated, and programs—often of national significance—mounted. For example, ThirdAge.com is a website welcoming some 500,000 visitors every month. This site is oriented to people who might be called seniors or older citizens, but a new, more upbeat designation (Third Age) has been chosen to represent their position. Databases of information and resources, experts, community forums, and shopping sites are all available. For example, a virtual bank offers retirement planning facilities, Toys 'R' Us offers an order service for grandparents, a nutritional database supplies information on vitamins and minerals, and IBM sponsors "E-Business Entrepreneur—a guide for those wanting to generate a Web business. Again, the powers of self-construction are augmented.

ROUTES TOWARD RECONSTRUCTION

As discussed earlier, the older population is expanding, its economic and political bases are stronger, and its technological sophistication is rapidly growing. We thus confront a population with enormous resources for self-construction, for generating and sharing conceptions of the self, age, and personal value among themselves. Here is a population that can increasingly resist the constructions of others—how students, middle-aged workers, television producers, or health care professionals construe their lives and dictate the terms by which they will understand themselves. In our view, this resistance to the dominant culture of meaning-makers is precisely what is taking place, and in steadily increasing degree. It is not a process that is

TABLE 6.1 Websites for the Aging

Senior Information Networks: The one-stop resource center for seniors.
  http://www.senior-inet.com/index.htm

Senior News Network
  http://www.seniorsnews.com

National Council on Aging
  http://www.ncoa.org/

Third Age
  http://thirdage.com

American Association of Retired People is a large lobbying group for older citizens in the U.S.
  http://www.aarp.org

Health and positive aging information from Novartis' Gerontology Foundation. The authors co-produce this site.
  http://www.healthandage.com/

equally effective across all sectors of the aging population, nor is it a process that can be completed. For any subgroup in the population, a total refusal of the majority's views of them is impossible to sustain. The challenge of supporting a viable alternative reality is continuous.

Most important for present purposes, there is no single, pervasive model for the New Aging. Rather, we find important manifestations of at least three significant images, each accompanied by particular patterns of living, and each with different implications for cultural futures. For analytic purposes we shall treat them as "pure types," recognizing that any single individual may represent a pastiche of multiple tendencies. We may distinguish, then, among emerging constructions of eternal youth, re-empowerment, and sybaritic expansion.

Eternal Youth

The most pervasive form of reconstruction derives from the long-standing binary of "old" versus "young" and the traditional privileging of the latter over the former. National surveys consistently find that in spite of calendar age, fewer than 10% of the population will identify themselves as "old." As Betty Friedan (1993) notes, in some senior citizens clubs members are fined for simply mentioning the word "old." Investigators have even coined the term "gerophobic" to describe the extreme fear of aging. Margaret Gullette (1997) proposes that age "internalized is a stressor, a depressant—what I want to call a psychocultural illness" (p. 193). With a prevailing fear of being "no longer young," it is scarcely surprising that the image of the aging body is a primary target for reconstruction. Such refusal to disappear silently into the night of old age is vivified in research carried out by Mary Gergen (1989) with a group of women between 42–48. The study took the form of a focus group, treating the issue of menopause. During the discussion the women recalled stories they head heard from others on the miseries related to menopause— women going crazy, drying up, losing their looks, getting divorced, becoming aggressive and angry witches, etc. However, in the course of their conversation they came to agree that such dire consequences of menopause would not mar their lives. They would refuse to be victims. Rather, they would construct another way out. As one discussant said, "We'll do it differently. There has never been such a good looking group of women our age. We are healthy, strong, athletic, and smart. We'll just play right through it!"

And it is this "playing through it" that occupies the time and efforts of an increasing segment of the older generations. As research on Americans' use of time indicates, life over 65 typically is marked by gains in disposable time. Most interesting for this image of aging is that, increasingly over the past 20 years, this time is being devoted to personal care and grooming (Robinson & Godbey, 1997). Nor are such practices limited to those entering their 60s. Fighting body fat, graying hair and balding pates, age spots, varicose veins, yellowing teeth, and facial wrinkles are pervasive behaviors even among those in their 30s and 40s. Charles Longino, formerly of the University of Miami's Center for Social Research in Aging, once coined the term "youth creep" to describe this condition of ever more youthful-looking older people. Using the rather unflattering terms of gerontology, he said, "The Old group seems younger as the decades pass. . . . The Old Old seem like the Young Old of a few decades earlier" (quoted in Margolis, 1990, pp. 112–113).

One of the chief reasons for the widespread popularity of the option to erase age markers derives from its support by a range of ancillary, profit-making institutions: self-help book publishers, pharmaceutical companies, plastic surgeons, dentists, opticians, beauticians, fitness centers, personal trainers, and more. All are economic stakeholders in agelessness. For example, popular spiritual advisor Deepak Chopra, in his volume *Ageless Body, Timeless Mind,* promises that "The field of human life is open and unbounded. At its deepest level, your body is ageless, your mind timeless" (1993, p. 7). The medical profession is an increasingly noteworthy participant in the economy of agelessness. In 1998, a convention of the newly created Academy of Anti-Aging Medicine, whose Board consists of academic scholars, medical doctors, and book publishers, hosted over 4,000 participants. Dozens of physicians have become certified experts in "anti-aging medicine," and the Academy now publishes the *Journal of Anti-Aging Medicine* http://www.liebertpub.com/jaa/default.htm). Concomitantly, a new medical field, *Cenegenics*—Greek for "new beginning"—is emerging, a field dedicated to the science of "youthful aging." The relationship between these institutions and the aging population is fully symbiotic: The quest for agelessness within this economically powerful segment of the culture creates a demand for new products and services and their creation (Viagra, laser skin removal, dental caps and crowns, hair transplants, miracle herbal supplements, skin creams, and hormonal replacement therapies); the existence of the products and services then function as an invitation to the population to remain youthful.

Yet, in spite of the compelling image of ageless adulthood, there are also important limitations to this life orientation. There is, for one, the continuous and increasing effort and expense required to "maintain the appearance," and the accompanying backdrop of anxiety over the accumulating indicators (both actual and imagined) that the youthful attributes are eroding. Further, if the defining physical indicators of youth remain fixed, the aspirant must inevitably fail. The supports for self-esteem are ultimately removed. At the same time, the picture may not be as dark as this scenario suggests. As we scan the horizons of various media, we begin to detect a new variation on the quest for eternal youth. Specifically, there are manifestations of a glamorization of age. In this case the attempt is not to emulate the young, but to employ certain vestiges or markers of traditional glamour to redefine age. For example, increasingly, we find the use of graying hair and mature, attractive older faces for marketing a product, as well as the presence of older models in ads for expensive luxury items—perfume, diamonds, watches, wines, cruises, exotic travel itineraries, exclusive residential units, and prestige sedans. The potentials for reconstructing the marks of age as beautiful are substantial.

Re-Empowering: Reclaiming Agency and Productivity

Earlier, we proposed that cultural investments in individual agency and productivity threaten the elderly with profound losses in self-worth: no longer are they in control of their lives or serving as productive citizens. Yet, in our view, the increasing degrees of economic power and self-organizing capacities among the elderly have precipitated strong moves toward the refusal of this characterization and the formation of alternative images and lifestyles. In part, the desire for control may be manifest in the increasing attempt by the elderly to function as masters of their own living spaces. As surveys show, some 85% of those over 65 wish to maintain their own private dwellings for as long as they can (Morris, 1996). The relatively recent emergence of retirement communities also helps speak to these needs for personal autonomy: here residents live fairly independent lives, with a great deal of choice concerning their living spaces, nourishment, entertainment, and social life. The shift to assisted living provides a buffer zone between complete independence and hospitalization or nursing home care.

Some of the most dramatic initiatives to reestablish control are taking place around issues of death. Increasingly, the elderly are seeking means of prolonging their lives and terminating them at their will. Prolongation frequently finds expression in fitness programs, dietary regimens, and pharmaceuticals for sustaining health. More symbolic are attempts to establish trust funds, wills, and endowments, to arrange for the disposition of one's personal belongings, and to plan one's own funeral services, all of which sustain control over one's resources after death. Most dramatic are explorations into regenerating a body that has succumbed to death (see, for example, http://www.cryonics.org/). Walt Disney, among several other imaginative men and women, have paved the way toward the potential of eternal life by having themselves frozen in specially designed vaults. Others have their eggs and sperm cells frozen for subsequent fertilization. Most well-known, perhaps, are the Nobel prize winners who have donated their sperm for artificial insemination. Equally controversial, but increasingly supported by the adult population, are initiatives to control the circumstances of one's death. For many, fears of aging center on the possible helplessness, pain, and personal indignities resulting from the deterioration of bodily functions as death approaches. Thus, movements toward living wills, doctor-assisted suicide, and euthanasia become increasingly commonplace as people find ways to extend their personal control to include their own manner of death.

Impulses toward asserting personal control are also manifest in movements toward reconceptualizing productivity—what it is to make a contribution to society. Material income in itself is a highly limited vision of productivity. And there are many precedents from history and culture of alternative means for contributions from aging participants to be regarded as productive. From councils of elders, elder statesmen, and ruling matriarchs in the West to the role of "peace chiefs" and "ritual leaders" in other cultures (cf. Guttman, 1987), images of elderly power are amply available. Thus, with sufficient resources of money, time, and conversational companionship, images of empowerment can be generated, vivified, and made actionable. Two of these reconstructions of aging are especially interesting.

Wisdom Refigured

Whether or not one subscribes to Carl Jung's (1928) theory of archetypes, we can be grateful to him for revealing the cultural and historical ubiquity of the image of the "old wise man." Religious institutions of today have also served to keep this tradition salient with strong presences of aged leaders—the Pope, Bishop Tutu, the Dali Lama, the Ayatollahs, etc. These images now serve as resources for reconstituting the aging self. Betty Friedan (1993) has written eloquently about the redrawing of the older population as venerable contributors to society.

> "In their 'late style' artists and scientists, creators and great thinkers seem to move beyond tumult and discord, distracting details and seemingly irreconcilable differences, to unifying principles that give new meaning to what has gone before and presage the agenda of the next generation."

And so, she says, all of us can locate in aging a "new wholeness, previewing in the serious or the seemingly irrelevant efforts of our late years new dimensions of life for the next generation." (p. 613)

It is in this vein that we find increasing media representations of and reliance placed on financially sagacious men (e.g., Alan Greenspan, Warren Buffett) and seasoned advisors and/or leaders of government (George Mitchell, Jimmy Carter, Henry Kissinger). Senator Strom Thurmond will reach 100 years of age if and when he completes his present term in the American Senate. At the age of 77, Senator John Glenn returned to Earth from his second space flight. There are heroes in other realms of life as well—sports, entertainment, literature, science, journalism, lifestyles, and fashion (Consider Billie Jean King, Walter Cronkite, Maya Angelou, and Dr. Ruth Westheimer). As the media rekindles the image of wisdom, so is the aging population offered new self-conceptions and social roles. The significance of wisdom as an attribute of aging is also flourishing among scholars as well (Baltes & Staudiner, 1993; Srivastva, 1998; Sternberg, 1989).

Historical Witnesses

As Alex Kucznyski recently lamented:

I used to feel bad about being born too late in the 1960's. The American generation I fell into grew up feeling a little bit like a bunch of left-out losers because the Baby Boomers would have you know that in order to understand the United States and politics and tragedy and intellectual freedom, you had to have lived through the demonstrations against the Vietnam war and the assassinations of the 1960's. The heroes of my generation were not murdered; we didn't discover LSD; we didn't protest wars. Our hero was the Six Million Dollar Man. All we got was disco, Ronald Reagan, chronic fatigue syndrome and a few halfhearted nostalgic strikes at Columbia University, 20 years too late. (1998, p. 12)

Manifestations of "age envy" can best be understood in terms of the way in which the same technologies that circulate the images of the new aging also function to thrust the past into present. Television, film, magazines, newspapers, books, and musical recordings all function to keep the past alive and vivid in the contemporary imagination. In part, the media continue to recirculate the past because elderly cohorts are a valuable market segment. This is their life, and it is to be savored, reflected upon, and interrogated for meaning. At the same time, for the culture at large, the past is a repository of drama—glamour, fame, victories, achievements—essential food for the enormous appetite of the contemporary entertainment business. This tapping of the past even extends to the incessant television reruns—*Gilligan's Island*, *Happy Days*, *Leave it to Beaver*, and *I Love Lucy*. In this context, the aging population increasingly serves the role of historical witness. They not only bear personal testimony to the past—replete with stories, insights, and the drama of "I was there"—but they come to symbolize important eras, events, and ways of life. This is most obviously true in the case of public icons—Ringo Star, the Rolling Stones, Johnny Cash, Joan Baez, and the never-aging Beach Boys. In *Time* magazine's (May, 1998) competition for the most significant musician of the century, Elvis Presley, an icon of the 50's, and Frank Sinatra, whose fame was installed in the 40's, were the primary contenders. James Dean's photo continues to adorn the cover of youth magazines. "Swing" lessons, to the tune of the "Big Band sounds," are offered in clubs across the country. A statue has been erected to Bert Parks in Atlantic City for his contributions to the Miss America pageant, and a red-sequined dress worn by Marilyn Monroe was sold at auction for over $1 million in October, 1999. With increased media representation, the role of historical witness is made available to the elderly population more generally—those who "were hippies," "went to Woodstock," "watched the first moon landing," and so on. As the media rhapsodize the past, so do they enable iconic roles to be played by those who "were there." The nostalgia for the excitement, opportunity, freedom, and achievements of the past sustains the value and significance of those who participated.

Sybaritic Selves: The Generation of Joy

A final reconstruction of aging places the central emphasis on pleasure. Owing in part to fortified economic resources, to biological health, and technologies of personal extension, an increasingly large segment of the aging population finds itself in a position to transform "empty hours" into rich and invigorating explorations. Whether in matters of sports such as golf, tennis, fishing, scuba diving, sailing, or bridge; or international travel, pleasure cruising, theater and concert attendance, and fine dining, the aging population is in increasing evidence. Increments in participation have also occurred in domains of personal development—in Yoga training, educational development (e.g., Elderhostel programs, university extension courses), explorations in nature (e.g., hiking, bird watching, rock climbing), and spiritual expansion (e.g., meditation, evangelical movements, retreats). As the advertising world now writes large, "Aging is fun and fulfilling." And, of course, the advertising business is essential to the circulation of these images, for these endeavors, like quests for eternal youth, are highly lucrative. Again, the financial power of the aging population facilitates the reconstruction of the images and activities. Economics, commerce, and self-restoration walk hand in hand.

One of the most important features of the sybaritic moment is its rewriting of cultural value. The work ethic has long functioned to degrade the value of pleasure. Not to be working is variously to be "goofing off," "loafing," or "wasting time." Yet, the unabashed seeking of pleasure now manifest by the aging—along with the absence of guilt—gives reason for pause. The sybaritic life style places the work ethic in critical relief; the process of reconstruction reverses the priority. Hard work for its own sake becomes increasingly questionable. We shall return to this issue shortly.

CULTURAL IMPACT OF THE NEW AGING

We began this analysis by pointing to the way in which the aging person had been traditionally situated within the culture, how the matrix of cultural values, economic conditions, and institutional life had given rise to a Dark Age of aging. Yet, this was also a period in which the construction of aging was largely a byproduct of mainstream culture. The aging themselves were essentially victims of a process over which they had little control. In this sense the aged were positioned similarly to other disadvantaged minority groups. Yet, powerful grassroots movements—now termed identity politics—

have begun to challenge the commonplace stereotypes, and to seek means for controlling the images that circulate in the media (cf. Fiske, 1996; Jewell, 1993). Issues of race, ethnicity, and gender are now all important considerations in determining who is cast in what media role. Similarly, the aging population has not only begun to challenge the constructions of traditional mainstream culture, but more importantly, to forge its own domain of meaning. In her 1986 volume, *The Ageless Self,* Sharon Kaufman commented that "Practicing gerontologists deplore the fact there is no . . . valued role for the aged in the United States" (p. 165). This judgment echoes the view of Robert Burgess, who once framed the role of the aging population as "roleless" (Burgess & Bushell, 1969). This era is ending. The aging have begun to generate new criteria of worth, of meaningful activity, and conceptions of age itself.

Additionally, in our view, this command of construction has not only had an impact on those over 50, but it has powerful reverberations outside the aging population itself. Over and above the enhancement of self-worth and the enrichment of lifestyles among the aging, these reconstructions now insinuate themselves into the greater society. They begin to drive mainstream values and practices in various ways. Two of these deserve special attention.

Aging and the Restoration of Civil Society

In his weathervane essay, "Bowling Alone: America's Declining Social Capital," Robert Putnam (1995) argues that voluntary participation in political participation, group membership, and informal socializing have steadily declined over the past quarter-century. He warns against the depleting stock of social capital, people who can contribute time and energy to sustaining norms, networks, and social trust necessary for a viable society. As Michael Walzer (1998) similarly argues, we must rediscover the importance of "the world of family, friends, comrades and colleagues, where people are connected to one another and made responsible for each other" (p. 86). Dialogue on the creation of civil society is now widespread. In our view, the images, values, and action potentials of the New Aging form a major answer to this quest. With an expanded population of the elderly, we have a significant expansion in the number of free hours available for use in the culture (Robinson & Godbey, 1997). Common wage-earners spend more than half of each waking day serving the institutions in which they are employed. Time is essentially converted to products or services. However, with an expanded number of retired persons, the reservoir of personally determined time is radically expanded. And this time is increasingly available for communal contribution.

Further, with the multiple moves toward re-empowerment discussed above, we find the basis for a renewed sense of competence and control. With the shift toward agelessness, there is also an increased sense of vitality. Thus, the aging population stands as a major resource for refurbishing the civil society. In our view, such moves are already significantly present. With the rise of both two-career and single-parent families, grandmothers and grandfathers are becoming increasingly central figures in the lives of developing children. Adult siblings—now consumed by occupations and geographically separated—increasingly rely on their parents to sustain their bonds. Increasingly, colleges and universities are pursuing the services, counsel, and endowment funds of the alumni who have long since graduated from their institutions. Community governments, civic organizations, and neighborhood security watches also depend increasingly on the services of retired persons. Charitable organizations depend upon the time and energies of older people, who often work in support of their less fortunate peers. Hospital auxiliaries, church thrift shops, and Sunday School programs, as well as senior center recreational facilities, mentally retarded centers, prison visitation programs, literacy programs, and other civic betterment activities are staffed in great measure by senior citizens. As Peterson and Somit (1994) conclude from their research on the elderly, among those who are educated and healthy, political knowledge and participation in civic affairs is steadily increasing.

Nor is communal contribution limited to the local arena. For example, the non-profit organization, RSVP International, has developed volunteer programs worldwide designed to enable older adults to use their skill, knowledge, and experience to better the human condition. For example, RSVP volunteers have participated in programs to improve drainage systems and increase forest growth in Gambia; developed and operated a paper recycling project in Bogota; installed locks and smoke detectors in seniors' homes in Belfast;

and taught children to read and write in Dakar. In the U.S., RSVP committees also engage in smaller projects, raising money for charitable affairs through bake sales, envelope-stuffing, and other activities.

The reverberations of this shift in the socioemotional functioning of society may be profound. We spoke earlier of the prevalent value of individualism in the U.S., touching on ways in which individualism and self-absorption were connected, and their detrimental implications for the aging. Yet, the contributions of the aging to the civil society stand in contrast to individualist values. Such activities are largely voluntary, and thus altruistic in tenor. As these activities gain increasing recognition, so do values of care and love for others become more salient within the culture. The banner of "relatedness" comes to stand as a significant and possibly superior alternative to the pervasive "me first." While it may seem that the sybaritic tendencies of the aging do not lend themselves so readily to these ends, there is good reason to believe that many enter retirement years not with an "either/or" but a "both/and" disposition. And there can be pleasure alongside practices of community contribution. In fact, pleasure is gained through community service.

The Refiguring of Productivity

As we have proposed, the powerful value placed on economic productivity in the U.S. has traditionally thrust the aging population into an alienated and denigrated status. At the same time, as the workplace demands increasing numbers of hours from employees, many in the younger generations find little remaining in the way of leisure time. Not only are there few hours for relaxed enjoyment, physical pleasure, and participation in nature, but little time for family, friends, or community, as well. For many two-career families, there is simply no "spare time" for rearing children and intimate connection (Hochschild, 1989). It is under these conditions that the insinuation of the sybaritic image of aging into the culture becomes significant. The widely circulated images of elderly persons strolling arm in arm, on beach holidays, golfing, fishing, cruising, dining, and enjoying grandchildren often stand in stark contrast to the arduous demands of the work world. Nor, given the companionate and equally pervasive image of agelessness, does it appear that such persons are at death's door. The dominant picture is one of decades of relatively unfettered enjoyment.

In our view, there are several interrelated effects of this dramatic contrast. First, there is increasing interest in early retirement. Middle-aged persons increasingly attempt to garner sufficient savings and securities that they may escape the workplace. In a related vein, the elderly come increasingly to serve as models for leisure time activity. One cannot overlook, for example, the fact that the game of golf—traditionally a game of the old—has now become ageless. As the young take up the game in increasing numbers, so do they emulate the elderly. And to enhance the image of the latter, young Tiger Woods competes with the elderly on even terms—often suffering defeat. And thus the youth/age binary becomes increasingly blurred. It is not the young resisting the image of becoming old so much as attempting to enter a category under transformation.

There is a further implication of this emerging complex that is more difficult to chart, and possibly more a favored fantasy at this juncture than a lived reality. While the cultural value placed on economic productivity has contributed to the prosperity of the nation, there are many who believe that we face the upward limits of economic growth. It is not simply that working hours seem to expand to fill all available space. Rather, it is the more general concern with the limits to growth and progress. The perils of a continuing surge toward increasing prosperity—with its attendant demands for increasing profits, markets, material supplies, and energy—have been widely documented. Interest in sustainable—as opposed to steadily expanding—economies is increasingly widespread. However, if sustainability is to be achieved, it will require a population oriented toward "satisficing" as opposed to "maximizing." And this is precisely the point at which the new images of age become important. If the values of relaxation, bodily expression, and participation in nature and in families become increasingly salient, then work in itself begins to lose value. Increasingly as the cultural image of the "good life" does not include a lifetime of servitude to reach some mythical "top," we move closer to sustainable growth. In our view, both the society and indeed the world would be the better for this.

IN CONCLUSION

In this analysis we have purposely chosen to focus on new and promising developments in the conception and practices of aging.

As survey research by the Drexel University Center for Employment Futures indicated (1998), approximately 90% of the people over 65 feel satisfied with their lives, feel they have contributed positively to society, and claim to be in good health. However, our focus is nevertheless selective; not all sectors of the aging population are equally satisfied. There is enormous heterogeneity within the aging population (Dannefer, 1987), and there remain significant sectors of the population in which abject poverty, loneliness, and ill health prevail (Angel & Angel, 1997; Margolis, 1990). We do not wish to invite neglect for the afflicted. However, so vast has been the attention devoted to the problems of the aging population, that the image has expanded to color an entire phase of life. In certain respects this emphasis on decline may reflect the needs of those professions—scientific, medical, social service—that depend on "aging as a problem" to remain viable. To emphasize the positive would be to lose their raison d'etre. Again, in no way do we wish to suppress support for those who need it. Rather, our purpose here has been to keep the specter of deficit appropriately in check, to reflect appreciatively on the opportunities for new forms of aging, and to hasten the expansion of more promising possibilities of self-construction.

REFERENCES

Angel, R. J., & Angel, J. L. (1997). *Who will care for us? Aging and long-term care in multicultural America*. New York: New York University Press.

Baltes, P., & Staudiner, G. (1993). The search for a psychology of wisdom. *Current Directions in Psychological Science, 2*, 6–27.

Bellah, R. N., Madsen, R., Sullivan, W. M., Swindler, A., & Tipton, S. M. (1985). *Habits of the heart*. Berkeley, CA: University of California Press.

Bengtson, V. L., Schaie, K. W., & Burton, L. M. (Eds.). (1995). *Adult intergenerational relations: Effects of societal change*. New York: Springer Publishing Company.

Burgess, R. L., & Bushell, D., Jr. (1969). *Behavioral sociology: The experimental analysis of social process*. New York: Columbia University Press.

Campioni, M. (1997). Revolting women, women in revolt. In P. Komersaroff, P. Rothfield, & J. Daly (Eds.), *Reinterpreting menopause* (pp. 22–41). New York: Routledge.

Chopra, D. (1993). *Ageless body, timeless mind*. New York: Harmony Books.

Cunningham, W. R., & Brookbank, J. W. (1988). *Gerontology: The psychology, biology, and sociology of aging.* New York: Harper & Row.

Dannefer, D. (1987). Aging as intracohort differentiation: Accentuation, the Matthew Effect, and the life course. *Sociological Forum, 2,* 211–236.

Dannefer, D. (1988). *Neoteny, naturalization, and other constituents of human behavior.* Unpublished manuscript, Warner Graduate School of Education and Human Development, University of Rochester, Rochester, NY.

Drexel Center for Employment Futures. (1998). Survey of aging suggests a bright future. *Philadelphia Inquirer,* p. D-1.

Dychtwald, K. (1999). *Age power: How the 21st century will be ruled by the new old.* New York: Penguin.

Erikson, E. E. (1963). *Identity and the life cycle.* New York: International Universities Press.

Fiske, J. (1996). *Media matters, race and gender in U.S. politics.* Minneapolis: University of Minnesota Press.

Frank, A. W. (1995). *The wounded storyteller.* Chicago: University of Chicago Press.

Friedan, B. (1993). *The fountain of age.* New York: Simon and Schuster.

Gergen, K. J. (1994). *Realities and relationships.* Cambridge: Harvard University Press.

Gergen, K. J. (1996). Beyond life narratives in the therapeutic encounter. In J. E. Birren, G. M. Kenyon, J-E. Ruth, J. J. F. Schroots, & T. Svensson (Eds.), *Aging and biography* (pp. 205–223). New York: Springer.

Gergen, K. J. (1999). *An invitation to social construction.* Thousand Oaks, CA: Sage.

Gergen, K. J. (2000). *The saturated self* (2nd ed.). New York: Basic Books.

Gergen, M. M. (1989). Talking about menopause: A dialogic analysis. In L. E. Thomas (Ed.), *Research on adulthood and aging: The human sciences approach* (pp. 65–87). Albany, NY: SUNY Press.

Gergen, M. M. (1990). Finished at forty: Women's development within the patriarchy. *Psychology of Women Quarterly, 14,* 451–470.

Gergen, M. M. (1992). Life stories: Pieces of a dream. In G. Rosenwald & R. Ochberg (Eds.), *Storied lives* (pp. 127–144). New Haven, CT: Yale University Press.

Gergen, M. M. (2000). *Feminist reconstructions in psychology.* Thousand Oaks, CA: Sage.

Gergen, M. M., & Davis, S. N. (Eds.) (1997). *Toward a new psychology of gender.* New York: Routledge.

Gubrium, J. F., Holstein, J. A., & Buckholdt, D. R. (1994). *Constructing the life course.* Dix Hills, NY: General Hall.

Gullette, M. M. (1997). Menopause as magic marker: Discursive consolidation in the United States, and strategies for cultural combat. In P.

Komesaroff, P. Rothfield, & J. Daly (Eds.), *Reinterpreting menopause: Cultural and philosophical issue* (pp. 176–199). New York: Routledge.

Guttman, D. (1987). *Reclaimed powers: Toward a new psychology of men and women in later life*. New York: Basic Books.

Hagestad, G. O. (1991). The aging society as a context for family life. In N. A. S. Jecker (Ed.), *Aging and ethics: Philosophical problems in gerontology: Contemporary issues in biomedicine, ethics, and society* (pp. 123–146). Clifton, NJ: Humana Press.

Harrington, M. (1969). *The other America*. Baltimore, MD: Penguin.

Hashimoto, A. (1996). *The gift of generations*. New York: Cambridge University Press.

Hazan, H. (1994). *Old age, constructions and deconstructions*. Cambridge, England: Cambridge University Press.

Helson, R., Mitchell, V., & Moane, G. (1984). Personality and patterns of adherence and nonadherence to the social clock. *Journal of Personality and Social Psychology, 46,* 1079–1097.

Hochschild, A. (1989). *The second shift: Working parents and the revolution at home*. New York: Viking.

Jewell, J. S. (1993). *From mammy to Miss American and beyond*. London: Routledge.

Jung, C. G. (1928). *Contributions to analytical psychology*. New York: Harcourt Brace.

Kagan, J. (1984). *The nature of the child*. New York: Basic Books.

Kaplan, E. A. (1997). Resisting pathologies of age and race. In P. Komersaroff, P. Rothfield, & J. Daly (Eds.), *Reinterpreting menopause* (pp. 100–126). New York: Routledge.

Kaufman, S. R. (1986). *The ageless self*. Madison, WI: University of Wisconsin Press.

Kuczynski, A. (1998, September 20). Somebody to love? *New York Times Review of Books*, p. 12.

Lasch, C. (1979). *The culture of narcissism*. New York: Norton.

Levinson, D., (1978). *The seasons of a man's life*. New York: Ballantine.

Margolis, R. J. (1990). *Risking old age in America*. Boulder, CO: Westview Press.

Martin, E. (1997). The woman in the menopausal body. In P. Komesaroff, P. Rothfield, & J. Daly (Eds.), *Reinterpreting menopause: Cultural and philosophical issues* (pp. 239–254). New York: Routledge.

Morris, C. R. (1996). *The AARP: American's most powerful lobby and the clash of generations*. New York: Random House.

Neugarten, B. (1969). Continuities and discontinuities of psychological issues in adult life. *Human Development, 14,* 121–130.

Neugarten, B. L. (1979). Time, age and life cycle. *American Journal of Psychiatry, 136,* 887–894.

Neugarten, B. (1980, August 11). When age doesn't matter. *Newsweek,* p. 73.

Peterson, S. A., & Somit, A. (1994). *The political behavior of older Americans.* New York: Garland Press.

Putnam, R. (1995, January). Bowling alone: America's declining social capital. *Journal of Democracy, 6,* 65–78.

Robinson, J., & Godbey, G. (1997). *Time for life: The surprising ways Americans use their time.* University Park: Pennsylvania University Press.

Rose, A. N., & Peterson, W. K. (Eds.). (1965). *Older people and their social worlds.* Philadelphia, PA: Davis.

Rubinstein, R. L., Kilbride, J. C., & Nagy, S. (1992). *Elders living alone: Frailty and the perception of choice.* New York: Aldine de Gruyter.

Sampson, E. E. (1988). The debate on individualism. *American Psychologist, 43,* 15–22.

Santrock, J. W. (1992). *Life-span development* (4th ed.). Dubuque, IA: Wm. C. Brown.

Shweder, R. A. (Ed.) (1998). *Welcome to middle age! (and other cultural fictions).* Chicago: University of Chicago Press.

Srivastva, S. (1998). *Executive wisdom and organizational change.* San Francisco: The New Lexington Press.

Sternberg, R. J. (1989). Intelligence, wisdom, and creativity: Their natures and interrelationships. In R. L. Linn, et al. (Eds.), *Intelligence: Measurement, theory, and public policy: Proceedings of a symposium in honor of Lloyd G. Humphreys* (pp. 114–143). Champaign, IL: University of Illinois Press.

Stewart, A. J., & Ostrove, J. M. (1998). Women's personality in middle age: Gender, history and midcourse corrections. *American Psychologist, 53,* 1185–1194.

Tiefer, L. (1997). Sexual biology and the symbolism of the natural. In M. Gergen & S. N. Davis (Eds.), *Toward a new psychology of gender* (pp. 363–374). New York: Routledge.

Time Magazine, May, 1998 cover.

Turnbull, C. M. (1984). *The human cycle.* London: Jonathan Cape.

Walzer, M. (1998). The idea of civil society: A path to social reconstruction. In E. J. Dionne (Ed.), *Community works-The revival of civil society in America.* Washington, DC: Brookings.

Young, K. (1997). *Presence in the flesh.* Cambridge: Harvard University Press.

Commentary

Are We Really Entering a New Era of Aging?

Neal Krause

INTRODUCTION

In their thought-provoking chapter, the Gergens (this volume) contrast the Dark Ages with an era of New Aging. The Dark Ages are based on stereotypes of elders as decrepit, unproductive, and passive. Under these circumstances, the self-concepts of older people will presumably suffer. In contrast, they argue we are now on the threshold of a New Era of Aging. Here, elderly people will be much more in control of their fate. Sweeping changes in society will soon usher in a time where elders will take a much more active hand in molding a new and more positive image of growing old. As a result, self-concepts are purported to flourish.

By casting their work in the context of two broad eras, the Gergens take an approach that is not often found in the wider literature on the self-concept. This is noteworthy because, for too long research in this field has been weighted heavily in favor of internal cognitions and informal social network influences. However, even though the analyses provided by the Gergens are challenging, they are not complete. Although some older adults may pursue the course outlined by the Gergens, this is far from true for all of them. This, in turn, raises serious questions about whether we are really at the dawn of a New Era.

In order to show why this is the case, the discussion that follows will address three issues. First, the factors thought to be driving the New Era of Aging will be examined closely. Second, some of the hallmarks or manifestations of this New Age will be explored. Finally, the implications of these changes for the self-concept will be reviewed. Here, an emphasis will be placed on self-esteem.

FACTORS PROMOTING THE NEW ERA OF AGING

According to the Gergens, the New Era of Aging is being driven by fundamental changes in demography, technology, and economics. The economic factors will be examined here. According to the authors, the financial situation of the elderly has improved dramatically, and these resources provide older adults with the leverage to take control of the images of aging. This assertion is supported with data showing that over time, the proportion of elderly people living below the poverty line has declined. This is true, but focusing solely on these figures does not tell the whole story.

Researchers have identified a number of problems with the poverty index. Three are reviewed briefly below. First, the poverty index is nutritionally based, and deals primarily with the amount of money needed to maintain a minimally adequate diet. Even the chief architect of the poverty index now questions its utility (see Schulz, 1997). As Schulz (1988) points out, the nutrition focus of this index is especially troublesome for studies in late life, because it doesn't capture the costs and expenditures that are central at this point in the life cycle. Chief among them are out-of-pocket medical costs and the costs of long-term care. As Binstock (1997) recently observed, nearly two-thirds of prescription drug expenses, not covered at all by Medicare, are paid out-of-pocket by older adults. In addition, about 24% of people aged 85 and older now live in nursing homes (Binstock, 1997). Yet, patients are not reimbursed by Medicare for long-term care. The upshot of this is significant. In 1993, the total cost of long-term care was $75.5 billion (Binstock, 1997). Forty-four percent of this amount was paid out-of-pocket by older people or by members of their family (Binstock, 1997).

The second problem with the poverty index is that it does not include all who are in need. In particular, it overlooks the near poor. Although the definition of near poor varies from study to study, many consider those with incomes of 150% of the poverty level to fall into this group. The statistics on the near poor are important because they paint a different picture of how the elderly are doing, relative to those who are young. In particular, Schulz (1997) reports that 27.6% of those 65 and over have incomes that are below 150% of the poverty level. In contrast, only 23.6% of those under age 65 fall into this group. This means that approximately 8.8 million older adults are poor or near poor.

The third problem with the poverty index arises from the fact that it describes a person's economic status at a single point in time. However, poverty is actually a dynamic phenomenon that changes substantially over time. In fact, the average spell of poverty lasts only about 2 or 3 years (Rank & Hirschl, 1999). Viewing poverty from a more dynamic perspective presents an economic picture of the elderly that differs dramatically from the view provided by the Gergens. Rank and Hirschl (1999) recently analyzed 25 years of data from the Panel Study of Income Dynamics. These investigators report that between the ages of 60 and 90, 40.4% of Americans experienced at least one year below the poverty level, while 47.7% experienced at least a year in which their incomes fell below 125% of the poverty level.

The Gergens acknowledge that there are some pockets of deep poverty. But this hardly does justice to the situation, because it tends to gloss over an unsettling aspect of income distribution in the United States. In particular, the odds of slipping into poverty are disproportionately greater for older women, especially those who are members of minority groups (Burkhauser, Butler, & Holden, 1991). Schulz (1997) points out, for example, that 66% of single, older women who are Black live below the poverty level. However, the data provided by Rank and Hirschl (1999) are especially startling. These investigators report that by age 85, 88.1% of Black women who are not married and who have less than 12 years of education will experience a bout of poverty. These are some deep pockets indeed. The comments made by Schulz (1997) regarding overly optimistic views of the financial situation of older people gets right to the heart of the matter: "In the future, when we read that the elderly are "better off," we should remember the situation of older women in particular, and not make the mistake of believing what is simply not true" (p. 11).

The New Era of Aging is supposedly fueled in part by economic advances among older adults. But as the data presented in this section reveal, many will miss the boat. This, in turn, places a heavy burden on the perspective developed by the Gergens. At best, it applies to some middle- and upper-class elders, while saying little about the situation of many who are not so well-to-do.

Hallmarks of the New Era of Aging

The Gergens identify a number of hallmarks or manifestations of the New Era of Aging. Two will be examined briefly below. The first has to do with health, while the second involves housing.

According to the Gergens, we will soon see a time when physical decline will be altered dramatically, if not eliminated entirely. This is captured succinctly in the following excerpt from their work: "In this sense there is nothing about changes in the human body that require a concept of age, of development, or decline. There is no process of aging *in itself* (emphasis in the original)." Although there are certainly social influences on the definitions and perceptions of health, this goes a little too far. The inescapable fact of life is that those who are not killed in accidents grow old, get sick, and die. The biological basis of inevitable decline and death is spelled out clearly in Nuland's (1994) compelling book, *How We Die; Reflections on Life's Final Chapter.*

The Gergens' views on the ever-improving health status of the elderly are consistent with a familiar concept in the literature—the compression of morbidity. Essentially, proponents of this view maintain that lifestyle changes and medical advances will lower mortality risks while simultaneously postponing the onset of many diseases that contribute to disability in late life (Fries, 1989). However, a number of investigators do not share this view. More specifically, some studies suggest that reductions in mortality rates may actually be accompanied by longer (not shorter) periods of time spent with disabling diseases (Olshansky, Rudberg, Carnes, Cassel, & Brody, 1991). But as Olshansky and Rudberg (1997) point out, longitudinal data necessary to conclusively examine the compression of morbidity are still not available. Even so, available data on age differences in health do not appear to support the Gergens' position.

The fact that aging and illness are inextricably linked can be readily demonstrated by quickly reviewing data provided by the National Health Interview Survey (NHIS) (U.S. Department of Health and Human Services, 1998). This extensive survey of the nation's health includes data on 65 chronic conditions. The findings reveal that the prevalence of these chronic health problems is higher for those aged 65 and over in 56 of the 65 conditions. In many cases the differences are dramatic. This is further illustrated by recent data published by the American Association of Retired Persons and the Administration on Aging (1998). This report reveals that 52.5% of those 65 and over have at least one functional disability (as assessed by activities of daily living and instrumental activities of daily living scales). Moreover, this report classifies fully one-third of older adults as having severe functional disability.

In the concluding section of their paper, the Gergens cite a survey claiming that 90% of older adults feel they are in good health. This is not what is reflected in the NHIS data. In particular, this survey reveals that 28.4% of people aged 65 and over rate their health as either fair or poor. In contrast, only 7.3% of adults aged 25 to 44 feel the same way (U.S. Department of Health and Human Services, 1998).

But the health problems identified above are not distributed evenly in the population. Instead, there are clear socioeconomic differences. Adler and her colleagues recently conducted a comprehensive review of the literature on socioeconomic status (SES) and health. They conclude that "SES differences are found for rates of mortality and morbidity from almost every disease and condition" (Adler et al., 1994, p. 15). These socioeconomic data are important because they reveal that those experiencing the greatest health declines come disproportionately from the lower classes. If the New Era of Aging is fueled in part by economic factors, then those in greatest need of these changing images will be those who are the least likely to possess the resources needed to get there.

Aside from health factors, the Gergens also argue that there will be changes in housing during the New Era of Aging. In particular, they envision a time when age-segregated housing becomes more prevalent. Here, contact with the young will be carefully controlled, thereby allowing elders even greater control over the images of aging. But what are the odds that all older adults will have access to these age-segregated communities? A recent paper by South and Crowder (1997) provides a discouraging answer. Using data from the widely studied Panel Study of Income Dynamics, these investigators examined patterns of residential moves over a 6-year period. Based on a sophisticated series of analyses, they calculated the probabilities of moving from a poor to a nonpoor census tract. Their data are presented by age and race. At age 20, the probability of Whites moving from a poor to a nonpoor census tract is good (.4553). But by age 65, it declines precipitously to .0322, suggesting there is little chance of a move. The situation for Blacks is even more dire. At age 20, the odds of a move are .2039. However, by age 65, the chance of escaping a poor census tract is virtually nonexistent (.0086). Once again, these data suggest that those who would benefit most will not be able to sit at the table of the New Era of Aging.

IMPLICATIONS FOR SELF-ESTEEM

Since the focus of this volume is on the self-concept, it is important to think carefully about how the New Era of Aging might influence this particular social psychological construct. The self-concept is a very broad and somewhat slippery conceptual domain. In his classic work on this topic, Rosenberg (1979) defines the self-concept as "the totality of the individual's thoughts and feelings having reference to himself as an object" (p. 7). This clearly covers an enormous amount of ground. Fortunately, Bengtson, Reedy, and Gordon (1985) provide a relatively straightforward way to organize the literature on the self-concept. In particular, they note that self-conceptualizations are comprised of three components involving attitudes toward the self: (1) a cognitive component containing more factual self-attitudes, (2) an affective component comprised of subjective self-evaluations, such as liking or disliking of the self as an object, and (3) a conative component, which includes specific behaviors or actions arising from conceptions of the self. Instead of trying to link the New Era of Aging with this each of these components, it makes more sense to focus instead on the affective component. This is more generally referred to as self-esteem in the literature, and has been linked with health and well-being more often than the other components identified by Bengtson and his colleagues (Bengtson et al., 1985).

The data presented up to this point would seem to imply two rather distinct implications for the effect of the New Era of Aging on self-esteem in late life. On the one hand, those with the resources necessary to partake in the New Era of Aging should enjoy the benefits arising from controlling the images of aging. This should, in turn, bolster feelings of self-worth. In contrast, it is unlikely that the poor and near poor will reap the same benefits. If this logic is valid, there should be clear socioeconomic variations in self-esteem. There is a fairly well-developed literature on socioeconomic status and self-esteem. In the discussion that follows, illustrative data from this field will be used to reframe the notion that we are on the verge of a New Era of Aging.

Two of the key markers of socioeconomic status are education and income. Gecas and Seff (1990) report the following bivariate correlations between self-esteem and these SES indicators: The correlation between education and self-esteem is .16, while the corresponding estimate for the relationship between income and self-esteem is .08. These data suggest that feelings of self-worth are indeed higher among those with more income and a better education. But it is the magnitude of these effects that is important. The relationship is strongest for education and self-esteem. Squaring this coefficient reveals that at the bivariate level, education explains a mere 2.6% of the variance in self-esteem in late life. Given the disturbing health and economic data presented earlier, it is initially hard to figure out why the SES gradient in self-esteem is not more pronounced.

Perhaps part of the answer lies in Kaplan's (1975) work on the self-esteem motive. He argues that one of the primary motivating forces in social life is the enhancement and maintenance of feelings of self-worth. This means that older adults will take active steps to avoid negative self-images and build positive views of the self. This, in turn, has two important implications for the proposed New Era of Aging. The first deals with the Dark Ages. As noted earlier, this is characterized by a number of negative stereotypes of aging. Since we are still at least partly in the grasp of these times, why don't we see the economically depressed and most ill elders suffering from the poorest self-images? Perhaps one answer may be found by turning to the lessons learned decades ago from labeling theory (Gove, 1980). Many elderly people do not now, nor have they ever, passively internalized negative views of aging. This leads to the second point. Rather than being passive receptacles that automatically accept whatever people say about the aged, older people are somehow able to turn to some source(s) of resilience. More importantly, given the weak relationship between socioeconomic status and self-esteem, the lower social classes may provide a good place to start looking for these sources of strength.

We still don't know enough about resilience in late life, but there are some intriguing possibilities. Two are discussed briefly below. The first has to do with social support, while the second is concerned with religion.

A vast literature indicates that older adults are immersed in vibrant social networks that provide considerable assistance in the face of adversity (Krause, 1986). Moreover, the support provided by others helps to replenish feelings of self-worth that have been eroded by stressful events (Krause, 1987). But elders do more than merely receive help from others—they provide assistance to their social network members as well. This, in turn, has been linked to enhanced well-being in late life (Krause, Herzog, & Baker, 1992).

An emphasis has been placed throughout this chapter on the influence of socioeconomic status in late life. Consequently, it is important to consider whether social support is an important source of resilience for older adults who are economically challenged. This issue was examined in a recent study by Krause and Borawski-Clark (1995). Their analyses were designed to see whether there are SES variations in 10 different types or dimensions of social support. Few systematic differences emerged in the data. Perhaps more importantly, the findings suggest that older adults in lower SES groups tend to receive as much tangible and emotional support from significant others as elderly people who are more well-to-do. This is impressive given the challenges facing lower-SES elders, and points to a potentially important source of resilience in economically depressed communities.

In addition to social support, there is some evidence that religion may also be an important source of resilience in late life. More specifically, a number of studies reveal that involvement in religion tends to increase with age, and that religious commitment is stronger in the lower social classes (Pargament, 1997). Perhaps religious themes provide alternative definitions of the self that allow lower-SES elders to transcend the negative images arising from the physical and economic challenges they face. But there may be much more to it than this. As eloquently discussed by Pargament (1997), religion imbues life with a deep sense of meaning and purpose. This is noteworthy because many developmental theorists have argued that one of the primary tasks in late life is the pursuit of meaning (e.g., Erikson, 1959).

The search for a deeper sense of meaning in late life and the drive to make sense of one's own existence stands in sharp contrast to the predictions made by the Gergens. In particular, they argue that one facet of the New Era of Aging will be the pursuit of eternal youth and the glamorization of age. This will be accomplished, they suggest, by greater access to plastic surgeons, fitness centers, and even cryonics. The increasing involvement in religion with age coupled with the insights from developmental psychologists suggests that instead of pursuing these shallow and superficial goals, many elderly people are concerned with deeper and more meaningful issues. The body is not their main concern—the soul is. Moreover, there is nothing new about the pursuit of these higher goals; it has literally been going on for thousands of years.

CONCLUSIONS

One of the most important contributions of social and behavioral gerontology has arisen from efforts to counteract negative stereotypes of aging. It is indeed true that there was a time when late life was viewed in unflattering terms that did not accurately portray the situation or the potential of the later years. But we must be careful not to swing too far in the opposite direction by painting portraits of aging that are too glowing and overly optimistic. Instead, it is important to begin by acknowledging the inescapable facts—people get old, they get sick, and they die. Then, taking this as a point of departure, the goal should be to carefully examine how people confront these critical issues. This examination will likely reveal a plethora of strategies. Some will be more successful than others, thereby producing the widely documented trend toward greater heterogeneity in late life (Nelson & Dannefer, 1992). The work of these investigators is important for the following reason. Nelson and Dannefer (1992) examined published research in order to see whether measures of dispersion for 16 different constructs increased with advancing age. Self-esteem was among the variables examined. Their analyses reveal greater dispersion (i.e., greater differences among people) in 65% of the study measures.

If differences among people become more pronounced as they grow older, then we must carefully reconsider whether it makes sense to think in terms of eras when discussing our aging population. By definition, an era refers to a point in time where people are engaging in similar types of behavior or sharing similar attitudes or cognitions. Implicit in this view is a sense of similarity or homogeneity. But instead of gravitating toward a period of greater homogeneity, the work of Nelson and Dannifer (1992) suggests that the opposite may be taking place in our aging population. This, in turn, implies that researchers should be searching for sources of diversity, not similarity. Rather than developing utopian images of a disease-free era, in which elders are the masters of their fate, it makes far more sense to explore and celebrate the myriad ways in which the indelible human spirit responds to the challenge of growing older.

REFERENCES

American Association of Retired Persons and the Administration on Aging (1998). *A profile of older Americans: 1998*. Washington, DC: Author.

Adler, N. E., Boyce, T., Chesney, M. A., Cohen, S., Folkman, S., Kahn, R. L., & Syme, S. L. (1994). Socioeconomic status and health. *American Psychologist, 49*, 15–24.

Bengtson, V. L., Reedy, M. N., & Gordon, C. (1985). Aging and self-conceptions: Personality processes and social contexts. In J. E. Birren & K. W. Schaie (Eds.), *Handbook of the psychology of aging* (2nd ed.) (pp. 544–593). New York: Van Nostrand Reinhold Company.

Binstock, R. H. (1997). Issues in resource allocation in an aging society. In T. Hickey, M. A. Speers, & T. R. Prohaska (Eds.), *Public health and aging* (pp. 53–72). Baltimore: Johns Hopkins University Press.

Burkhauser, R. V., Butler, J. S., & Holden, K. C. (1991). How the death of a spouse affects economic well-being after retirement: A hazard model approach. *Social Science Quarterly, 72,* 504–519.

Erikson, E. (1959). *Identity and the life cycle.* New York: International University Press.

Fries, J. F. (1989). The compression of morbidity: Near or far? *Milbank Quarterly, 67,* 208–323.

Gecas, V., & Seff, M. A. (1990). Social class and self-esteem: Psychological centrality, compensation, and the relative effects of work and home. *Social Psychological Quarterly, 53,* 165–173.

Gove, W. R. (1980). *The labeling of deviance.* Beverly Hills, CA: Sage.

Kaplan, H. B. (1975). *Self-attitudes and deviant behavior.* Pacific Palisades, CA: Goodyear.

Krause, N. (1986). Social support, stress, and well-being among older adults. *Journal of Gerontology, 41,* 512–519.

Krause, N. (1987). Life stress, social support, and self-esteem in an elderly population. *Psychology and Aging, 2,* 349–356.

Krause, N., & Borawski-Clark, E. (1995). Social class differences in social support among older adults. *The Gerontologist, 35,* 498–508.

Krause, N., Herzog, A. R., & Baker, B. (1992). Providing support to others and well-being in later life. *Journal of Gerontology: Psychological Sciences, 47,* P300–P311.

Nelson, E. A., & Dannefer, D. (1992). Aged heterogeneity: Fact or fiction? The fate of diversity in gerontological research. *The Gerontologist, 32,* 17–23.

Nuland, S. B. (1994). *How we die: Reflections on life's final chapter.* New York: Alfred A. Knopf.

Olshanksy, S. J., & Rudberg, M. A. (1997). Postponing disability: Identifying points of decline and potential intervention. In T. Hickey, M. A. Speers, & T. R. Prohaska (Eds.), *Public health and aging* (pp. 237–251). Baltimore: Johns Hopkins University Press.

Olshansky, S. J., Rudberg, M. A., Carnes, B. A., Cassel, C. K., & Brody, J. (1991). Trading off longer life for worsening health: The expansion of morbidity hypothesis. *Journal of Aging and Health, 3,* 194–216.

Pargament, K. I. (1997). *The psychology of religion and coping: Theory, research, practice.* New York: Guilford Press.

Rank, M. R., & Hirschl, T. A. (1999). Estimating the number of Americans ever experiencing poverty during their elderly years. *Journal of Gerontology: Social Sciences, 54B,* S184–S193.

Rosenberg, M. (1979). *Conceiving the self.* New York: Basic Books.

Schulz, J. H. (1988). *The economics of aging.* New York: Auburn House.

Schulz, J. H. (1997). Ask older women: Are the elderly better off? *Journal of Aging and Social Policy, 9,* 7–12.

South, S. J., & Crowder, K. D. (1997). Escaping distressed neighborhoods: Individual, community, and metropolitan influences. *American Journal of Sociology, 102,* 1040–1084.

U.S. Department of Health and Human Services. (1998). *Vital and health statistics: Current estimates from the National Health Interview Survey, 1995 (Series 10, Data from the National Health Survey, No. 199).* Hyattsville, MD: Author.

Commentary

The "New Aging": Imagining Alternative Futures

Martha B. Holstein

undamental questions about social and cultural transformation, in particular as they affect the conditions in which people experience aging and old age, are obviously both significant and complex. In their chapter, Ken and Mary Gergen (this volume) offer a conception of what that transformation might be like. Further, they describe the preconditions that support their belief that these specific transformations are not only possible but, one would assume, desirable. Their conceptual framework is social constructionism, laced with all the markings of a growing trend in the cultural studies of aging to assume the "postmodern life course" as a given. Whether used descriptively or normatively, the postmodern life course is peculiarly free-floating. Divorced from old structural, economic, or bodily concerns, it sees, among other things, liberation from the bureaucratic life course, plurality, openness, contingency, and possibility. The danger is that while dancing along the yellow brick road, the liberated few can easily marginalize the many.

My response, growing out of a background in the humanities, critical gerontology, and feminist social ethics, rather than the social sciences, focuses on three broad themes: the content of the images the Gergens propose and their implications; their approach to the preconditions that support these new images; and their view of the "Dark Ages" of aging as the foil for the "New Aging." The Gergen chapter and my response are about alternative understandings of what is "real," about ideas of what constitutes the good life in old age, about who decides and on what grounds, about ways to think about an imagined future, and about what factors ought to count as we celebrate the possibilities for a modestly, if not radically, different future.

I view, for example, their image of a glamorous old age as oppressive, not emancipatory, but I would like to hear voices speaking directly from the vantage point of age to tell me what it's like and what a "New Aging" ought to be about, for the Gergens are raising important moral questions about the nature of the good life in old age. Nor can I share their optimism about a better future without at least alluding to the structural constraints, power relationships, class, race, gender, social attitudes, and other factors that stand as barriers to the good life (however defined) for so many older people. Inequalities are profound, and significantly affect the conditions of our old age, and so the aged alone cannot be expected singularly to create the "New Aging." While a vision of the wholly "other" as a goal toward which to strive is vital, we also need a sense of possibility, and that requires careful analysis of the contemporary sociopolitical environment and resistance to barriers whenever and wherever possible. If (and I say this cautiously) the postmodern life course is to be truly emancipatory for the many, rather than the marketer's dream for the few, good old-fashioned political action will be needed.

If these are elements I miss, there are things I appreciate in what the Gergens are doing. I value their efforts to disrupt theoretical and empirical claims that construct and discipline aging and old age through the assertion of truths grounded in certain methodologies and texts. I also welcome their image of technology's potential to create many simultaneous conversations in which older people become the subjects of their own lives. I do, nonetheless, worry that participation, while large, will not reflect what I would guess are contrasting perspectives of a grandmother from the Robert Taylor

Homes (a low-income housing project) on Chicago's South Side and a grandfather living in the exclusive suburb of Kenilworth on Chicago's affluent North Shore. While the Web has become an important symbol of the consumerist "postmodern" representation of aging, access to the Web is sharply distinguished by race and class. According to a recent report (National Public Radio, August 12, 1999) less that 12% of African-American families have such access. One might wonder who among these users are over 65 and how many beyond 75. Growing technological sophistication and the quotidian aspects of its use further marginalizes those without a computer, Web browser, or technological know-how—a clear example of the dominant culture's exclusionary powers. So one must ask, which voices and with what degree of articulateness, will dominate the computer conversation?

At bottom, however, I am unsettled by this chapter, for the reasons noted above and for the same reasons that I find certain aspects of postmodernism so troubling. Most simply, the Gergens reflect an all too easy acceptance of postmodernism's lightheartedness, life as an aesthetic creation, that leaves little critical space to politically challenge "real" tragedy and suffering. And related to these aesthetic conceptions is their resistance—another facet of postmodernism—to making any defensible claims about the social or physical world, at least as the starting place for counterarguments. Without staking out some middle ground between traditional scientific claims of objective realism and pure social constructionism (McCarthy, 1991), it is too easy to be intellectually and politically irresponsible, to not take one's own claims seriously. As social constructionists, the Gergens disclaim that they are offering "accurate and objective reports on what is the case;" yet, they present what might otherwise be considered "evidence" for their case, claims as to why the "New Aging" they envision can come to fruition. I think we have much to learn from critical social analysis about how the world is, and I am sufficiently modernist to believe that these grounds bear close scrutiny as do the conclusions drawn from them. And if what the Gergens hope is that "this particular form of understanding will harbor promising potentials for our collective future," then I must take issue both with its "reality" for other than the most privileged older people and its desirability as a goal. In what follows, I will turn first to their vision of the "New Aging" and then turn to an analysis of the assumptions and arguments on which they ground its possibilities.

THE SYBARITIC SELF

Starting with their last category—sybaritic selves—I think how nice it would be if the aged could teach us that life was meant not singularly (or almost singularly) for work, but also for pleasure *and,* which they do not address, that the workplace and the reward system it cultivates would respond appropriately. To make leisure respectable without expecting a 50-plus-hour work week as its price will rely on structural alterations, institutional support, and collegial acceptance. So far few signs suggest that even the Family Leave Act—which addresses not leisure, but matters like parenting and family caregiving already deemed truly important—have affected the way market values shape our lives. But maybe it is too soon; these transformed values have not yet had their chance to work their magic. Yet, what task could be as important (and pleasurable) than for parents to raise the next generation jointly? Instead of that occurring, one hears of women (but not men) reducing their working hours, rejecting career possibilities, and calling it a "choice." The democratization of leisure across the life span (is raising children a leisure-time activity?) cannot occur in a vacuum. It would demand a radically altered workplace; a more equitable distribution of pension and other benefits; excellent and easily available child care; and other structural changes that would support the possibilities for work, leisure, and family life for both men and women. Values transformation may be a cultural product, but putting ordinary food on the table demands a materialist foundation.

The sanctification of leisure directly contradicts market values as they now exist. We encounter value conflicts, for example, in which the value of balance confronts the marketplace. At a small start-up company, where I consult about organizational ethics, we opened a discussion about the central values held by the executive staff. The first value articulated was one of balance between home and work. When I asked what it would take for the company to respect this critically held value, it rapidly became clear that, in practice, work would need to take priority. Americans are becoming more, rather than less, busy and technology, while liberating, not only reinforces busyness, but through items like the cell phone also take away the small islands of solitude or quiet we may once have had in our day. Young executives may look longingly at the golf greens, but know that these are well into their future if they are to be a possibility at all.

POLICY, CULTURE, AND THE SYBARITIC LIFE

The sybaritic life, rather than representing a more general cultural transformation, may represent a fragment in time for certain current retirees. Proposed changes in the Social Security system, defined contribution rather than defined benefit pension plans, and remaining earnings differentials by gender and race can mean that voluntary early retirement may be an option only for high earners. For many others it will become a forced decision, as American businesses ease them out of the workplace just as the Social Security retirement age climbs. Few will have the resources to live sybaritically. To affect not only people now retired, but also the larger society, this kind of cultural transformation will take much more that the reinvention of aging selves and the images it suggests to the young.

Consider the deeply embedded economic definitions of productivity (see Holstein, 1999, for the gender implications of this view) as an example. Why and how would older people comfortably surrender the very cultural norms of productivity and individualism that have defined for them over the course of their lives what constitutes meaning and value? While the Gergens propose an alternative definition of productivity that might emerge, in essence, turning it on its head, what evidence would suggest that this definition would carry any weight or credibility in a society that judges itself by hours worked (see Hochschild's [1997] recent book about the avoidance of home). While I appreciate the effort that so many gerontologists have made to enlarge the meaning of productivity, which the Gergens take even further, I am skeptical that the aged, even as their numbers grow, can redefine a term so laden with cultural meanings and values—self-worth, citizenship, activity, economic growth. As noted above, the frequently mentioned "postmodern life course" in which aging has indeed become irrelevant seems more a wish of the educated middle class, and perhaps the healthy old, than a reality in the lives of most men and women.

Currently, there is little evidence that American society is moving away from the dominant values the Gergens associate with the "Dark Ages" of aging. Even in the general area of "ethics and long-term care," client self-determination and autonomy are central ethical values and not, for example, continued responsibility for and accountability to others. Cost containment in medicine does not speak the language of sustainability, asking what we may have to do without so that more of us might be served. Thus, the argument that the future aged may represent a new force for re-creating the civil society (a relatively new revival of interest in nongovernmental organizations and individuals resolving problems through civic action and civic conversation), however desirable, is tenuous. Even in the oft-quoted article, "Bowling Alone," Putnam (1995) finds that the WWII generation, not the baby boomers, have been the most socially committed. The men and women now retired came of age during the Depression and the Second World War. They learned to live with little, to save, and to believe in something profoundly like America's efforts to defeat the Axis powers. They are also benefiting from a thriving economy. While it is possible that the generation now old may refurbish civil society, subsequent generations have experienced a very different value environment. And, despite their history, we have little substantial evidence that even the current elderly are ready to abandon the individualistic norms and values that dominated their childhood and young adulthood and replace them with more communal values. The preoccupation with self-maximization is almost a cult message in our society today, as witnessed by efforts to reduce taxes. Recreating civil society requires virtues for which many may yearn, but which seem to have little salience in contemporary society, while productivity, competition, the Dow-Jones averages, and globalization continue to have broad prominence. The vision of sybaritic men and women, moreover, taking responsibility for the re-creation of civil society is an irony that cannot pass unnoticed. I picture guests at the great house parties in Edwardian England, devoted to the pursuit of luxury, self-indulgence, discrete adultery, and glamour, taking time out from the hunt to address the needs of working men and women or the plight of the homeless.

The new image of the glamorous old or the new athleticism—mountain-climbing grandmothers and scuba-diving grandfathers—is even more disturbing than the sybaritic life style for a vision of the whole of life. This image of youth and glamour, which I find deeply troubling, has both normative and descriptive dimensions. If we are thinking about it normatively in terms of the aging self, then I would want to know: Does this image perpetuate oppression, deepen marginalization, or enhance hegemonic power? Has this new story line made the old, especially women, feel more or less invisible? What will this image do for the aging person who is chronically ill or otherwise disabled, a time when the sense of self is dramatically challenged? What would it mean if this became one of the dominant narratives about old age in American society? Can it provide sources of meaning to any but the relatively few? Is this a story line that we (and I won't try to define we at this time) ought to resist? I would also ask: Who is telling this story? Are they credible speakers?

THE BODY AS A SOURCE OF MEANING

For many older people, the body has become the literal grounding of social identify. Repressive norms of youth and beauty, physical prowess, and glamour can further harm older people who cannot measure up to those norms. Such repressiveness may, in particular, affect women who have for so long been identified with their bodies. Preoccupation with weight and appearance are sufficiently oppressive for young women; how much more damaging for older women, who have a harder time resisting the forces of gravity, years of exposure to work and the elements, and other causes of physical change. Many older women have identified with dominant cultural meanings, and thereby they are rendered outsiders when they cannot live up to those ideals. As Frida Furman (1997) noted in her ethnographic study of older women, "inhabiting an older body—*being* an older body—comes to rob older women of respect and public visibility. The cultural values and social relations that have shaped their moral identities often make such women feel like moral failures; weighted down by guilt, shame, or the experience of insufficiency: for having wrinkles, for not being thin enough, or for their inability to continue caregiving tasks" (p. 168). These women are not the perpetual middle-agers, nor are they the glamorously old; they are many of us, just a few years further down the line.

Instead, we might want to grant cultural approbation for the moral terrain women already occupy so well—attentive and loving concern for their families, friends, and often their communities. Simultaneously, structural supports in the form of child care, equal pay for equal work, benefits for women in lower-wage occupations, and related changes might allow women to choose, as they cannot now do without long-term penalties, how to balance roles. In our autonomy-driven society, autonomy is essentially a procedural value. It supports the right to chose how we wish to live without outside interference, but also with limited attention to the conditions that make meaningful choice possible. It rests upon a view of the self that is atomistic and driven by self-interested values (though one can choose otherwise, it is not morally blameworthy to refuse commitment to others). How we define our identity cannot be separated from our moral vision of what constitutes a good life (Taylor, 1989). The contemporary conceptual framework leaves no opening to either challenge selfish choices or to hold out as morally praiseworthy the lives that many women have lived. As feminist philosophers (and some are male) continue to critique these traditional notions of the self and the ethical positions they support—and if these views gain some degree of cultural endorsement—then the likelihood of socially contributing selves will increase. So far, once again, the evidence that these conversations are gaining ground are scanty.

While I applaud the Gergens' views about economic sustainability over maximization, it is strangely absent from our cultural conversation. The drive for bigger and better—cars, houses, genetic composition, perfectibility—seem to be accelerating rather than declining. What else would it take in addition to images of white, white-haired, well-coifed, well-dressed, agile and slim couples walking hand in hand in some old-age Eden to lead us to these ends? Once again, I am less than sanguine that the affluent elderly alone have the power to implement such cultural redefinition. Postmodern consumer culture would, moreover, seem to contradict the very idea of economic sustainability.

As the above comments suggest, I am deeply skeptical about the prediction that the directions the Gergens propose will reflect the next wave of aging. To voice a trusim, cultural change is an extraordinarily complex phenomena. To accept the Gergens' view, one would have to take several questionable assumptions as articles of faith: 1) that the elderly (somehow viewed monolithically with many overlapping values) alone can create change; 2) that they will be sufficiently powerful to override many countervailing pressures; 3) that they favor the notions the Gergens prefer; and 4) that someone else, like advertising executives, will define old age—up to the point that illness and disability set in. If one cannot accept the first three of these assumptions, it becomes vital to analyze the historical conditions that have favored change—or at least a more positive view of the aged—in the past, a topic beyond the scope of this commentary, but certainly a subject of debate among historians of aging (see, for example, Achenbaum, 1978; Cole, 1992; Haber, 1984). The historical metaphor—the Dark Ages of aging—is useful rhetorically, but inadequate historically. It erases complexity, implying a uniformity that never existed. Aging has always served important and context specific cultural functions. Neither a "Golden Age" nor a "Dark Age" can capture the resulting historical complexity. The dialectical interplay between older people as subjects and the social processes around them help guarantee that few, if any, social transformations will have single causes.

Even the demographic shift, which the Gergens highlight, has Janus-like features. Should it be translated into actual political power, the immediate context should alert us to possible dangers. The very existence of elderly enclaves in Florida or Arizona, while certainly a source of value generation, cannot speak for all elderly, for example, for those who live in Brooklyn's Bedford-Stuyvesant neighborhood or in the South Bronx. Hence, if anything like political change is to occur, its initiators would be the "snowbirds" or other two-home families; one would thus wonder at the saliency of the images and the legislative initiatives produced—private contracting for Medicare or Medical Savings Accounts, for example. The once-powerful National Council of Senior Citizens, labor-based and the force behind Medicare, has been completely eclipsed by the more middle-class and conservative AARP. Is there any indication that the aging organizations and aging voters articulate the good of the commons?

The perceived political power of the elderly already has had negative ramifications. The media, organizations of generation Xers, and others have accused elders of having too much power; this assumption leads to charges of selfishness, rather than social favor, and also tends to focus attention on the so-called affluence of the elderly. The Gergens accept the affluence of the aged as a given, and use it as a positive phenomenon to ground the potential for important changes while ignoring its negative uses. Yet, the aged's economic status is surprisingly complex; advocates for one or another interpretation tend to stress different data or present it in different forms. We do know, however, that many elders live in precarious economic straits. Recent data (Rank & Hirschl, 1999) suggest that "poverty is an experience that at some point can touch a surprisingly high percent of Americans during their elderly years . . . on average, 29.7% of 60-year-old Americans will experience poverty at some point in their elderly years, and 36.4% will experience poverty at the 125% level" (p. S191). Many older people hover at or near the poverty line as their life circumstances change with advancing age, a factor that cross-sectional data hides. A 1995 Kaiser Family Foundation Report place 42% of Medicare beneficiaries in the income range of $10,001–$25,000; 18% have incomes between $25,001 and $50,000, and only 5% have incomes in excess of $50,000.

At a minimum, then, if the authors are to rely on the preconditions that they describe, a tighter argument, based on more evidence, is necessary to conclude that increased political power, improved economic status, and the power of technology are real enough or potent enough to support the potential of self-definition and to avoid the negative implications so far evident by political and economic shifts. In the end, most elderly may be poorly, rather than well, served by these new powers of self-definition that the Gergens so favorably describe. Given what we know about cultural marginalization, "public" man may define old age, once again presuming as universal the moral values they embody while setting aside alternative moral identifies that many women have nourished for many years.

CONCLUSION

Let me close with some questions, and, perhaps, some challenges that, if addressed, would make the case for the Gergens' thesis stronger or, in some cases, challenge it even further. As the descriptions emerge, how can one remedy the differential power to create norms as forged through the filter of class, race, or gender? As the history of the women's movement makes clear, changes brought about are best suited to the lifestyles and values of White, middle-class women. The authors would do well to consider the arguments for justice that political philosopher Iris Marion Young (1990), for example, offers that show why some are so often excluded. She effectively argues that justice is far more than distributional formulas; it requires a place at the table for the culturally marginalized and oppressed when problems are defined and responses promulgated. Without such a richer notion of justice (in the cultural as well as the political sphere), will the values established be normative, representing cultural ideals for old age in all its different manifestations? And, if so, who will sit at the proverbial table as decisions are made?

Assuming, in agreement with the Gergens, that the life course is socially and not naturally constructed, how will we change the very structures and institutions that created the normalized life course? Is there still a special place for aging in a human life and the life of a society? I would argue that we as individuals and as a society lose something of considerable importance by trying to reduce old age to the wide and widening expanse of middle age. Life can end badly—and does, for large numbers of people, no matter what we do; we are vulnerable as Oedipus was vulnerable; we are vulnerable to the deepest terrors of the soul, to use the words of Reinhold Niebuhr; we are vulnerable to a loss of dignity, a deeply held need to be held in high regard by those we value. What would it take to assure that the aged man in the wheelchair, who may have the wisdom that the Gergens touch upon, can be seen and heard, and not reduced to his physical limitations? It is indeed important to attach different meanings to conditions of physical and mental change, as they suggest, and as medical anthropolgists have long argued (see Kleinman, 1988, for example). But our understandings of illness are culturally shaped; hence, older people alone cannot achieve that transformation. It requires, at a minimum, the support of biomedicine, social policy, and the helping professions.

But even if life doesn't end badly, it is different than it was before. Writing in her 80s, Jungian analyst, Florida Scott Maxwell (1979/1968), laments that she has the duty to all who care for her—not to be a problem, not to be a burden.

Disabilities crowd in on the old; real pain is there, and if we have to be falsely cheerful, it is part of our isolation. Another secret we carry is that though drab outside—wreckage to the eye, mirrors a mortification—inside we flame with a wild life that is almost incommunicable. In silent, hot rebellion we cry silently, "I have lived my life haven't I? What more is expected of me?" She observes so well: "The woman who has a gift for old age is the woman who delights in comfort. If warmth is known as the blessing it is, if your bed, your bath, your best-liked food and drink are regarded as fresh delights, then you know how to thrive when old." (p. 88)

Perhaps society needs to hear this kind of message more often.

What counterpressures represent the contextual half of the dialectic between individual agency, subjectivity, and context? What kind of social, institutional, and attitudinal changes will be necessary to facilitate the "New Aging"? We must combine social opportunities and support with individual change. In addition, cultural and social recognition for changing images seem to be critical if we think about the conditions of self-respect as being typically "gained and sustained only in on-going and mutually supportive interpersonal relations" (Flanagan, 1991, p. 133). It is no secret that women have been taking care of children and grandchildren for generations. It has never before resulted in a transformation of their image. In their new aging, will women alone still be left with most of the unchosen obligations?

As a long-time advocate for empowerment, especially of older women, behind the arguments the Gergens raise, I hear the refrain, "But we are invisible." Visibility cannot be restored by elders alone. Like dignity, it is relational. I may feel powerful; I may have the capacity and the knowledge to act; but if I have no listeners, my power is immediately circumscribed. In the same way, the possibilities for older people to be the icons of wisdom are probably more specific than their age or white hair alone. Certain people have lifelong panache that transcends age, but is it transferable to the aged in general? What would it take beyond Walter Cronkite to create cultural images of the aging as wise women and men, images that are sufficiently inclusive to extend to the bent-over old woman in the Medicaid facility?

Let me end by suggesting that I support counterstories that tell a different tale about aging, but that I believe the task will require much more than a select group of older people with the collusion of the media and economic interests to make that happen. The work to be done is intense and complex, because the counterstories must include the poor and the frail as well as the elegant and the healthy. We must acknowledge the losses that may indeed be part of our aging, without translating those losses into narratives of decline (see Gullette, 1997). For many losses, indeed, there might be gains. We must resist by not tolerating the ageist remarks that our age peers or others make, consistently point out how and when cultural images render us invisible or show us on a downward slope, reject the myth that somehow, if only we did everything right, we could somehow never age. We can document how master narratives of decline serve powerful and vested interests. We can turn to our religious traditions that offer powerful messages that fail to reach the larger society or even most congregants. The prophetic tradition, for example, offers commanding messages of resistance. What else can we call upon to present many different images, at the same time that we address cultural ideals that are directly contrary to the virtues we might wish to highlight in old age.

REFERENCES

Achenbaum, W. A. (1978). *Old age in the new land: The American experience since 1790.* Baltimore: Johns Hopkins University Press.

Cole, T. (1992). *The journey of life: A cultural history of aging in America.* New York: Cambridge University Press.

Flanagan, O. (1991). *Varieties of moral personality: Ethics and psychological realism.* Cambridge, MA: Harvard University Press.

Furman, F. (1997). *Facing the mirror: Older women and beauty shop culture.* New York: Routledge.

Gullette, M. (1997). *Declining to decline: Cultural combat and the politics of midlife.* Charlottesville, VA: University of Virginia Press.

Haber, C. (1984). *Beyond sixty-five: The dilemma of old age in America's past.* Cambridge, England: Cambridge University Press.

Hochschild, A. (1997). *Time bind: When work becomes home and home becomes work.* New York: Henry Holt.

Holstein, M. (1999). Women and productive aging: Troubling implications. In M. Minkler & C. Estes (Eds.), *Critical gerontology: Perspectives from political and moral economy* (pp. 227–244). Amityville, NY: Baywood.

Kaiser Family Foundation. (1995, October). *Medicare chart book.* Washington, DC and Menlo Park, CA: Kaiser Family Foundation.

Kleinman, A. (1988). *The illness narratives: Suffering, healing, and the human condition.* New York: Basic Books.

Maxwell, F. S. (1979). *Measure of my days.* New York: Penguin Books. (originally published 1968).

McCarthy, T. (1991). *Ideals and illusions: On reconstruction and deconstruction in contemporary critical theory.* Cambridge, MA: MIT Press.

Putnam, R. (1995, January). Bowling alone: America's declining social capital. *Journal of Democracy, 6,* 65.

Rank, M., & Hirschl, T. (1999). Estimating the proportion of Americans experiencing poverty during their elderly years. *Journal of Gerontology: Social Sciences, 54B,* S184–S193.

Taylor, C. (1989). *Sources of the self: The making of the modern identity.* Cambridge, MA: Harvard University Press.

Young, I. M. (1990). *Justice and the politics of difference.* Princeton, NJ: Princeton University Press.

Author Index

Subject Index